CO-AYS-420

POLISH FOREIGN
POLICY RECONSIDERED

POLISH FOREIGN POLICY RECONSIDERED

Challenges of Independence

Edited by
Ilya Prizel and Andrew A. Michta

St. Martin's Press
New York

POLISH FOREIGN POLICY RECONSIDERED
Copyright © 1995 by Ilya Prizel and Andrew A. Michta

ISBN 0-312-12293-4

Library of Congress Cataloging-in-Publication Data

Polish foreign policy reconsidered : challenges of independence /
    edited by Ilya Prizel and Andrew A. Michta
        p.   cm.
    Includes bibliographical references and index.
    ISBN 0-312-12293-4
    1. Poland—Foreign relations—1989- 2. Poland—Politics and
government—1989- 3. National security—Poland. I. Prizel, Ilya.
II. Michta, Andrew A.
    DK4450.P65   1995
    327.438'009'045—dc20   94-35327
                                                        CIP

Book design by Acme Art, Inc.

First Edition: June 1995
10 9 8 7 6 5 4 3 2 1

To Chelsea, Lauren, Natalie, and Peter

CONTENTS

ACKNOWLEDGMENTS

The editors wish to thank Simon Winder and Michael Flamini of the Scholarly and Reference Division of St. Martin's Press for encouraging this project and for seeing it through to completion.

Andrew A. Michta would like to thank his wife, Cristina, and his daughter, Chelsea, for their encouragement, patience, and senses of humor. Special thanks go to Mertie W. Buckman and her son, Robert Buckman, of Memphis, Tennessee, for their commitment to research in International Studies. A word of sincere thanks goes to Michta's student assistants, Yohaan Demel and Brian Kuns, for their help, and to Brenda Somes, whose assistance has been invaluable.

Ilya Prizel would like to express his gratitude to his wife, Kate, and children, Peter, Natalie, and Lauren. In addition he would like to acknowledge his gratitude for the help and support of his colleagues at the Paul H. Nitze School of Advanced International Studies at the Johns Hopkins University, especially that of Bruce Parrott and Florence Rotz.

Finally, the editors would like to express their thanks to the contributors, who managed to accommodate this project in their crowded schedules.

INTRODUCTION

Ilya Prizel and Andrew A. Michta

Only a few years ago a discussion of Polish foreign policy would have been a spurious exercise, for although Moscow allowed its communist satraps in Eastern Europe a modicum of autonomy on matters of economic and social policy, all key foreign and security policy questions were decided by the Soviets. The collapse of the Berlin Wall and the disintegration of the Soviet empire freed Moscow's former clients to define their place in the international arena. For the Poles the regained freedom and national sovereignty have created a new imperative to articulate their country's vital national interests and to devise a foreign policy to secure them.

In this century Poland had experienced independence for only two decades, so it is not surprising that the current debates on foreign policy cannot escape history. The Poles realize quite well that, as in the past, they are no match for their powerful neighbors, and their ability to influence the direction of the continent's transformation is limited. Still, enough has changed in Poland's domestic politics and in the country's international position to warrant measured optimism.

This book revisits the history of Polish foreign policy and examines changes in Poland's international position since the collapse of Communism. We see the restructuring of post–Cold War Europe as a significant opportunity for Poland to break out of its centuries-old dilemma of being a medium-sized and a relatively weak power located at a critical juncture of Europe's geopolitics, between Germany and Russia. In this century Poland paid a terrible price when it was either an outpost of the West against the East or a buffer state of the Soviet Union against the West. Today, more than at any juncture in its history, Poland has a chance to escape its historical dilemma and to gain leverage in its relations both with the West and with Russia. It is our position that the long-term success of Poland's efforts to protect its newly-gained sovereignty and to secure prosperity for its people will depend on Poland's ability to turn its geopolitical liability into an asset.

The nature of Poland's future relationship with the West depends on whether the post–Cold War European order will include or exclude Russia. The new order can be established without Russian participation, but for Poland the exclusion of Russia will mean the difference between being a bridge between Western Europe and Russia and becoming a frontier outpost of the West against the East. Worse yet, in the end Poland may find itself isolated from both, facing a hostile Russian state and a disunified and disinterested Western Europe. It is our view that the opportunities still inherent in the current transitional phase in post–Cold War Europe make a reassessment of the historical argument possible. United Germany today is not a threat to Poland; instead, it is the greatest advocate of Polish interests in Western European institutions and a powerful force behind the Polish bid for membership in the European Union and NATO. Likewise, Poland is not directly threatened by Russia, although the continuing crisis in the East makes the final outcome unpredictable. Today, more than at any point in the last two hundred years, the Poles can reasonably hope to rejoin Europe. This historic opportunity is as much a function of the changed international environment as it is due to the new way the Poles see their state and its place in the international system.

Inasmuch as the Polish People's Republic of the half century of communist domination was a break with Polish history, the Third Republic of today *(Trzecia Rzeczpospolita)* need no longer be bound by the legacy of the past. In terms of its geography and its ethnic composition, the independent Polish state of the late twentieth century is different from the historical Commonwealth of Poland-Lithuania and from the interwar Second Republic. Today Poland is ethnically homogenous. It no longer needs to define its destiny as an imperial civilizing force controlling the Eastern Borderlands *(Kresy)* or as a bastion of the West against Russia. Poland has become a modern-day nation state whose traditional ethnic composition and class structure have been shattered by the legacy of World War II and Communism. It is a state where the rising middle class battles for influence against the traditional peasant interests and those of the urban proletariat of the communist era. It is a country where, the incessant debates on domestic political issues notwithstanding, democratic institutions are taking hold, where free elections have resulted in an orderly transition of power, and where there is a broad-based consensus among the elite on the key issues of economic reform and foreign policy.

Perhaps more than most other European states, Poland is a captive of its tortured history when its independence was interrupted by its more powerful neighbors. Today the strengths of the restored Polish state must be balanced against the danger that the country may once more be confronted by international developments that it cannot control. In addition to the legacy of its history, Poland is forced to contend with two unknowns, each with potentially fateful consequences for the future of the Polish state. First, it remains unclear whether Russia's experiment with democracy and a market economy is a fundamental break with its thousand-year-long historical experience, or whether it is yet another "false spring" likely to be followed by yet another version of traditional Russian authoritarianism cum expansionist messianism. The second unknown is whether a reversal in Russia will inevitably result in a new bi-polar world, or whether the Western alliance system deprived of its past unifying impetus will itself atrophy. Should the latter happen, it would allow the Kremlin to exploit the differing agendas and threat perceptions in the various Western capitals which could leave Poland on the margins of the West's security concerns. If the history of the last world war has taught the Poles anything, it is that a rising threat to the European order may not necessarily generate a unified and resolute Western response.

Today the ever-present awareness that a severe reversal in the geopolitical fortunes of Poland is possible has forced Warsaw to pursue a subtle and, at times, contradictory foreign policy. Earnestly anxious to avoid turning Russia into a pariah state bent on undermining the international system, Poland has championed Russia's integration with the rest of Europe. At the same time, cognizant of the danger should a revisionist Russia reappear on the international arena (especially if unchecked by a coherent Western alliance system) Warsaw has become the most eager and persistent applicant to join NATO. While Poland has made strenuous efforts to accommodate its large and difficult neighbor to the East, at the same time it has persevered in its endeavors to join and preserve the Western alliance as a coherent body able to deal with the contingency of a resurgent Russia.

The greatest challenge facing Warsaw today is to resolve the tension inherent in the two-pronged design of Polish foreign policy. It is our view that in the long run Poland stands to benefit the most if its reintegration in the West is not purchased at the price of unyielding Russian hostility, for such an outcome would not only deny Poland potential leverage in the West, but also, if NATO loses its ability to speak with one voice on matters of European security, it would leave Poland with paper-thin security guarantees. It is certainly true that in the final analysis, the task of forging a stable Central Europe will require leadership on the part of the Western powers and a dose of realism in Moscow. Still, Poland has an independent albeit limited role to play in the process of post–Cold War restructuring in the region. It is our hope that as this book examines the evolution and adaptation of Polish foreign policy to the new and unpredictable environment, it will begin articulating an alternative to the historical dilemmas that had determined Poland's fate in the past.

POLISH FOREIGN POLICY RECONSIDERED

1

In the Shadow of the
Second Republic

John S. Micgiel

At a meeting in Manhattan in June 1994, the chairman of the Polish Parliament's Foreign Affairs Committee, Bronislaw Geremek, averred that in terms of foreign policy, Poland has never been in as fortuitous a situation as it is today.[1] Professor Geremek expounded on a number of issues, most of which could have applied to any other democracy: the latest public opinion polls, the latest government crisis, inflation. How different these issues were from those in Poland just a few short years ago. How has Poland's geopolitical situation changed since? The purpose of this brief survey is to examine the history of Polish foreign policy in the twentieth century. By concentrating on how Poland fared within an international system that existed for only two decades before it once again tore itself apart, and on how Poland has dealt with foreign policy in the period since 1989, we shall see whether the effects of decisions made decades ago are apparent today.

The first official document in the foreign policy of independent Poland is a communication from the Polish head of state to foreign powers dated 16 November 1918. It speaks of justice and democratic principles and, not surprisingly, reflects Poland's overarching foreign policy goal in the interwar period: to safeguard its all too fragile independence.

As the Commander in Chief of the Polish army, I wish to notify combatant and neutral governments and nations of the existence of an independent Polish state, comprising all lands of unified Poland. The political situation in Poland and the yoke of occupation have not allowed the Polish nation to express itself freely concerning its fate. Thanks to the changes that have occurred as a result of the splendid victories of the allied armies, the restoration of an independent and sovereign Poland has become an accomplished fact. The Polish state is being established by the entire nation and is based on democratic principles. The Polish government will replace the rule of coercion, which weighed heavy upon Poland for 140 years, with a system based on order and justice. Supported by the Polish army under my command, I trust that, from now on, no foreign army will enter Poland without our first expressing our formal approval. I am convinced that the great Western democracies will lend their assistance and fraternal support to the reborn and independent Polish Commonwealth.[2]

In the eighteenth century, Poland had been a major European state, second only to France in population and to Russia in territory. Partitioned by Russia, Prussia, and Austria, Poland ceased to exist as a state for 123 years. The outbreak of World War II pitted the partitioners against each other and offered the Poles new opportunities, although very few people believed at the time that independence could be achieved. One such person was Jozef Pilsudski, a former Socialist, who considered the Russian state the greatest threat to the Polish nation. A different conclusion was reached by Roman Dmowski, a National Democrat, who saw in Germany the same threat.

Pilsudski believed that ultimately the Russians would be defeated by the Central Powers, and that, in turn, the Central Powers would be so fatigued by the struggle that Polish military formations might be able to achieve power at a critical juncture in the hostilities. He therefore formed a legion to fight alongside the Austrians against the Russians. Dmowski, meanwhile, left for the West to try to secure as much as he could for Poland by tying Poland's future to the Franco-Russian alliance. He soon became the leading spokesman for the Polish cause in the West, where his diplomatic campaign against Germany found fertile ground. As the head of the conservative Polish National Committee (Polski Komitet Narodowy-PKN),[3] which was formally recognized by the Allied Powers in late 1917, he and his colleagues achieved a virtual monopoly over representation of Poland abroad.[4]

It would surely be an exaggeration to impute a cause-and-effect relationship between President Wilson's pronouncements concerning the establishment of an independent Poland and Allied support thereof to the influence of Dmowski and Ignacy Paderewski, the renowned pianist and composer, among Allied leaders. Yet these and other statements would hardly have been made without such diplomatic pressure.[5] Even so, independent Poland was not born solely because of diplomatic declarations made on foreign soil. They were, however, an important element in a complicated scenario that included the collapse of the old established order and the transfer of power to Pilsudski, whose credo had always been independence.[6]

After 14 November 1918, Pilsudski was indeed in charge in Warsaw and Central Poland. However, the victorious Allies refused to recognize his regime, and with the support that the Polish National Committee enjoyed, there was little chance of this happening without Dmowski's approval, which was not forthcoming. In the meantime, the Left Wing government of Jedrzej Moraczewski installed by Pilsudski was quickly recognized by the German government, which sent a legation to Warsaw on November 20. Diplomatic relations with Germany were perceived by the Polish government as crucial at this stage, given the large number of German troops occupying the Ober-komando-Ost, a vast area east of the Bug River. Still controlled by the German government, these troops physically separated the Poles from the advancing Bolsheviks; a withdrawal would facilitate Russia's westward expansion. More-over, the impact of a German withdrawal across Central Poland, both politically and socially, would have unforeseeable consequences for the weak Polish state. A cautious policy toward the German government was therefore adopted. Proponents in Poland of closer relations with the western Allies opposed Pilsudski's relations with the Germans, seeing them as a distinct liability in the peace talks that were to take place in Paris shortly and were expected to settle such important matters as Poland's borders with Germany.[7] They demanded that the Moraczewski government break relations with Germany, discounting or disregarding the consequences that this would have in Poland should the German troops retreat across Central Poland and the Soviets move westward to fill the void.

For his part, Pilsudski saw the Paris talks and recognition by the Entente as important; his emissaries were told by the French, however, that recognition was contingent on his coming to terms with Dmowski's Polish National Committee and the formation of a new government. Indeed, the Moraczewski government was losing ground within Poland; the struggle culminated in a coup d'état attempt by supporters of the right on 4-5 January 1919, which ultimately failed. Negotiations between the two sides continued until a compromise was finally reached; a compromise government was installed on 16 January 1919, two days before the opening of the peace conference in Paris. Ignacy Paderewski was appointed prime minister[8] and foreign minister. The Entente powers quickly recognized the new government, thereby ending the dualism in Polish foreign policy.

Paderewski also served as the chief delegate of Poland during the Peace Conference in Paris. Despite his reputation, enormous charm, and access to the leaders of the victorious alliance, Poland did not obtain all that it wanted in the West.[9] Part of the reason was that the Polish approach, formulated by Dmowski, was to build a large Polish state that would incorporate areas not predominantly ethnically Polish and whose inhabitants would be absorbed and assimilated. This was contrary to Wilson's ideal of self-determination. Futhermore, ceding industrial and mining areas that were important to German economic well-being was contrary to British interests. Pilsudski favored a federalist approach, in which Poland would be allied with smaller states carved out of former imperial Russia.[10] Although Pilsudski's approach was more of a trend than a blueprint, many important people in Poland supported federalist principles,[11] and Pilsudski's appeal to the population of the former Grand Duchy of Lithuania in April 1919, was well received by the Entente. But fear that Dmowski's policy of incorporation would prevail hurt the Polish cause both in Paris and in the so-called borderlands, or Kresy.

Having been engaged in hostilities with the Bolsheviks since early 1919, with the promise of little support from the French and none at all from the British, and believing that Poland was in mortal danger from the Bolsheviks, notwithstanding their appeals for peace, Pilsudski decided to settle the territorial conflict with Soviet Russia militarily. On 21 April 1920, he concluded a pact, followed three days later by a military convention, with the Ukrainian Peoples' Republic (led by Semyon Petlura) and embarked on a campaign to inflict the maximum possible damage on Bolshevik forces in the Ukraine. By May 7, his troops had thrust to Kiev, although they were soon driven all the way back again. By August 1920, it seemed that Pilsudski's fortunes were lost, with five Soviet armies deep in ethnically Polish territory, at the gates of Warsaw, with the avowed goal—to paraphrase Marshal Tukhachevsky's order—of marching over the corpse of Poland to carry revolution into Western Europe. With modest assistance from France, for whom Poland constituted a cordon sanitaire against the Bolsheviks, Pilsudski executed a boldly conceived counterattack, smashing the Soviet offensive and driving Tukhachevsky eastward. The Treaty of Riga of 1921 ended the Polish-Soviet armed conflict and set the Polish eastern borders until 1939.[12] It also ended Pilsudski's dream of an East-Central European federation of independent states. Regardless of Plisudski's rhetoric about the self-determination and independence of Ukraine and Byelorussia, he realized that those states would soon be swallowed by Soviet Russia.[13]

Although Polish borders reached to within an average of 50 miles of the historic 1772 borders of prepartition Poland,[14] the area they outlined was at the same time too little and too much. Poland received substantial areas with a predominantly non-Polish population, including Eastern Galicia, which proved too small to form the basis of a federal structure yet too large to be successfully absorbed into a centralized nation-state.[15] The Ukrainians in particular, with their demands for cultural and political autonomy in the late 1920s and 1930s, would test the mettle of Polish politicians and bureaucrats who saw autonomy as a luxury that a Poland surrounded by dangerous neighbors could ill afford.[16] By 15 March 1923, when the Allied Council of Ambassadors recognized the border established by the Treaty of Riga, all of Poland's borders were fixed.[17]

Poland was not alone in its problems with obtaining or keeping territory. Most if not all of the successor states in East-Central Europe had territorial problems with their neighbors following World War I, some of which erupted into armed conflicts. However, it seemed that only Poland had such a large number of hostile neighbors, two of whom had been and would again be major powers bent on recouping territory lost to Poland. Indeed, the Polish-Soviet War of 1920, in which Bolshevik armies were routed at Warsaw while Germany and Czechoslovakia refused to allow passage of supplies from France to Poland, soon reaffirmed the perils of geographic location.[18] After 1923, the twin principles of peace and territorial integrity were stressed by all foreign ministers of the interwar Polish governments throughout frequent cabinet changes.[19] The question, of course, was how best to achieve these goals.

Poland had acted to improve its security by signing a pact with France in February 1921. Directed mainly against Germany, the pact also obligated the French to help Poland, albeit not militarily, in the event of hostilities between the Poles and the Soviets. Together with a military pact signed with Romania, this formed, as Pilsudski put it, a canon of Polish foreign policy.[20] While French support in particular was welcome, it was not entirely sufficient, especially in the event of hostilities with Soviet Russia. Additional safeguards were required. Essentially, three options were available to Poland's foreign policy makers: (1) an alliance with either of its two neighbors, (2) neutrality between the two, reinforced by a regional system, and (3) neutrality strengthened by an alliance with France.[21] Partnership with one neighbor against the other seemed logical to outside observers. Alliance with Germany, however, would have entailed cession of territory and in the early postwar years would have meant a break with France. Because of Poland's smaller size and weak economic condition, such a relationship would be analogous to, as one historian put it, that between a person and a slice of bread: Poland would have been easily consumed.[22] Alliance with Soviet Russia probably would have meant a break with the West and complete isolation. Experience predicted that sooner rather than later the country would have been completely subordinate to the Soviets. Clearly, neither of these options was acceptable to the vast majority of Poles. Neutrality or balance between the two powers was the only option left.

Although the attempt to create conditions for a federation had failed, new efforts were undertaken to create an East-Central European regional defensive system. One possibility was a Baltic bloc. While Poland's relationship with Latvia was solid, the seizure of Wilno/Vilnius in October 1920 by the ostensibly mutinous Polish General Lucjan Zeligowski understandably soured Polish-Lithuanian relations. The failure of efforts aimed at reaching a compromise between the two sides and the subsequent incorporation of the area into Poland in April 1922 completely alienated Lithuania.[23]

Although Poland did cooperate with Finland, Estonia, and Latvia, the Polish-Lithuanian issue made the establishment of a Baltic bloc in the interwar period impossible. Moving southward, Poland engaged Czechoslovakia and Romania in talks, and while a deal was struck with the latter, no arrangement with Czechoslovakia was possible. This was true partly because of that country's sympathetic policy toward Russia and partly because of mutual mistrust stemming from the dispute over Cieszyn/Teschen. While the two sides did negotiate on several more occasions in the future, the results were anything but encouraging. By 1926, it was clear that neither a Baltic nor a Danubian bloc would arise.

It was also clear by that time that French statesmen believed that their allies in East- Central Europe did not offer adequate security guarantees against Germany at a time when both Britain and France were revising their policies toward that country. The French felt that a political and economic rapprochement with Germany was necessary and recognized Britain's unwillingness to enter into commitments in East-Central Europe. Negotiations among the two Allies and Germany eventually resulted in the Locarno Treaties.[24] From the Polish point of view, the Locarno Treaties undermined the Franco-Polish alliance to achieve partial guarantees of France's western borders. Austin Chamberlain, Aristide Briand, and Gustav Stresemann, the principal architects of the Locarno Treaties, each received a Nobel Prize for their work.[25] On 16 October 1925, Poland signed a new treaty with France, ostensibly guaranteeing its security, and a nonterritorial arbitration treaty with Germany. However, an analysis of the pacts soon showed that the balance between Eastern and Western Europe had been distorted and that a security gap still existed, since it did not commit Germany to its Eastern border.

The Locarno Treaties also resulted in Poland's being allotted a semipermanent seat in the Council of the League of Nations in September 1926, over the objections of Germany, which had received a permanent place in the

Council following Locarno.[26] This was important for reasons of prestige and was unquestionably a diplomatic victory. As a supranational forum, however, it proved to be of little use to the Poles, particularly to Pilsudski. This was brought home in an incident involving Lithuania. On 16 December 1926, Augustinas Voldemaras, who became the new Lithuanian prime minister as a result of a coup, set off to sharpen the feud with Poland. Lithuania had cut off diplomatic relations and closed its borders with Poland following the Polish incorporation of Wilno. Voldemaras now announced that as far as he was concerned a state of war would exist between the two countries until Wilno was returned to Lithuania. His government proceeded to close several Polish language schools and to disaccredit teachers. The Polish government responded in kind toward the Lithuanian schools in the Wilno region. German and Soviet support for Lithuania made the matter internationally significant, and on 15 October 1927, the Lithuanians brought the matter to the League of Nations, alleging Polish violation of the Versailles Minority Treaty and a plot against Lithuania's existence. A confrontation between Pilsudski and Voldemaras occurred at the meeting of the Council on 10 December 1927. Interrupting Voldemaras's presentation of his case, Pilsudski asked bluntly whether war or peace prevailed between their countries. Voldemaras hesitantly conceded that it was peace, whereupon Pilsudski concluded: "In that case I have nothing more to do here." Hailed by public opinion at home, Pilsudski's display of theatricality achieved nothing. No improvement in relations was forthcoming, the border remained closed, and diplomatic relations remained nonexistent.[27] He made no demands on the Lithuanians, toward whom he displayed a certain tolerance and understanding that was sadly lacking in many of his colleagues. In retrospect, it was the first of several demonstrations of a new, tougher foreign-policy stance that actively opposed decisions made without Polish acceptance.[28]

Relations with Poland's eastern neighbor, the Soviet Union, changed suddenly in 1929. By 1931, when the Japanese occupied Manchuria and the Soviets moved many of their troops east to meet the potential challenge, Stalin had become interested in a nonaggression pact with the Poles. Although Pilsudski was not convinced of the sincerity of the offer, he realized the effect that such a pact would have on Germany and on the rest of Europe. After much haggling, the three-year pact was signed on 25 January 1932, with both states reaffirming their promise to renounce war as an instrument of policy. The first leg on which the policy of equilibrium between Germany and Russia was rested in place. Next, something had to be done about Germany, with whom Poland had been engaged in a long economic battle designed to elicit political and territorial concessions from the Poles.

At the end of his career, Pilsudski's closest foreign-policy aide was Jozef Beck, who was appointed foreign minister in late 1932, just prior to Hitler's rise to power in Germany. It was a dangerous time for Poland in European politics. In March 1933, Benito Mussolini floated the idea of a Four Power Pact that would give Britain, France, Germany, and Italy the right to make decisions that would be binding on other European nations. The Italian draft specified that treaties could be revised in cases in which there was a possibility that conflict would ensue. The Poles realized that this placed their border with Germany in Pomerania, the so-called Corridor, in peril. After all, the British had been consistently critical of Poland, the Italians would be anxious to indulge the Germans, the Germans themselves were anxious to take back these territories, and the French had proven how malleable and elastic their alliance with Poland could be. The building of the Maginot Line was evidence enough of the defensive posture that France had adopted. Poland quietly floated trial balloons concerning a defensive war against Germany and just as quietly was refused. Direct negotiations with Hitler were the next step, which, to everyone's surprise, succeeded.

Hitler acceded to the Polish request of affirmation of Polish rights in Danzig and issued a communiqué on May 3. A détente in Polish-German relations ensued. After all, Hitler was not after territorial concessions, but rather the dismantlement of the entire European order established at Versailles. The first and most important step was to rearm Germany, which is why Germany withdrew from the League of Nations on 14 October 1933. At the same time, Hitler sought to allay fear by indulging the Poles in discussions about a nonaggression treaty. As a result, on 26 January 1934, the Declaration on Nonaggression and Understanding was signed by both parties in Berlin, and the two nations' parliaments ratified the document the next month. The agreement ruled out the use of force to resolve disputes between the two states, and was to remain in effect for ten years.

The declaration, like the nonaggression treaty with the Soviets two years earlier, was a spectacular accomplishment, the second leg of the equilibrium that Pilsudski sought. In fact, it was precisely this policy that caused the Poles to decline to participate in the Franco-Soviet pact that the French proposed in the spring of 1934. Yet Marshal Pilsudski's oft-quoted statement of early 1934 that Poland had bought four years' peace illustrates his deep-seated mistrust of both neighbors.

Notwithstanding its new relationship with Germany, Poland stood ready to fulfill its treaty obligations toward France and support the existing status quo in Europe during the crisis caused by Hitler's remilitarization of the Rhineland on 7 March 1936. France, however, refused to take up the challenge. Germany thereby improved its strategic position along its western border, and, more important, France demonstrated to its allies that it was unable to defend its own national interests. This was no doubt one of the reasons for the Belgian decision to leave the French orbit in October 1936 by declaring neutrality.

As Europe became more tense in the late 1930s, Poland continued its policy of trying to stay neutral toward its two great neighbors.[28] But after Pilsudski's death on 12 May 1935, it was more flexible about its smaller neighbors. On the eve of the Anschluss, Germany's occupation of Austria in March 1938, Minister Jozef Beck took advantage of an incident on the Lithuanian border to hand the Lithuanian government an ultimatum to open its border with Poland and begin diplomatic relations. The Lithuanians were forced to comply. During the Munich crisis of September 1938, the Poles demanded and received cession of Teschen and other areas in Spisz and Orawa by the Czechoslovaks. In this latter case particularly, in which a four-power pact, exactly like the one that Poland had objected to in 1933, decided on the borders of a neighboring country, Beck's policy is difficult to fathom. A few hundred square miles of land were regained along with a mixed population. But all of Europe now saw the Poles as Germany's accomplices, and, more important, Poland's strategic situation, now worse than before, would be worse still in six months.

In fact, the strategic relationship between Poland and Germany, which had been weighted in Poland's favor in 1934, had long since shifted. Germany's strength far outstripped Poland's when Hitler began his campaign in October 1938 to intimidate the Poles on the pretext of obtaining Danzig and extraterritorial rights for a highway and railroad from Danzig to Germany. The danger of Poland being cut off and thus economically strangled by these terms was obvious; moreover, no government that accepted such terms would long survive in Poland. German pressure on the Polish government increased as the months wore on. When the Germans occupied Bohemia and Moravia on 15 March 1939, Poland's strategic situation was tragic: the Nazis were now on three sides of Poland and exerted a great deal of influence on Poland's other neighbors to the south, Slovakia, Romania, and Hungary. Eight days later, on March 23, the Germans seized Klajpeda (Memel) from the Lithuanians.

Considering that the British had maintained their policy of noncommitment on the continent, their guarantee to defend the territorial integrity of Poland on 31 March 1939, was quite astounding. In response, Hitler declared the Polish-German Declaration of Nonaggression to have been violated by the Poles and no longer in existence. Jozef Beck was undaunted; having witnessed German propaganda campaigns throughout his career as foreign minister he was prepared for the German verbal onslaught. And he responded in kind, with the most impressive remarks ever uttered by a Polish foreign minister. On 5 May 1939, responding to Hitler's allegations and demands, he concluded:

> Peace is a valuable and desirable thing. But peace, like almost everything in this world, has its price, high but definable. We in Poland do not recognize the concept of peace at any price. There is only one thing in the life of men, nations, and states that is priceless, and that is honor.[30]

Could or should Beck have sought an alliance with the Soviet Union? Should he have relied on his French and British allies as he did? Just as Polish public opinion would not have tolerated capitulation to German demands, it would not accept the presence of Soviet troops on Polish territory, which is what Stalin demanded during the Franco-British-Soviet negotiations in the summer of 1939. Moreover, given the history of Polish-Russian and Polish-Soviet relations, it is highly unlikely that Poland's leadership would have entertained such a radical idea. The horrors of the World War I were quite recent, and even British and French leaders did not believe that Hitler would actually risk engaging their countries in military hostilities over Poland and advocated calling Hitler's bluff. Unfortunately, probably even fewer people believed that a pact between Germany and the Soviet Union was possible. Caught between two aggressive great powers, Poland faced a situation in 1939 similar to the one it had faced in the late eighteenth century. Although Poland had allies this time, the results were unfortunately the same.[31]

Germany's September Campaign was disastrous for Poland. Despite plans that called for a French offensive on Germany's western border within 15 days of the outbreak of war,[32] Poland was left to go it alone. The Germans, irrespective of their overwhelming superiority in weaponry, did not have to do so. On September 17, the Red Army crossed Poland's eastern frontier and fought westward to the demarcation line that had been established beforehand with the Germans.[33] The Polish government thereupon crossed the border into Romania and was interned, along with President Ignacy Moscicki. Poland was partitioned again, with Germany annexing the western areas and deporting Poles and Jews from those areas into what was central Poland and was now called the General Gouvernement. The Polish elite, and almost all of Poland's 3 million Jews, were hunted down and slaughtered. The Soviets held a plebiscite in the areas they occupied in order to provide a pseudolegal basis for incorporation. Between 1 million and 1.5 million Poles, Ukrainians, Jews, and Byelorussians, all former Polish citizens, were deemed undesirable or dangerous and arrested, jailed, or simply deported. Most never returned. Polish officers who had the misfortune to become Soviet prisoners of war—as well as border guards, policemen, and various state officials totalling over 21,000 people, the cream of Poland's educated class—were quietly executed in April 1940 on the Politburo's orders. The murders were kept a dark secret, protected by the NKVD.

Meanwhile, a new Polish government was formed in France, led by General Wladyslaw Sikorski, who was also commander in chief; Wladyslaw Raczkiewicz became president. The legal continuity of the Polish state thus continued in exile. A new army participated in the campaign against the invading Germans in spring of 1940. The government, and what was left of the Polish army, was then evacuated to Great Britain, which also hosted the Czechoslovak and Yugoslav governments in exile, and the "Free French." Polish pilots soon played a key role in the Battle of Britain, and Polish soldiers and sailors distinguished themselves in all theaters of operation. The Polish underground, the Home Army, was the largest in Europe; it was also under orders from the government in exile.

The German attack on the Soviet Union soon brought the latter into the anti-German alliance. Prime Minister Sikorski quickly signed an agreement with Soviet Ambassador Ivan Maisky on 30 July 1941 that mandated the amnesty and release of all Polish prisoners of war and detainees. Those released were to form the core of a Polish army that was to be established in the Soviet Union and participate in the fight against the Germans. Polish leaders were divided on the wisdom of joining forces with Hitler's accomplice, and both the Poles and the Soviets were suspicious of each other. Although the pact annulled the Ribbentrop-Molotov agreement under which Poland had been divided in 1939, no mention was made of restoring the prewar borders.

Polish apprehensions grew as efforts to locate the officers presumed to be held captive in the vastness of the Gulag met with evasiveness. It was not until April 1943, when the Germans discovered some 4,000 bodies in the woods at Katyn, that the awful secret was revealed. The Polish called for an International Red Cross investigation, and Stalin used the pretext to sever relations with the London government in exile. By that time, almost the entire army formed by General Anders had been evacuated to the Middle East and went on to fight in the Italian campaign. In May 1944, the Polish Second Corps won a major victory by breaking the German defenses at Monte Cassino and opening the road to Rome.

The political arena, however, was more difficult. General Sikorski recognized that the Soviet Union had hegemonic designs on East-Central Europe, and he tried to obtain British and, especially, American support for Poland. In these discussions he raised the issue of territorial compensation from Germany with a border along the Oder-Neisse Rivers but received no firm assurances regarding Poland's postwar frontiers.[34] Together with Edvard Benes, he drew up plans for a Czechoslovak-Polish confederation that would be able to withstand German pressure in the future in East-Central Europe.[35] The bedrock on which all Polish plans were constructed was status quo antebellum in the East, which clashed with Stalin's plans for the area. Many of Sikorski's troops came from the area that had been annexed by the Soviet Union in 1939, nearly half of Poland's prewar territory, and the pressure on the Polish government to refuse to give up these areas increased even further when the Katyn forest massacre was discovered. Sikorski was killed in a mysterious plane crash at Gibraltar in July 1943, and it fell to his successor, Stanislaw Mikolajczyk, to tackle the myriad problems that Polish diplomacy faced. The underlying truth was simple and unpleasant: the British and the Americans were unwilling under any circumstances to support Polish territorial claims in the East or in the West, for that matter. The Soviet Union was far more important to the war effort, and keeping the Soviets in the war and away from a possible separate peace with Germany far outweighed any argument that Poland's representatives could offer.

After diplomatic relations with the Polish government were suspended by the Soviet government in 1943, Great Britain, in the form of Winston Churchill, came to play the role of arbiter and counselor to the Poles, not always honestly or without ulterior motives. For example, at a meeting of Churchill, Roosevelt, and Stalin in Teheran in December 1943, it was Churchill who proposed to Stalin that Poland be moved westward to the Oder. Both before Teheran and after October 1944, when the Moscow talks concerning the makeup of the Polish postwar government failed, the British were opposed to giving the Poles what they considered to be too generous a frontier. But between Teheran and the Moscow talks, Churchill applied tremendous pressure on Prime Minister Mikolajczyk to accept the arrangement. Mikolajczyk, in turn, knew of the adamant opposition to territorial concessions by all parties in the government except his own. He also knew that time was on Stalin's side. The Soviets had installed the Lublin Committee as a rival government on 22 July 1944, and pushed the Germans back across the Vistula River. Soviet behavior during the Warsaw Uprising in August and September was unappetizing even to the Polish Communists in Lublin, although they directly benefitted from the destruction of a large segment of the Home Army, whom they had great difficulties in suppressing in the areas east of the Vistula. No amount of pressure from the British or the Americans could prod Stalin into alleviating Warsaw's plight.

Mikolajczyk resigned as prime minister on 24 November 1944, and was succeeded by Tomasz Arciszewski, whose government continued the policy of refusing to submit to Soviet and British pressure. Soon, however, the exercise was a dead letter. The Great Powers decided at Yalta, without the participation of the Polish government-in-exile, that the eastern territories of prewar Poland had been irrevocably ceded to the Soviet Union; that in return the country would receive "substantial accessions of territory in the north and west" and that the western frontier would be formally delimited at the peace conference; and finally that the then-functioning provisional government in Warsaw would "be recognized on a broader democratic basis with the inclusion of democratic leaders from Poland itself and from Poles abroad." A commission composed of Ambassadors Vyacheslav Molotov, Averell Harriman, and Clark Kerr were to consult in Moscow with the provisional government and with these other Poles with the aim of establishing "a Polish Provisional Government of National Unity which would hold unfettered elections as soon as possible on the basis of universal suffrage and secret ballot."[36] Independent of their political orientation or place of residence, Poles regarded the Yalta accords as proof of their having been given up to the Communists by the Western Allies.[37]

The Arciszewski government protested, to no avail. Mikolajczyk, on the other hand, announced his acceptance of the accords and travelled to Moscow in late June to participate in negotiations concerning the makeup of the new government. (Ironically, the talks took place during the trial of Underground Poland's leaders—known subsequently as the Sixteen—who had been arrested by the NKVD and flown to Moscow; they received stiff sentences.) The negotiations were successful, and the composition of the government was announced on June 28, with 14 of the 21 cabinet posts, including all of the key ministries, going to representatives of the Lublin Poles. One week later, on 5 July 1945, the new government was officially recognized by both the United States and Great Britain.[38] In so doing, these countries withdrew their recognition of the government in exile, depriving its officials of their diplomatic standing. Its members refused to surrender their cause, however, and remained at their posts until December 1990 when its president returned the Polish Republic's insignia to Warsaw following the election of Lech Walesa as president of Poland.

Piotr Wandycz has written that "the western powers aimed at a postwar world based on cooperation with Russia and they were unwilling to compromise this objective by confronting Moscow over the Polish rights."[39] But just as Britain shattered its canon of noninvolvement in continental affairs by its guarantee to Poland in 1939, so, too, the United States and Britain would suddenly change their policies following the Polish parliamentary elections in January 1947 and confront the Soviet Union. Like the referendum,[40] the elections were hardly "free and unfettered," and the official results showed that the Communists had won. Poland had entered a dark period in which none of its foreign policy decisions, and few of its domestic policies as well, originated in Warsaw. And while its eastern border had been set (with one minor modification in 1951) by treaty with the Soviet Union in August 1945, no peace treaty was made with Germany because the Allies could not reach an understanding. Subsequently, Germany was split in 1949, and on 6 July 1950, the German Democratic Republic signed a treaty with Poland at Zgorzelec recognizing the new border. Of the Allies, only France recognized the arrangement.

Was Poland truly independent following World War II? The Polish government did sign state treaties, such as those with the Soviet Union that delimited the state's eastern and western borders, and it was a member of the United Nations, where its voting record mirrored those of the Soviet Union, Ukraine, and Byelorussia. But it also allowed the forced resettlement of its citizens, permitted Soviet military tribunals to abduct and try its nationals, and was dominated by Soviet advisors who served at all levels in the army, ministries, and even smaller state enterprises. Moscow passed on all state decisions, including and perhaps especially those that concerned the countries of the Soviet bloc. And if something were found to be outside the party line, the Soviets were quick to take action, as in the cases of Tito and, in the Polish context, Wladyslaw Gomulka.[41] Poland was nominally independent but not sovereign; until the 1956 thaw, one really cannot speak of an independent Polish foreign policy, and not much afterwards.

Shortly thereafter a remarkable plan—and one which was indubitably to Poland's advantage—was presented to the XII Session of the UN General Assembly by Adam Rapacki, the Polish minister of foreign affairs. On 2 October 1957, Rapacki submitted a proposal to establish a denuclearized zone in Central Europe comprising Poland, Czechoslovakia, the German Democratic Republic, and the Federal Republic of Germany. According to the plan, nuclear weapons would be neither manufactured nor stockpiled in these states, no service installations or equipment would be located there, and the use of nuclear weapons against those countries would be prohibited. The plan was rejected by the United States on the grounds that it would undercut the America's tactical nuclear capability without affecting the Soviet Union's superiority in long-range missiles; it would also prevent the United States from someday arming the West Germans with nuclear weapons.[42] Rapacki's plan, in somewhat changed form, was discussed at the United Nations and in other international forums until 1962. When it met with no interest Poland unsuccessfully tried to arouse interest in a conference on European security.[43]

The citizens of neighboring Czechoslovakia were certainly less happy with Poland's next foray into international politics. In August 1968, in the name of Socialist unity and the Brezhnev Doctrine, Polish forces participated in the

Warsaw Pact invasion of Czechoslovakia, another dark spot on the history of relations between these two countries.[44]

Yet Brezhnev's détente and the emergence of the West German *Ostpolitik* in the mid-1960s fostered an environment in which both the Catholic Church and the Polish government were interested. In the "Letter of the Polish Bishops" to their German counterparts, dated 18 November 1965, the Polish Catholic hierarchy appealed for an end to the historic enmity between the two nations, forgave the Germans, and asked for forgiveness. In 1969, First Secretary of the Polish United Workers' Party Wladyslaw Gomulka sought a rapprochement with the Germans—and a confirmation of Poland's western border with the German Democratic Republic. To everyone's astonishment, his efforts were rewarded, first by the remarkable sight of Chancellor Willy Brandt kneeling in atonement before the Memorial to the Victims of Nazi Oppression,[45] and then by the Treaty of Warsaw, which was signed by both governments on 7 December 1970. No peace conference had as yet taken place (and therefore the accord was not officially sanctioned by the Allies), nevertheless, it was a remarkable diplomatic achievement both for the Poles and for Brandt's *Ostpolitik*.[46]

The miracle year of 1989 changed many things in Poland and in other countries of the region. One of the first acts undertaken by the Polish parliament, newly elected in semifree elections, was to issue an apology to the Czechoslovaks for having participated in the Warsaw Pact's quashing of the Prague Spring 21 years earlier.

Slowly but surely, a truly independent Polish foreign policy developed. One of its most important elements was the international recognition of Poland's western frontier. A veritable barrage of diplomacy ensued, resulting in the German Bundestag passing a resolution on 21 June 1990 recognizing the Polish-German border. Shortly thereafter, Poland was invited to participate in the so-called 2 + 4 Peace Conference, at the conclusion of which a treaty was signed on 12 September 1990, in which Poland's western borders were recognized by the four Allied Powers and by Germany. The border was again acknowledged in the Polish-German border agreement of 14 November 1990, and in the Polish-German Treaty on Good Neighborly Relations and Friendly Cooperation of 17 June 1991, settling the issue on a bilateral basis.

The recognition that the establishment of a stable democracy and economic prosperity demand good relations with one's neighbors has placed Poland in the forefront of countries seeking and attaining good relations with the states of the former Soviet Union and Germany.[47] In fact, Poland has Good Neighbor Treaties with all seven of the states that now adjoin it (the other six being Belarus, the Czech Republic, Lithuania, Russia, the Slovak Republic, and Ukraine).[48] Lithuania was the last country to sign such an accord. The negotiations lasted for well over two years. The delay was caused in large part by the Lithuanian demand that in the treaty the Poles condemn General Lucjan Zeligowski's seizure of Wilno and Poland's possession of the Wilno region until 1939. Historical concerns had earlier been expressed by the Poles themselves in their treaty negotiations with Germany and Russia, but without incurring such long delay. Ultimately, both sides compromised and the treaty was signed on 26 April 1994. This is qualitatively a very different eastern policy than that practiced in the interwar period.

Poland has had other recent foreign policy triumphs, including attracting economic assistance from the World Bank, the International Monetary Fund, and the Paris and London clubs; negotiating an end to the Warsaw Pact; finally reaching agreement with the Soviet Union on the withdrawal of its combat troops; and full or associate membership in multilateral organizations such as the Central European Initiative; the Visegrad Triangle (later Quadrangle); the Central European Free Trade Association; the Conference on Security and Cooperation in Europe; the North Atlantic Cooperation Council; the Council of Europe; and the Western European Union.

Not all its efforts have been entirely successful. For example, Poland has been actively lobbying for relatively quick entry into the European Union and the North Atlantic Treaty Organization, with only modest results. The dissolution of the Council for Mutual Economic Assistance (CMEA), the demise of the transferable ruble and paucity of hard currency, and an inability to agree on a clearing system for old debt all caused trade with the Soviet Union's successor states to plummet. Economic relations with Russia, once Poland's largest trade partner, showed some improvement when the two countries bestowed most favored nation status on each other and signed an agreement to build a natural gas pipeline—a ten billion dollar investment—across Poland. In the near term, however, only modest progress in improving trade seems to have been made. And despite statements to the contrary by Russian president Boris Yeltsin, Russia's negative attitude toward Polish participation in NATO is well known and likely to withstand Polish attempts at neighborly persuasion. Still, with one traditionally hostile Great Power, Russia, in temporary political and economic disarray, and with Germany a friendly liberal democracy, no serious external threats exist. As Bronislaw Geremek implied, this is a luxury to which the Poles have been unaccustomed.

Sarah M. Terry offered the following comments in her 1983 analysis of Polish wartime foreign policy:

> During the war . . . the London Poles were variously described as unrealistic, nationalistic, reactionary and, most of all, troublesome. The Poles were also "troublesome" in 1919 at Versailles. Since the end of

World War II, they have proved "troublesome" on no less than four occasions—1956, 1970, 1976, and now since August of 1980. Indeed, over the last two hundred years, every ruler of Germany from Frederick the Great through Hitler, like every ruler of Russia from Catherine the Great through Brezhnev, has found the Poles "troublesome." Yet, in those same two hundred years, the basic decisions concerning Poland's fate have almost always been made by someone else, by the Great Powers of the time. The Poles themselves, when given a say at all, have generally been able to make only the smaller decisions, within the established framework or in response to it—decisions that, to be sure were not always wise, but that have repeatedly been thrown back at them as evidence of their folly and as the cause of their misfortunes.[49]

Poland's success in meeting foreign policy challenges in the new European geopolitical situation since 1989 has made that accurate analysis a historic one. Today, Poland is well on the way to achieving the paradigm described by Pilsudski in his telegram announcing the establishment of a new commonwealth.

Notes

1. Meeting with Professor Bronislaw Geremek, held at the Polish Daily News-*Nowy Dziennik,* on Wednesday, 1 June 1994.
2. Telegram from Jozef Pilsudski to the president of the United States and to the governments of England, France, Italy, Japan, Germany, and all combatant and neutral states, in *Powstanie II Rzeczypospolitej: Wybor dokumentow 1866-1925,* ed. Halina Janowska and Tadeusz Jedruszczak (Warsaw: Ludowa Spoldzielnia Wydawnicza, 1984), pp. 441-442.
3. The Committee set up a ministry of foreign affairs, which had representatives in Paris (Erazm Piltz), London (Wladyslaw Sobanski), Rome (Konstanty Skirmunt), and Washington (Ignacy Paderewski).
4. In the United States, the Committee's efforts were opposed by the National Defense Committee (Komitet Obrony Narodowej-KON), which supported Pilsudski's efforts. Pilsudski sought to explain his policies and influence the Allied powers through his own representatives: August Zalewski in London, Wladyslaw Baranowski in Rome, and Aleksander Debski in the United States. His support for a Provisional Council of State, and later a Regency Council in Warsaw, was, of course, difficult to accept. The Regency Council had representatives in Vienna (Stefan Przezdziecki and Tytus Filipowicz), Berlin

(Adam Ronikier), and Sofia (Tadeusz Grabowski). Like Pilsudski's emissaries and their counterparts in the Polish National Committee, their experience and talents would later be put to good use in the diplomatic service of their country.

5. Piotr Wandycz, *Polish Diplomacy 1914-1945: Aims and Achievements* (London: Orbis Books, 1988), p. 10.

6. On 11 November 1918, the Regency Council gave Pilsudski command over Polish military forces, and three days later, assigned all of the Council's authority to Pilsudski before dissolving itself. See Decree of the Regency Council on the Transfer of Authority over the Military to J. Pilsudski, and Letter of the Regency Council to the Commander in Chief of the Polish Army, Jozef Pilsudski, transferring state authority to him, in Janowska and Jedruszczak, eds., *Powstanie II Rzeczypospolitej*, pp. 436, 440.

7. See Przemyslaw Hauser, "Leon Wasilewski," in *Ministrowie spraw zaqranicznych. 1919-1939*, ed. Janusz Pajewski (Szczecin: Polskie Pismo i Ksiazka, 1992), pp. 25-28.

8. At the time, the official designation was minister-president.

9. Thanks to a successful uprising in Wielkopolska, the Poles received Poznan province and a corridor of land in Pomerania separating Germany from Danzig, which was declared a Free City under the protection of the League of Nations. Plebiscites were to be held in Upper Silesia, where three uprisings eventually took place, and in the Allenstein and Marienwerder provinces of East Prussia, resulting in one million Germans being left within Poland and two million Poles in Germany. In addition, Poland and seven other countries reluctantly signed a convention guaranteeing the rights of national and religious minorities. For a competent summary of the Polish problem at the Versailles Peace Conference, see Jan Karski, *The Great Powers and Poland, 1919-1945: From Versailles to Yalta* (Lanham, MD: University Press of America, 1985), chapter 2.

10. For a detailed study of Pilsudski's ideas on federalism, see M. K. Dziewanowski, *Joseph Pilsudski: A European Federalist, 1918-1922* (Stanford, CA: Hoover Institution Press, 1969).

11. Pilsudski himself later fueled skepticism concerning his own commitment to these principles as applied to the eastern territories: "We enter them with weapons in our hands, which is contrary to the principle of federation. Besides I did not see there the people who would want to join us in a federation." Jozef Pilsudski, as cited in Piotr Wandycz, "Polish Federalism 1919-1920 and Its Historical Antecedents," *East European Ouarterly* 4, no. 1 (March 1970): p. 31.

12. For very readable accounts of the war and Soviet-Polish relations during this period, see Norman Davies, *White Eagle, Red Star: The Polish-Soviet War*

1919-20 (London: Orbis Books, 1983), and Piotr S. Wandycz, *Soviet-Polish Relations 1917-1921* (Cambridge, MA: Harvard University Press, 1969).

13. The Polish betrayal of Petlura at Riga discredited him in the eyes of many Ukrainian nationalists and undermined the notion of a federation with the Poles. It also weighed heavily on Pilsudski; when visiting his former allies at a camp in Szczypiorno, Poland, in May 1921, the marshal was reported to have apologized to the Ukrainian troops interned there. Dziewanowski, *Joseph Pilsudski,* p. 335.

14. Richard M. Watt, *Bitter Glory: Poland and its Fate, 1918-1939* (New York: Simon and Schuster, 1939), p. 151.

15. Sarah Meiklejohn Terry, *Poland's Place in Europe: General Sikorski and the Origin of the Oder-Neisse Line, 1939-1943* (Princeton, NJ: Princeton University Press, 1983), p. 23.

16. Polish colonization of ethnically Ukrainian areas, assimilation policies, Ukrainian resistance, and subsequent repression escalated in the interwar period. Bad sentiments would have tragic consequences for the Poles during World War II, when many Ukrainian nationalists collaborated with the Germans. Ukrainian massacres of Poles began in Volhynia in 1943, the beginning of an effort by the Ukrainian Partisan Army (UPA) to push ethnic Poles out of areas considered to be Ukrainian. The bloody struggle between the UPA and the government in Warsaw between 1944 and 1947 led to deportations of the Ukrainians to the Soviet Union and later, for those who refused to leave, to forced resettlement in western and northern Poland. For a compilation of documents on this subject see Eugeniusz Misilo, ed., *Akcja Wisla* (Warsaw: Archiwum Ukrainskie, 1993).

17. The Upper Silesian plebiscite on 20 March 1921, was disputed by the Poles, who launched an uprising against the German authority in May. In October, the League of Nations awarded the Poles about one-third of the area, containing some 40 percent of the population and much of its mineral resources. The dispute with Czechoslovakia over Teschen was settled by Allied decision in August 1920, when Poland was preoccupied with the presence of Soviet armies bearing down on Warsaw. The decision awarded most of the area, along with 139,000 Poles, to Czechoslovakia, and placed a pall over relations between the two neighbors for the rest of the interwar period.

18. Anna M. Cienciala and Titus Komarnicki, *From Versailles to Locarno: Keys to Polish Foreign Policy, 1919-1925* (Lawrence, KS: University Press of Kansas, 1984), p. 4.

19. Between 1918 and Pilsudski's coup d'état in May 1926, 14 cabinets had held power.

20. Piotr Wandycz, "Polska wobec polityki Locarnenskiej Brianda," *Z dziejow dyplomacji* (London: Polonia Book Fund, 1988), p. 73.

21. Wandycz, *Polish Diplomacy,* p. 17.

22. Interview with Professor Anna M. Cienciala, "Sprawa historycznego ob-iektywizmu," *Nowy Dziennik,* Przeglad Polski, 2 June 1994, p. 5.

23. In fact, there were numerous incidents along the Polish-Lithuanian border as late as early 1923. See Piotr Lossowski, *Po tej i tamtej strony Niemna* (Warsaw: Czytelnik, 1985), pp. 195-196.

24. For a full discussion of the complicated course of these events, see Cienciala and Komarnicki, *From Versailles to Locarno,* pp. 223-279.

25. Ibid., p. 275.

26. Poland was reelected for membership in the Council in 1929 and 1932.

27. Joseph Rothschild, *Pilsudski's Coup d'État* (New York: Columbia University Press, 1966), pp. 305-307, and Watt, *Bitter Glory,* p. 255.

28. Others included the case of the Polish destroyer *Wicher,* which entered Danzig harbor on 15 June 1932, on Pilsudski's express orders in demonstration of Poland's refusal to tolerate even a minor transgression of its rights. And on 6 March 1933, Danzig was the scene of yet another incident in which Polish troops were put ashore at the Polish arms depot and garrison at Westerplatte in response to a unilateral change in status for Danzig's harbor police. *Bitter Glory,* pp. 312-316.

29. Field Marshal Herman Göring sought to distract the Poles in August 1938 with vague allusions to Poland's "interests" in the Soviet Ukraine. Ambassador Jozef Lipski refused the bait, however. See Waclaw Jedrzejewicz, *Diplomat in Berlin, 1933-1939: Papers and Memoirs of Jozef Lipski Ambassador of Poland* (New York: Columbia University Press, 1968), pp. 377, 387. Foreign Minister Joachim von Ribbentrop reported in his minutes of a discussion with Minister Jozef Beck in Warsaw on 1 February 1939, that Beck had spoken of Polish aspirations toward the Soviet Ukraine. See A. J. P. Taylor, *The Origins of the Second World War* (New York: Atheneum, 1961), p. 196. However, Polish undersecretary of state Jan Szembek's notes do not bear this out. Anna M. Cienciala, *Polska polityka zagraniczna w latach 1926-1932* (Paris: Instytut Literacki, 1990), p. 241.

30. Jerzy Marek Nowakowski, "Jozef Beck," in Pajewski, ed., *Ministrowie spraw zagranicznych,* p. 197.

31. For a very critical view of Beck's foreign policy, see Taylor, *The Origins of the Second World War.*

32. According to the Polish-French military convention signed in Paris on 19 May 1939. For its text see Cienciala, *Polska polityka zagraniczna,* pp. 389-390.

33. For an interesting study of the almost unknown Polish-Soviet War of 1939, see Karol Liszewski, *Wojna Polsko-Sowiecka 1939* (London: Polska Fundacja Kulturalna, 1988).

34. For a full discussion of Poland's postwar borders with Germany, see Terry, *Poland's Place in Europe.*

35. For the definitive treatment of this partnership see Piotr S. Wandycz, *Czechoslovak-Polish Confederation and the Great Powers, 1940-1943* (Bloomington, IN: Indiana University Press, 1956).

36. For excerpts from the text concerning Poland, see *Documents on Polish-Soviet Relations 1939-45, Vol. II 1943-45* (London: Heinemann, 1967), Document 308, pp. 520-521.

37. For reactions in the press, see Edward J. Rozek, *Allied Wartime Diplomacy: A Pattern in Poland* (New York: Wiley, 1958), pp. 352-354.

38. The Soviet Union, of course, had recognized the Provisional Government in January 1945. The following countries recognized the new Polish Government as follows: France, 29 June 1945; the United States, Great Britain, and China, 5 July; Norway, 6 July; Canada, Switzerland, Sweden, and Italy, 7 July; Denmark and Mexico, 9 July; Finland, 14 July; Bulgaria, 16 July; Turkey, 18 August; Romania, 12 September; Luxemburg and Syria, 22 September; Albania, 22 December; Bolivia, Peru, and Venezuela, 29 December. From that date on, only Spain, Ireland, Cuba, Lebanon, and the Vatican continued to recognize the government-in-exile. Jozef Szaflik, *Historia Polski 1939-1947* (Warsaw: Wydawnictwo Uniwersytetu Warszawskiego, 1979), p. 174.

39. Wandycz, *Polish Diplomacy,* p. 48.

40. Documents demonstrating conclusively that the results of the vote were falsified have recently been published. See Andrzej Paczkowski, ed., *Dokumenty do dziejow PRL. Referendum z 30 czerwca 1946 r.* (Warsaw: Instytut Studiow Politycznych, 1993).

41. Yet, paradoxically, given the vehemence with which the Communists took power in Poland in the mid-1940s, fewer Communists in Poland were subjected to the repressions stemming from Stalin's paranoia in the late 1940s and early 1950s than in any other country in the Soviet bloc. Gomulka's insistence on pursuing his own brand of national Communism resulted in his being removed from party and state functions, but neither he nor other purged Polish Communists were subjected to the show trials and executions that took place in the other "Peoples' Democracies." Stalin's death may have prevented these actions (some Communists were indeed being prepared for show trials); it did not immediately have an impact on repressions against anti-communist opponents of the regime.

42. Adam Ulam, *Expansion and Coexistence,* 2nd ed. (New York: Praeger, 1974), p. 612.

43. Wandycz, *Z dziejow dyplomacji,* p. 18.

44. The standard work on the Czechoslovak crisis is Jiri Valenta, *Soviet Intervention in Czechoslovakia 1968: Anatomy of a Decision,* rev. ed. (Baltimore, MD: Johns Hopkins University Press, 1991). For personal narratives by Polish officers who participated in the invasion, see Lech Kowalski, *Kryptonim Dunaj* (Warsaw: Ksiazka i Wiedza, 1992).

45. Otherwise known as the Heroes of the Ghetto Monument.

46. The average Pole was far less pleased with German chancellor Helmut Schmidt's reaction to the implementation of martial law in Poland in December 1981. For a detailed description of *Ostpolitik* and Polish reactions to it, see Timothy Garton Ash, *In Europe's Name: Germany and the Divided Continent* (New York: Random House, 1993).

47. Gales Stokes, *The Walls Came Tumbling Down: The Collapse of Communism in Eastern Europe* (New York: Oxford University Press, 1993), pp. 210-211.

48. For a highly informative survey of contemporary Poland's relations with its neighbors, see Czeslaw Mojsiewicz, et al., *Polska i jej nowi sasiedzi (1989-1993)* (Torun: Wydawnictwo Adam Marszalek, 1994).

49. Terry, *Poland's Place in Europe,* p. 357.

2

Domestic Politics and Foreign Policy, 1989–1993

Louisa Vinton

Foreign policy is the single issue on which Poland's fractious and divided political scene has managed to reach a lasting consensus. In the four years that followed the negotiated demise of communism in 1989, Polish foreign policy was guided by a single, steady hand. Foreign affairs minister Krzysztof Skubiszewski was the only Polish cabinet member to hold his post for this entire period, from the formation of the first noncommunist government in 1989 until the defeat of the Solidarity parties in the 1993 elections. In these four years, Skubiszewski survived five prime ministers, four changes of government, three national elections, and virtually unending political upheaval. Skubiszewski's consistent and principled conduct of Polish foreign policy made him the dean of Central European foreign ministers; it also won him lasting popularity among the public. Even after the assumption of power by the two "postcommunist" parties following the 1993 elections, which ended his term of office, the principles of *raison d'état* established by Skubiszewski remained the guideposts of Polish foreign policy. In presenting the outgoing foreign minister with a national medal of honor on 27 October 1993, the day the new, "postcommunist" government took office, President Lech Walesa aptly noted that "future students of Polish foreign policy will doubtless refer to the 'Skubiszewski era'—an era of assiduous effort to win Poland its worthy and rightful place on the international and European political scene."[1]

Consensus on foreign policy in the "Skubiszewski era" did not mean a lack of conflict, however. Foreign policy often sparked passionate political debates on both the substance and the conduct of foreign relations. More often than not, however, questions of substance were used as vehicles by Polish parties in their efforts to carve out a place for themselves on the domestic political scene rather than as tools to articulate demands for specific changes in foreign policy. The political parties had little effect on the practical conduct of Poland's foreign relations. This process of self definition was particularly evident in discussions of Poland's place in Europe and the nation's "Eastern policy."

Similarly, questions of institutional control over the definition and implementation of foreign policy reflected battles on the Polish political scene over the nature of the new democratic political system, the contours of which still lacked final definition when Skubiszewski left office. Tension between presidential and parliamentary systems of government emerged with particular force in the struggle over the right to define security policy and guide the military. Institutional conflict over this issue came to a head in early 1992 and provided the single occasion on which domestic infighting threatened the Skubiszewski consensus. The engine of conflict here was friction over domestic political prerogatives rather than rival foreign policy visions.

THE SKUBISZEWSKI CONSENSUS

The chief preoccupation of Polish foreign policy in the Skubiszewski era was to buttress the sovereignty regained with the collapse of communism. In a country whose historical experience had so often been one of limited sovereignty or outright foreign domination, the imperatives of *racja stanu [raison d'état]* induced a solemnity among politicians that other issues failed to command. An independent professional among well-meaning Solidarity amateurs, Skubiszewski likewise won a political respect that few could challenge or rival. These factors helped build consensus around the three goals that guided Skubiszewski's foreign policy: securing and strengthening independence, instituting Poland's "return to Europe," and pursuing friendly relations with all neighboring states based on equality, international standards, and the inviolability of borders.

The constancy of these goals did not mean that Polish foreign policy was stable in this period. Poland's international environment changed dramatically between 1989 and 1993. Although these changes had Polish roots—they were in large part the result of the peaceful revolution initiated in Poland that, with the sanction of Soviet Communist Party General Secretary Mikhail Gorbachev, set in motion a reverse "domino effect" in the communist bloc—they reflected processes that Poland had little or no power to influence. Having begun the postcommunist period with three countries on its borders, by 1993 Poland had seven independent states as neighbors. Looking eastward, Poland's situation seemed almost to come full circle in this period, as a resurgent Russia began in 1993 to emit "neo-imperial" signals reminiscent of the final phases of Soviet domination. Given Poland's still elusive goal of integration with Western security and economic structures, this shift created a new sense of threat. Looking westward, the new star in Poland's constellation was its exemplary relations with a reunited Germany: a reversal of potentially momentous significance in the history of Polish-German relations. These new external opportunities and constraints were far more important than domestic political concerns in determining shifts in Polish foreign policy.

Poland's foreign policy between 1989 and 1993 can be divided roughly into four periods. With the exception of the initial, transitional period following the elections of 1989, in which Poland succeeded in uncoupling its domestic political system from its position in international relations, the different stages in Poland's often dramatic political evolution into a multiparty democracy do not follow this structure.

The initial transitional period of cautious self-limitation, in 1989 and early 1990, reflected the delicate position in which the nation found itself after the roundtable talks and the "contractual" elections of 1989. At this time, continued allegiance to the Warsaw Pact and the Council for Mutual Economic Assistance (CMEA) was the price Poland paid for the right to undertake its domestic experiment in the peaceful transfer of power to a noncommunist government. From the very start, however, Poland signaled its determination to "hollow out" these alliances, to disengage their ideological functions from their role in providing security.

As Poland's neighbors likewise undertook to dismantle communism, ending Poland's international isolation, this initial caution evolved into a pioneering "dualism" in relations with the Soviet Union. In promoting this "dualism," Skubiszewski strove to balance the desire to recognize the strivings for independence of the Baltic States and Ukraine with the pragmatic need to avoid antagonizing the central Soviet authorities, particularly given the ongoing attempt to negotiate the withdrawal of Soviet troops from Polish territory. This dualism was evident during Skubiszewski's first official visit to the Soviet Union in October 1990, when the Polish foreign minister signed separate declarations of friendship with the Russian Federation and with Ukraine.[2] Poland was particularly concerned to show support to Lithuania, which declared independence in March 1990. Without moving to resume formal interstate relations, Skubiszewski made clear that Baltic "aspirations to independence enjoy Polish support—within the bounds set by international law." By this, the foreign minister meant that Lithuania should negotiate Soviet assent to its new status. This delicate policy of "dualism" was called overly meek by some domestic critics, but Skubiszewski consistently argued that Poland was testing the limits with this innovation. In addition, he stressed, quiet pragmatism was more useful than gestures and empty declarations.

The dismantling of the Soviet Union offered Poland a real window of opportunity. Russia's early attempts to comply with Western standards of international conduct, in the period from late 1991 through 1992, allowed Poland new room to maneuver and seemed to clear the way for Poland's integration into Western European security and economic structures. Having successfully negotiated the withdrawal of former Soviet (later Russian) troops, Skubiszewski concentrated on building the legal framework for relations with each of Poland's neighbors. With the exception of Lithuania, new bilateral treaties confirming mutual sovereignty, the inviolability of borders, and the rights of ethnic minorities were signed with all neighbors by mid-1992.[3] Poland strove to "Europeanize" its foreign relations with its newly independent eastern neighbors. The drafting of treaties based on European standards was seen not only as a means of ensuring a secure international environment but also, by expanding the web of European standards eastward, as a form of preparation for Poland's membership in Western European structures. Similarly, Poland's efforts to coordinate with Hungary and Czechoslovakia within the Visegrad "triangle" in this period were viewed as means of demonstrating maturity on the international stage—as a form of practical entrance exam for the European Community.

By the end of the Skubiszewski era, however, Poland's room to maneuver had narrowed once again, due to the rise of "neo-imperial" trends in Russia on the one hand and growing isolationist sentiment in Europe on the other. These changed circumstances presented Skubiszewski's successor, Foreign Affairs Minister Andrzej Olechowski, with new challenges and encouraged a more cautious and explicitly pragmatic approach to Russia. Still, the political consensus as to Poland's foreign policy priorities remained intact. The return to power of the "postcommunist" parties—whose predecessors had embodied Poland's subjugation to Soviet dominance—did not alter foreign policy goals, despite the parties' prior criticism of some of Skubiszewski's policies. The leaders of the Social Democracy of the Polish Republic (SdRP), the direct successor to the Communist Party, for example, were part of a parliamentary delegation that traveled to Moscow in March 1994 to emphasize that Poland's goal of joining both the European Union (EU) and the North Atlantic Treaty Organization (NATO) remained unchanged. Similarly, receiving a delegation from the North Atlantic Assembly on 18 April 1994, Sejm speaker Jozef Oleksy, a leader of the ruling Democratic Left Alliance (SLD), picked up precisely where the Solidarity forces had left off, pressing for a timetable and clear criteria for Polish membership in NATO. "Full membership in NATO and the EU are the best guarantee for Poland," Oleksy said.[4]

THE IMPERATIVES OF TRANSITION

The strength of Poland's foreign policy consensus in the Skubiszewski period owed much to the novelty of having a foreign policy at all. Until the roundtable breakthrough in 1989, foreign policy was circumscribed by Poland's subordination to the Soviet Union, which dictated the country's domestic political structure as well as its place in the international order. Membership in the Warsaw Pact was synonymous with Communist Party rule. In its domestic structure, of course, Poland had always been a fairly heretical member of the Communist bloc, as the party strove to neutralize the persistent disaffection of workers and intellectuals. The experience of the Solidarity movement of 1980-81 had boiled down the Polish definition of communism to a bare minimum: the "leading role" of the Communist Party in Poland; state control of all but a margin of economic activity; and obeisance to the Soviet Union in foreign policy. As Gorbachev undertook cautious reformist steps in the Soviet Union in the mid-1980s, the Polish United Workers Party (PZPR) gained new room for "socialist renewal," its attempt to revive the moribund command economy while at the same time marginalizing the Solidarity opposition. But such experimentation was still conducted within the framework of one-party rule, the sine qua non of communism; there was no question of devolving power to independent forces.

Until 1989, then, any change in Poland's domestic political arrangement had severe external repercussions. The threat of a Warsaw Pact invasion loomed in the background whenever the party's domestic policing was insufficient to limit challenges to the system, at least until Gorbachev introduced his "new thinking" in foreign policy. The uncoupling of the domestic political system from Poland's international entanglements was thus a major breakthrough. This departure did not take place by plan; it was the unforeseen result of the PZPR's strategy to neutralize the Solidarity opposition by drawing it, in a marginal role, into the official structures of power. At the roundtable talks of 1989, the party offered the opposition a key bargain: the PZPR would agree to legalize the independent trade union and other organizations in exchange for the opposition's agreement to take part in fixed elections, in which only 35 percent of the seats in the parliament, or Sejm, would be open to independents. The opposition was also asked to accede to the creation of a strong presidency, which both sides assumed that PZPR First Secretary General Wojciech Jaruzelski would fill. The presidency was viewed as the guardian of the existing system, with powers designed to prevent change from assuming revolutionary proportions. To sweeten for Solidarity the bitter pill of participation in undemocratic procedures, the party also offered to hold fully free elections to a newly created upper house of parliament, the Senate.

The roundtable talks were themselves a bold innovation in communist practice. In sitting down at the bargaining table with Solidarity, the PZPR implicitly recognized the autonomy of organizations independent of its control. But even this revolutionary departure paled in comparison to the "contractual" elections that followed the talks. These elections overturned the calculations of both sides, landing a fatal blow to Polish communism.[5] Both the PZPR and the moderate opposition grouped around Solidarity chairman Lech Walesa had assumed that the legalization of the union was the opposition's chief gain in the roundtable agreement; Solidarity's participation in fixed elections was seen as the opposition's chief concession. The opposition believed the roundtable talks would open the way for a slow, evolutionary process, in which the now legal independent union would organize on the sidelines in preparation for eventual free elections, tentatively planned for 1993, while the Communist Party would push ahead at the center with economic and social reforms.

The elections quickly became a plebiscite on communism, however, and the outcome was a landslide victory for Solidarity. Voters seized on the requirement that they cross out all but the names of the candidates they wished to support and drew an assertive x through all the establishment candidates. All but one of Solidarity's 161 Sejm candidates and 92 of its 100 Senate candidates breezed to victory in the first round. In contrast, only five of the 299 candidates for seats controlled by the PZPR and its allies won the required 50 percent in the first round; three of these had an endorsement from Solidarity, while the other two ran unopposed on the ill-fated "national list." In the second round,

Solidarity completed its triumph by picking up all but one of the seats for which it was allowed to compete. The rest of the party's seats were duly filled, but with humiliatingly low support. PZPR Central Committee spokesman Jan Bisztyga appeared on television to concede defeat. The elections had a "plebiscitary character," he acknowledged, "and Solidarity won a clear majority."[6]

The election outcome suggested that the roundtable contract was already obsolete, a realization that nevertheless took weeks or even months to sink in. At first, the two sides attempted to push on as they had anticipated they would before the elections: the opposition turned to the task of rebuilding the independent trade union, while the party undertook to form a new government. But the revelation of public hostility to communism in the elections was too powerful a force; life could not go on as before. The PZPR began rapidly to self-destruct. The party's prearranged majority in the Sejm was insufficient to prevent a power vacuum from emerging. In order to remain true to the letter and spirit of the roundtable bargain, the Solidarity opposition found itself forced again and again to shore up the weakened party. The last straw was the election of the president on 19 July 1989. Only the collaboration of a handful of Solidarity deputies made Jaruzelski's victory possible; even then, his margin of victory was a humiliating single vote. At this point, despite the Solidarity leader's initial hesitance to accept a formal role in government, Walesa moved to bring the political situation into alignment with the postelection balance of power. "When an opposition wins an election so convincingly, it takes over the entire government," he said in a statement on 25 July. "If the [PZPR-led] coalition has not matured to this decision, we will remain an opposition and create a shadow cabinet. It's all or nothing."[7]

Once Walesa had hammered together a coalition with two erstwhile allies of the communist party—the United Peasant Party (ZSL) and the Democratic Party (SD)—the PZPR did in fact mature to this decision. Tadeusz Mazowiecki was confirmed as Poland's first noncommunist prime minister on 24 August 1989; his four party coalition government was voted into office on 12 September 1989. As the price for its agreement, the PZPR demanded a hefty share of ministerial posts, including the strategic defense and internal affairs portfolios. This configuration made the first Solidarity government a hybrid creation, part opposition, part establishment. On taking office, it thus faced many unknowns. Would the PZPR accept defeat gracefully, or would it make a subversive attempt to roll back Solidarity's gains? Would the new government be able to exercise its will? Would the security apparatus, formerly under the PZPR's exclusive control, demonstrate loyalty? Would the Warsaw Pact accede to the party's decision to yield power? It was these uncertainties that had made the opposition hesitant to take formal power in the first place; at each step it was creating situations for which there were no precedents. In particular, Poland's abandonment of the party's "leading role" provided a practical test of the Warsaw Pact's tolerance for deviations from established practice.

The communist surrender of power was an outcome that neither side had foreseen or intended; indeed, it seems unlikely that the roundtable strategy would have been attempted had the PZPR had a more realistic sense of its chances in the elections. The accidental nature of Solidarity's triumph had important foreign policy consequences: it offered the first clear proof that the Brezhnev doctrine was, in fact, dead. Despite soothing statements from Gorbachev as the process was unfolding, Poland had no real guarantee against outside intervention—until it did not take place. While Soviet signals were reassuring and at times even encouraging in 1989, many of Poland's other communist neighbors were openly hostile to the appointment of a Solidarity prime minister.[8] The Romanian Communist Party issued what amounted to an appeal for Warsaw Pact intervention to prevent the PZPR from yielding power to "reactionary circles" and thereby undermining socialism and lending support to the NATO enemy.[9] While this was the most extreme declaration, unease at the Polish precedent was deep elsewhere, especially in Czechoslovakia and the German Democratic Republic (GDR).

The desire to shelter Poland's opportunity for domestic change led Solidarity to embrace, from the outset, the existing international order, including Poland's membership in the Warsaw Pact and the CMEA.[10] Mazowiecki accepted this equation upon taking office. In his address to the Sejm after winning confirmation as prime minister on 24 August and again in his inaugural address on 12 September, Mazowiecki pledged to uphold Poland's current commitments, at least as far as the country's external behavior was concerned.

> Our opening to Europe as a whole does not mean we are discarding the ties and obligations we have had until now. If we repeat today that the new government will respect Poland's alliance obligations, that is not a tactical maneuver of appeasement. It derives from our understanding of Polish raison d'état and our analysis of the international situation. If there comes a day when European security will not require military blocs, we will bid them farewell without regret. We believe that this will happen. Today, it is important that all pacts and military alliances affect only the external security of the countries involved and not their domestic political or economic order. The government that I head will respect the international agreements binding on Poland and fulfill all the obligations stemming from them.[11]

The point, Mazowiecki indicated, was to hollow out the Warsaw Pact, to neutralize its ideological control functions without explicitly rejecting them.

This was the reasoning behind the new government's oft-repeated distinction that "spheres of security can never mean spheres of influence." Whether the Warsaw Pact was viable without its domestic controlling functions was another question—one the Polish government chose not to address head-on. Similarly, although Solidarity was committed to the ideal of national self determination, the Mazowiecki government signalled its disinclination to export Polish innovations to neighboring states, lest this invite the early demise of Poland's experiment. Gestures of support for opposition movements in other countries were left to the efforts of public diplomacy, and Solidarity activists were frequent guests in Kiev and Vilnius.

The same self limitation was at work in Mazowiecki's allocation of the ministries of Defense (MON) and Internal Affairs (MSW) to the PZPR. This arrangement, insisted on by the party as a precondition for its assent to a noncommunist government, reflected the opposition's awareness that the military and police were considered to embody the "continuity of the state." They were the pillars of domestic party control; the army was also subordinated to the Soviet command via the Warsaw Pact. Leaving "insiders" in charge of the two ministries was seen as a way to insure that the security forces did not rebel against the new order, although at the cost of insulating them, at least temporarily, from reform. As Mazowiecki told the new Solidarity parliamentarians, "the party that controls the army and the police cannot remain in the opposition."[12] The prime minister nonetheless fought for the right to choose from the party's candidates to head these ministries.

The PZPR did not maintain control over the Ministry of Foreign Affairs (MSZ), however, although leading figures in both the party and the opposition had initially assumed that the MSZ would be part of the party's non-negotiable minimum. The bargaining over the foreign affairs portfolio was heated and protracted. The Solidarity side won out in the end, in large part, it seems, because of Mazowiecki's personal determination to begin laying the foundation for a sovereign foreign policy. Mazowiecki's closest associate during the government's formation, Waldemar Kuczynski (who was later named Poland's first privatization minister), has written in his memoirs that the new prime minister "attached great importance to foreign policy, and thus to the MSZ; in a certain sense, he considered it a sphere reserved for himself. Foreign policy was an instrument to rebuild independence and Poland's image as an independent state."[13] Kuczynski notes that Mazowiecki hoped to "bite off" as much as possible of the party's "key triangle: MSW-MON-MSZ." Of these three, Mazowiecki believed that foreign affairs was the ministry with which the PZPR would most readily part. Part of the bargain that granted Solidarity the MSZ, however, was that PZPR figures stay on as deputy ministers.

The prime minister's selection of Skubiszewski, a political independent, for the ministerial post in the MSZ eased some of the party's objections. A respected professor of international law with deep roots in Poznan, Skubiszewski had agreed in late 1986 to join the Consultative Council set up by Jaruzelski in his role as head of state. The council, a strictly advisory body, met irregularly until 1989.[14] In a way, it was a timid precursor to the roundtable talks, as it was designed to win the authorities credibility by suggesting that they were consulting with respected figures on the pressing problems of the day. In practice, the council amounted to little more than a talking shop; it had no real power or influence. The one innovation was that its deliberations were published in uncensored form in the low circulation journal *Rada Narodowa*. Much of the democratic opposition criticized those who joined the council, as it was seen as a decorative body designed to sow the seeds of hostility between the opposition's "realists" and its "radicals." The handful of independents who joined the council defended their decision as presenting an opportunity to voice public concerns directly to the authorities. Shortly after agreeing to join the council, for example, Skubiszewski and another controversial member, Wladyslaw Sila-Nowicki, a one time legal advisor to Walesa, appealed to the Constitutional Tribunal to repeal the 1982 law dissolving Solidarity, on the grounds that it violated international labor conventions ratified by Poland. The Solidarity underground nonetheless continued to regard the council's independents with considerable suspicion.

Skubiszewski also had ties with the Church hierarchy, having served on the Primate's Social Council from 1981 to 1984. These ties placed Skubiszewski in the ranks of those who strove to pursue change in the 1980s in a pragmatic, positivistic, even legalistic way. In the bipolar conditions of 1989, he was neither fish nor fowl, at least in terms of affiliation. As Kuczynski puts it, "Professor Skubiszewski . . . was not so clearly identified with the opposition, but he was 'ours' and not 'theirs.'"[15] Skubiszewski's desire to pursue a sovereign foreign policy was clear from his first actions on taking office, which included a stiff reprimand issued to Romania for its suggestion of "fraternal assistance" on the day after the government took office.

HOW BINDING A BARGAIN?

Only months after Mazowiecki had negotiated the construction of a government that respected the prerogatives of the Communist Party and elaborated the tenets of a self-limiting foreign policy, much of the rest of the region was racing ahead unhindered by any such encumbrances. Poland's breakthrough set in motion revolutionary changes in the rest of the bloc, but, ironically, the self restraint that made Poland's initial compromise possible soon began to act as a brake on progress toward the goals of democracy and full national sovereignty. Poland's transitional structures were an advance over communism but soon appeared outmoded given what neighboring countries managed to attain once barriers previously perceived as insurmountable were removed. This crumbling of the old order occurred with a speed and scope no one had anticipated. In the most glaring example, most of Poland's neighbors staged free elections, the most obvious precondition for democracy, in 1989 or 1990, while the roundtable timetable had assumed that Poland would stage free elections, at the earliest, in 1993 (in fact, they were held in October 1991). The nagging sense that Poland was lagging behind set the stage for the decisive political dilemma of the first postcommunist years: when—if ever—to abandon the substance and, more important, the self-limiting philosophy of the roundtable bargain?

The crux of the problem was that the institutions created to fulfill the purposes of the roundtable talks were ill-suited to the challenges that emerged when the Solidarity forces took power rather than remained, as anticipated, a vocal opposition on the sidelines. Despite Solidarity's election "landslide" and subsequent assumption of a controlling role in the government, the political proportions in the "contractual" Sejm remained those prearranged at the roundtable. The electoral law, with its provisions allowing the state authorities to assign seats to particular parties, was meant to be valid only for a single term; but, until a new law could be drafted, it remained in force. The presidency was structured to enable Jaruzelski to guard the fundamental principles of the socialist system and guarantee Poland's adherence to the Warsaw Pact. The constitution was still the Stalinist version from 1952; although it was amended to introduce the presidency and the Senate in 1989 and again at the end of the same year to remove the most offending "communist" clauses, it was hardly suited to a nation with a new democratic order. Finally, the political bargain entailed in the roundtable agreement implied that the Communist Party and its allies would not face collective retribution, or even lose their acquired privileges, provided they yielded their power without violence or any attempt to subvert the new order.

The roundtable thus cast a long shadow. The Mazowiecki government could initially count on loyal cooperation from the "contractual" Sejm; this multiparty consensus helped Poland to embark on the ambitious program of economic transformation that was designed by Deputy Prime Minister and Finance Minister Leszek Balcerowicz. As the "Balcerowicz plan" began to exact social costs, however, the parliament grew restless. The party ferment begun with the 1989 elections soon rendered the parliament strangely amorphous, as the original parties to the roundtable agreement dissolved and metamorphosed. Under democratizing pressure from below, the PZPR and the United Peasant Party changed their names and elected new "reformist" leaders; the Solidarity forces represented in the Citizens' Parliamentary Caucus (OKP) began to divide into rival factions. The question thus arose: When should Poland stage fully free elections? Would it be better to clear the air and elect a fully legitimate and representative parliament? Or to push on with an arrangement that seemed to be working and hold off on elections until the Balcerowicz plan had had enough time to show results?

The same dilemma—when to draw a line and end the transition—was reflected in dozens of issues. On taking power, Mazowiecki had elevated to a guiding principle the "rule of law." The rigorous application of this principle led the government at first to shy away from attempts to divest the PZPR of its vast assets, except where it could be proven that these had been unlawfully appropriated from the state. The state halted subsidies to political parties; but what of the disproportionate wealth acquired over 40 years by the former "official" parties? What of the PZPR's vast publishing empire, RSW "Prasa," which controlled virtually all of the nation's newspapers and the "Ruch" press distribution system? Here Mazowiecki was only driven to take action—to ask the Sejm to nationalize the party's assets—when it came to light that the PZPR had been secretly parceling out its property to loyal followers.[16] And what about President Jaruzelski? He proved a loyal and cooperative partner for the government and made no effort to disrupt democratic reform. But to many in the Solidarity camp, he remained an unacceptable symbol of martial law and, given his power to veto legislation, a potential impediment to far-reaching reforms. As Poland's neighbors elected standard bearers of the democratic opposition to fill their presidencies, his status was increasingly an embarrassment. Should Jaruzelski be forced to step down to allow Lech Walesa, a leader with genuine national support, to take his place? Or was this premature?

The battle over these issues took place exclusively within the ranks of the former opposition, as the PZPR and its allies had withdrawn from the field and seemed (at the time) to be in their death throes. Personified in the growing friction between Mazowiecki and Walesa, this conflict eventually erupted with full force in the presidential campaign of 1990, initiated with Walesa's famous call for a "war at the top."[17] In the battle between Walesa and Mazowiecki, questions of personal power were intertwined with policy differences. One of the driving forces behind Walesa's campaign for the presidency was resentment that the prime minister and his associates were failing to acknowledge the Solidarity leader's political preeminence. Walesa complained that Mazowiecki's supporters were attempting to control all the leadership posts in the new political system, an approach, he argued, that threatened "to replace one monopoly with another." Mazowiecki's followers countered with appeals for unity, arguing that a moratorium on divisions in the Solidarity movement was essential to maintain public tolerance for the hardships of the government's economic transformation program.

But more was at work than rivalry for the upper hand in the Solidarity camp; the presidential contest also centered on the proper tempo of political and economic change. Walesa's campaign slogan was a call for *przyspieszenie*, or to "speed things up," whereas the Mazowiecki campaign proclaimed its faith in *sila spokoju*, or "the force of calm," that the prime minister embodied. Walesa's followers charged that the Mazowiecki government was moving too slowly to take advantage of the opportunities presented by the collapse of communism. The Center Alliance, the coalition set up in mid-1990 as a political base for Walesa's campaign, argued that a Walesa presidency would prevent "the petrifaction of the transition."[18] Jaruzelski's continued tenure, they charged, symbolized the hybrid arrangement that left much power in communist hands.

Mazowiecki's camp countered that Walesa's call to speed up change raised unreal expectations about the speed with which economic prosperity could be attained. Mazowiecki stood for evolutionary, gradual, and, above all, legal means of procedure, whereas Walesa argued for pragmatic shortcuts, such as the granting of "special powers" to the government to enable it to bypass the roundtable Sejm. Walesa demanded a decisive break with the past; Mazowiecki emphasized the need for stability. Eschewing "witch hunts," Mazowiecki's supporters depicted demands for a blanket ouster of the former *nomenklatura* as an unhealthy lust for revenge, while Walesa's supporters argued that leaving former officials in positions of power jeopardized reform.

The Walesa-Mazowiecki conflict cleaved the Solidarity movement in two. The two sides long traded blame for the breach, never resolving the issue but leaving much bad blood. With the benefit of hindsight, Walesa has conceded that opening the division may have been unwise, as it left the Solidarity camp too weak and too preoccupied with infighting to ward off competition for public support from the "postcommunist" forces. Because the division took place along the lines of personal allegiances rather than deep-seated policy differences, moreover, it exacerbated the political fragmentation that was probably inevitable in the initial postcommunist period. Walesa's victory did not markedly accelerate change or generate a promised "breakthrough," mainly because the economic issues most important to the public were too complicated to solve overnight. To the dismay of his supporters, the president, once in office, backed away from "speeding things up" and chose to buttress Balcerowicz's position, blocking overhasty tinkering with the transformation program.

In the process, Walesa staked out an independent, if increasingly isolated, position in Polish politics. He remained the pivotal force in politics, relying more on his presidential powers and tactical skills than on consistent backing from any of the Solidarity parties or the public. As Walesa pursued his own agenda from Belweder (the presidential palace) with support from shifting political alliances, the battle between the "accelerators" and the "evolutionists" raged on, even as these two groups each splintered into ideologically diverse political parties. It lost none of its ferocity until the Solidarity forces were elbowed off the political stage. The Sejm elections of 1991, like the presidential elections of the preceding year, were fought out over the central question of whether to "complete" the Solidarity revolution. The Solidarity parties gave this issue varying definitions. The conflict increasingly focused on the "Balcerowicz plan," with the "accelerators" pledging to supersede it with speedier remedies for the pains of nascent capitalism and the "evolutionists" stressing the need for patient continuity. The "accelerators" also turned to anticommunist rhetoric, proposing to "decommunize" state structures and the economy. Mounting a persistent challenge from the political margins, meanwhile, the postcommunist forces echoed the accelerators' attacks on the Balcerowicz plan but shared the evolutionists' disinclination to attempt a final reckoning with communism. This combination ultimately proved a winner in the 1993 elections.

Foreign policy issues were not central to any of Poland's four national elections in the period from 1989 to 1993. In fact, they were all but absent, a powerful testimony to the strength and durability of the foreign policy consensus built by Skubiszewski. Where foreign policy did emerge as a contested issue was as a reflection of the domestic battle between the "accelerators," or "radicals," and the "evolutionists," or "realists," over the need to make a clean break with the past. As was typical in this contest, the accelerators, who exercised power only briefly, during Jan Olszewski's term of office, were more concerned about symbolic issues, national self assertion, and the traditional definition of sovereignty—a strong army—while the "evolutionists" were more pragmatic and defined a strong economy as the basis for an independent state.

SOVIET TROOPS AND POLISH SOVEREIGNTY

The Soviet troop withdrawal exposed the foreign policy dimension of the battle between the accelerators and the evolutionists. By mid-1990, part of the Solidarity camp—for the most part those activists associated with Walesa's presidential campaign who later broke off to form "center-right" parties—had begun to criticize Skubiszewski for what they charged was a lack of dynamism in Polish foreign policy. Skubiszewski's priorities, such critics argued, reflected a self-limiting set of assumptions that left Poland able to react only passively to foreign policy developments, rather than to anticipate and steer them in a direction beneficial to Poland. This approach, critics argued, was particularly evident in Poland's "Eastern policy"—the term used to describe relations with the Soviet Union and its restive constituent republics. As political divisions sharpened within the Solidarity camp on the one hand and the Baltic States' efforts to regain sovereignty met with resistance from Moscow on the other, criticism of Skubiszewski began to focus on his presumed willingness to subordinate Poland's interests to Soviet priorities. Skubiszewski's policies were mired in roundtable thinking, such critics charged; this wrongly assumed that Soviet interests were immutable. But Poland's international environment was changing rapidly; the time had come for the sort of departures that Poland could not afford to risk in 1989, they said, extending as far as the formal recognition of Lithuania.

Such charges that Skubiszewski had "roundtable blinders" with respect to the East were persistent, but they always reflected a minority viewpoint. The specific issues to which they referred changed over time, but the remedy the critics proposed was constant: a more assertive, or even hard-line approach to Moscow (whether the central Soviet authorities or, later, the Russian government), combined with more explicit encouragement for the non-Russian neighboring states striving to establish their sovereignty. Skubiszewski was urged to more strongly demonstrate democratic Poland's commitment to the right of national self-determination. Before Poland recognized the independence of the Baltic States in the wake of the failed coup of August 1991, for example, the government's foreign policy was criticized for missing a historic opportunity to redress Lithuania's resentment at the treatment it had received at the hands of interwar Poland. Slightly later, the same claims were made about Ukraine. The government was attacked for dragging its feet on the abolition of the Warsaw Pact and the CMEA, and later, in early 1992, it was criticized for adopting too timid an approach in seeking membership in NATO. Perhaps most controversial, the government was accused, in late 1990 and 1991, of having failed to expedite the departure of the 50,000 Soviet troops that were stationed on Polish territory when communism collapsed.

Poland's approach to the Soviet Union and, later, Russia was consistently cautious and pragmatic. It was—and remains—a matter of heated debate, however, how much this caution was the result of "objective" constraints and how much the lingering effects of a roundtable mindset. Dissenting views on foreign policy often seemed to reflect differences (or simple ignorance) as to the style appropriate to the conduct of diplomacy. Skubiszewski was a firm believer in the art of the possible and always eschewed loud declarations and demonstrative gestures. It was not enough to make demands, he argued; one also had to have the capacity to achieve them. For this reason, Skubiszewski expressed occasional impatience with Lithuania's repeated pleas for international recognition throughout 1990 and 1991. Sovereignty was to be attained not through declarations, he insisted, but rather through the arduous process of securing the "attributes of statehood." The foreign minister was also adept at protocol, the subtleties of which his critics seemed not to grasp or appreciate. There was much quiet symbolism, for example, in Skubiszewski's "dualistic" approach to the Baltic States, Belarus, and Ukraine, which involved giving officials from these countries nearly the same diplomatic treatment as would be extended to official visitors from recognized states. In addition, most criticisms of Skubiszewski's policies were made well after the fact, with the benefit of hindsight. This practice, which often served purely domestic political purposes, suggested that judging the limits of the feasible in relations with the Soviet Union (or Russia) was no simple task. Finally, and most important, Skubiszewski's critics often seemed to be venting frustration at Poland's inability—as a medium-sized country with a weak economy, wedged between Germany and the Soviet Union—simply to impose its will on the outside world.

The difficulty of distinguishing between the two factors—objective constraints and domestic political priorities—is evident in the controversy over the withdrawal of Soviet troops from Poland. For the new democratic leaders of Hungary and Czechoslovakia, the speedy withdrawal of Soviet troops was a priority, whereas the Mazowiecki government chose not to press the issue. With evident Soviet assent, Czechoslovakia concluded an agreement on the troop withdrawal in February 1990. Hungary signed a similar accord in March 1990. The last Soviet troops left both countries by the end of June 1991. In contrast, negotiations on Poland's troop withdrawal dragged on for more than a year after they opened in November 1990. A final agreement was signed only in May 1992; the last Russian troops did not leave the country until 17 September 1993.[19] By the time the Polish government moved to open official talks on the withdrawal, the Soviet stance, initially accommodating, had hardened, as Soviet politics underwent a creeping conservative reorientation in late 1990 and 1991 that culminated in the botched August coup. Particularly when the outcome of the negotiations was still in doubt, members of the Walesa camp tended to cite this apparent miscalculation by the Mazowiecki government as a glaring example of an overly conciliatory attitude toward the Soviet Union.

Mazowiecki's stance on Soviet troops reflected security concerns arising from German reunification. The foreign policy priority for 1990 was to secure internationally binding guarantees for Poland's western border on the Oder-Neisse line; this issue overshadowed all others. When reunification emerged as an imminent prospect, the government mounted a massive diplomatic offensive to ensure that Poland was able to present its views during the "2 + 4" talks between the two German states and the four Allied powers. This offensive had Jaruzelski's wholehearted support. Poland's chief concerns were to eliminate the remaining legal ambiguities in the stance of the German Federal Republic (FRG) and to secure a binding treaty to regulate the border issue as a precondition for reunification. Polish officials were careful to stress that, in Poland's view, the German nation had a right to determine its own fate, but at the same time they demanded that the new country be safely imbedded in a security arrangement that would protect Poland's interests. Poland achieved its goals, and a treaty confirming the permanence of the existing western border was signed in Warsaw on 14 November 1990.

There was virtually unanimous support for the government's diplomatic offensive. Memories of the Nazi occupation were still very much alive among the public. One of the central themes cultivated by communist propaganda, moreover, was the danger of German "revisionism"; the party had often used alleged threats to the Oder-Neisse border as a realpolitik style argument to justify Poland's alliance with the Soviet Union. Still, Mazowiecki and Skubiszewski did face some domestic criticism for the vehemence with which they addressed the border issue. Few in Poland believed that a reunited Germany would actually challenge the existing border. German chancellor Helmut Kohl's ambiguous statements and omissions caused considerable concern, but they were generally attributed to a desire not to antagonize the expellee lobby in the advance of elections rather than seen as a sign of revisionist thinking. The Polish government took the long view, however. Poland's historical experience with a unified German state had not been positive, Skubiszewski stressed. Moreover, an internationally guaranteed agreement would remove the prime strategic reason for Poland's reliance on the Soviet Union and thus, willy-nilly, draw Poland into West Europe's orbit. When it came, the breakthrough represented "the true end of Yalta,"[20] as the government's spokesman put it, because Poland's borders ceased to be the disputed outcome of third party agreements.

The government's tactics in its border offensive implied that Germany posed a bigger potential threat to Poland than did the Soviet Union. It was here that critics found fault with the government's approach, as Mazowiecki allowed settlement of the "German question" to overshadow the Soviet troops issue. Indeed, while asserting the inevitability of an eventual withdrawal, the government indicated that the troops would have to stay on until an acceptable alternative security arrangement was found. At a press conference on 21

February 1990, Mazowiecki was asked about Gorbachev's recent offer to discuss the terms of the troops' departure, "if the government of the Republic of Poland expresses a corresponding desire."[21] Mazowiecki responded that "like every nation we would prefer that there were no foreign armies on our territory, but like every nation we must also look at our security realistically, from the perspective of the balance of forces, from the perspective of alliances, and we must assess from that perspective the continued presence of the [Soviet] forces."[22]

The thinking implicit in the government's approach was taken a step further in a front-page article in *Gazeta Wyborcza* by Janusz Reiter, a young opposition journalist who was later named Poland's ambassador to Germany.[23] The article, entitled "Why Those Troops," was published just as Poland was demanding a right to take part in the "2 + 4" talks. Reiter posed a provocative question: "Will we be more independent when the Soviet army leaves Poland?" The Soviet troops had always fulfilled a dual function, Reiter argued: as enforcing the communist order and as "part of the balance of power in Europe." The troops' domestic policing function had come to an end, he said, but they still had a role in the European security alignment that had become more crucial owing to the challenges posed by German reunification. "As paradoxical as it sounds," he said, "the Soviet troops in Poland could be an asset"—a counterbalance to the new Germany and a bargaining chip for future negotiations on European security. Accompanying Reiter's article was an illustration showing a man in a raincoat holding an umbrella in the shape of a five pointed Soviet star over his head.

The Mazowiecki government had from the outset put the troops issue on the back burner. The presence of the troops was regarded as an anomaly, and Skubiszewski emphasized in his address to the Sejm on 26 April 1990 that their removal was a "foregone conclusion."[24] But the government indicated that the withdrawal would be a long and gradual process, stretching over years. In the meantime, negotiations were opened to secure the removal of especially burdensome units and to revise the anachronistic legal agreements governing the "temporary stationing" of Soviet troops in order to ease the financial and ecological burden they imposed on Poland. Despite growing public impatience, the Mazowiecki government doggedly maintained its position until September 1990, when Skubiszewski presented the Soviet government with a note proposing the rapid staging of negotiations on a troop withdrawal treaty. This note merely made "concrete" the positions the government had presented in previous bilateral talks, Skubiszewski said.[25] Subsequent statements by Polish officials indicated that Mazowiecki was relying on informal assurances from Gorbachev and Soviet foreign affairs minister Eduard Shevardnadze that, whenever Poland thought the time was right for the withdrawal, the Soviet Union would respond favorably. Deputy Defense Minister Janusz Onyszkiewicz told an interviewer in January 1991,

> The Soviet side constantly assured us that we could count on their understanding whenever the Polish government expressed its expectations with regard to the withdrawal of Soviet troops and the timing of the withdrawal. These explanations reassured us. Unfortunately the stance of the Soviet side has hardened enormously.[26]

In retrospect, the Mazowiecki government may have misjudged the stability and durability of the reform process in the Soviet Union. For final resolution, the troop withdrawal issue had to wait until the Soviet Union disintegrated and Boris Yeltsin came to power. In the intervening 18 months, Polish negotiators were forced again and again to backpedal, as the Soviet side ignored or rejected their proposed deadlines, and to declare their flexibility on the timing of the withdrawal.[27] The Soviet command did formally initiate the pull-out on 8 April 1991, but this was a unilateral decision that thwarted the Polish goal of securing a mutually agreed timetable. Meanwhile, Soviet forces commander Colonel General Viktor Dubynin raised hackles with his criticism of Polish ingratitude for the Soviet "liberation" in 1944 and statements to the effect that his troops would leave Poland when and how they themselves chose.[28] The outcome of the August coup broke this stalemate, and a withdrawal treaty was initialed in December 1991. A few remaining contested issues were settled during Walesa's May 1992 visit to Moscow, when the treaty was signed; the troops departed slightly ahead of schedule. But the experience was a frustrating one for Polish diplomacy.

The difficulties encountered when Skubiszewski finally opened talks explain why the troops became a slogan used to criticize as overly timid both the government's foreign and domestic policies. The issue in fact occasioned one of the first rifts between Walesa (then still Solidarity chairman, with headquarters in Gdansk rather than in Warsaw) and the Mazowiecki government. For Walesa, the government's stance on the troop withdrawal was evidence that the process of change in Poland was moving too slowly and that "acceleration" was necessary. During a meeting with Soviet ambassador Vladimir Brovikov in Gdansk on 18 January 1990, Walesa abandoned all diplomatic niceties and, before Brovikov could say a word, demanded flatly that Soviet troops leave Poland by the end of the year. The Solidarity leader's press secretary noted that Walesa "spoke to a representative of the Soviet authorities in a tone for which all Poles were waiting."[29] Indeed, the call for a swift withdrawal proved popular with a public that identified the troops as an infringement on Polish sovereignty. As on many other occasions, Walesa meant this statement as a signal for the government to take action; in his parlance, he was passing the soccer ball to the forward to set up a goal.

But Mazowiecki failed to heed Walesa's prodding—and indeed seems to have resented it, for both substantive and power political reasons. It clashed with the government's ordering of Poland's strategic priorities; it deviated from the cautious and gradual philosophy of change; and, finally, it infringed on the prime minister's ambition to steer the ship of state himself, without prompting from figures and forces outside of Poland's purely constitutional structures (even from someone as important as Walesa). Increasingly frustrated at being excluded from the government's major decisions and feeling himself to be the proper center for Polish politics, the Solidarity leader continued to push his own agenda. In February 1990, at the very point that the government's diplomatic offensive on the border question was picking up speed, Walesa told reporters that a reunited Germany posed no danger to Poland and that Soviet forces should be withdrawn from Poland "as soon as possible."[30] Walesa quickly reversed part of this statement to give wholehearted support to the government's demands for participation in the German reunification talks, but his reservations on the troops remained.

They were one of the many themes voiced in Walesa's successful presidential campaign of 1990, although Walesa himself did not spotlight the issue. The troops issue was a focus of concern for the Center Alliance and their mouthpiece, *Tygodnik Solidarnosc.* The presidential race, and the need to counter charges that Mazowiecki was moving too slowly to dismantle the vestiges of communism, may well have prompted the government to reverse its stance and open official withdrawal talks with the Soviet authorities in September 1990. Skubiszewski has conceded that this reversal was made under public pressure rather than as the result of any sense on the government's part that the troop presence posed a threat to Poland.[31]

The lesson that the "center right" forces drew from Poland's troop withdrawal experience was the need for an assertive, activist policy toward the Soviet Union (as well as its Russian successor). Aside from dwelling on lost opportunities and urging staunchness and dynamism, however, they did not have specific advice to offer on how to deal more effectively with an uncooperative Soviet side. As the troop talks ultimately suggested, the stance of the Polish government was largely irrelevant to the success of the withdrawal; the crucial variable was the attitude of the Soviet leadership (and their Russian heirs). The real lesson of the troop experience, then, was that Poland's ability to guide events was extremely limited and depended on the international alignment of forces. As Skubiszewski noted in response to criticism of the government's actions on the troops, "the issue was not to be solved by a demand from the Polish side, no matter how important the person voicing it."[32]

Walesa, now president, was himself to echo this argument in the aftermath of the failed Soviet coup in August 1991. Poland's reaction to the declaration of a state of emergency was sober and extremely cautious.[33] There was no condemnation of the coup attempt, no fiery rhetoric, and no declaration of support for Gorbachev or Yeltsin; both the president and the government seemed to be waiting for the outcome before acting. Walesa called for calm and stressed Poland's desire for friendly relations with the Soviet Union. "As a sovereign state we will continue to build democracy and carry on reforming our economy," he said. The government's statement said Poland's response to Soviet developments would rest on two principles: the defense of Polish national security and respect for the sovereignty of other countries. It also issued an understated warning of the futility of any resort to force, drawing on the experience of Solidarity in Poland: "We are firmly convinced that the course of history cannot be reversed," the statement read. Even as the coup collapsed, Walesa expressed only "cautious sympathy" in a ten minute telephone conversation with Yeltsin.

This caution infuriated Walesa's own camp—especially critics from his own advisory council—who squared off with the president during a discussion of "the Eastern crisis and Poland" on 28 August 1991.[34] The advisory council was composed of "center right" activists and experts who had backed Walesa's presidential campaign. It was headed by Zdzislaw Najder, the outsider Walesa had appointed to head the citizens' committee movement early in 1990 when he was mounting his offensive against the Mazowiecki camp. Over the course of 1991, Walesa's supporters gradually parted company with him, as it became clear he was unwilling to make dramatic policy departures (indeed, the creation of the advisory council was meant to serve as a political consolation prize after Walesa decided not to allow his supporters to dominate the government that was formed after Mazowiecki resigned). At the Belweder session, Najder launched a broadside against the foreign policy priorities then in force, arguing that Poland had wasted two years in "passive" and "reactive" behavior when "independent thinking" was essential. Skubiszewski's foreign policy had perpetuated a "client" relationship with the Soviet Union. In relations with the Baltic states, Belarus, and Ukraine, "we always lagged behind," waiting for a green light from Moscow. Jan Parys (who was later named defense minister in the ill-fated Olszewski government) charged that the errors in Polish foreign policy were so great that "someone ought to commit hara-kiri." "We must distinguish between what we want and what we can do," Walesa responded. A swift Soviet troop withdrawal, he added, "is our desire, not something we have the power to realize."[35]

This clash of views was typical of conflicts over foreign policy in Poland during the Skubiszewski era; it pitted a minority of "radicals" or "independence-oriented" activists *(niepodleglosciowscy)* against the governing "realists" or "pragmatists" supporting the Skubiszewski line. It matched the divide in domestic politics that deepened as the 1991 parliamentary elections approached. The radical dissenters differed with the realists not so much in terms of policy options but rather in the determination and resolve they felt could achieve them more quickly. Essentially, they urged Polish diplomacy to stand up and say "no" to the Soviet Union. Skubiszewski, for his part, argued that "those who criticize me do not have any alternative [proposals]," except, perhaps, "adventurism."[36] That this was in fact the case was suggested by the experience of the Olszewski government, which, having pledged to enact a "breakthrough" in foreign policy as well as in economics, was no more successful in achieving its goals than its predecessors. That government's efforts to move beyond the principles established under the first two Solidarity prime ministers managed only—through the work of the defense and internal affairs ministries rather than the MSZ, which remained in Skubiszewski's hands—to create an embarrassing sense of chaos and confusion that helped speed the government's downfall.

THE INSTITUTIONAL QUESTION:
WHO SETS FOREIGN POLICY?

In his brief term of office, in fact, Prime Minister Jan Olszewski orchestrated a crescendo of conflict that climaxed with the release of lists of alleged secret police collaborators holding public office to the Sejm on 4 June 1992. Among those identified as collaborators were Walesa, Skubiszewski, and some 60-odd members of the parliament. Shortly after midnight the same day, on an emergency motion from President Lech Walesa, the Sejm voted to oust Olszewski and his government: it was a bitter fate for the first postwar government to enjoy a mandate from a fully legitimate parliament. In the aftermath, each side accused the other of contemplating a coup d'état, and calm was restored only with the creation of the seven party coalition government headed by Prime Minister Hanna Suchocka in July 1992.[37] This dramatic turn of events broke the deadlock that had emerged in the contest between the government and the president for the upper hand in politics. This battle, which centered on the defense ministry and the armed forces, had effectively paralyzed the executive branch and brought Poland its most unstable moment since the roundtable elections. The experience offered ample illustration of the potential for conflict inherent in the hybrid constitutional structure that Poland inherited from the roundtable talks.

In four years of Solidarity governments, the parliament failed to give final definition to the Polish political order. Despite numerous amendments, including a major overhaul in late 1992 to clarify the division of power between the executive and legislature branches, the constitution still dates back to the 1952 Stalinist version. Poland's makeshift political edifice mixes presidential and parliamentary systems; it also reflects the legal tinkering and ad hoc adaptations made to smooth the transition. The lack of clear rules on the division of power has proved a recipe for conflict in the institutional triangle of president, parliament, and government. As conflict seems a permanent feature of Polish politics, of course, there is no reason to assume that even the most precisely formulated constitution would guarantee stability. Polish democracy has demonstrated a chaotic vitality even without a democratic constitution. Still, the lack of clear lines of constitutional authority has allowed practical precedents to assume great importance, encouraging a free for all whenever conflicts arise. At the same time, political interests have had several years to take root and seem likely to stymie any attempt to draft a constitution that does more than simply reflect the vested interests of the parties then in power. The chance for a "pure" constitution, conceived to serve the Polish national interest and stand the test of time, may already have receded into the past. The dissolution of the parliament in May 1993 set the timetable back yet again, and Poland is unlikely to adopt a new, democratic constitution before 1995. Its drafting is already caught up in the political battles associated with the presidential elections scheduled for that year.

This failure to decide once and for all on a constitutional order left foreign and security policy in institutional limbo. Institutional cooperation depended more on good will and the political balance of forces than on unambiguous legal rules; it thus varied considerably over time. As far as foreign policy is concerned, the primary arena of potential conflict was within the executive branch, where there was considerable overlap in the authority of the president and the government. Since 1989, the president has had the right of general supervision over foreign policy and national security, while the government has had responsibility for the day-to-day execution. This allocation of rights and privileges was implicit in the roundtable amendments; the "little constitution" adopted in 1992, after the Olszewski debacle, made it explicit. Conflict was not incessant, however; during the Skubiszewski era, in fact, it was extremely rare, and almost never involved the MSZ. But problems did arise in relations between the president and the government, in particular when Olszewski challenged Walesa's conception of the presidency as the constitutionally dominant voice in defense policy and national security.

AN APOLITICAL MINISTRY

Skubiszewski's personal authority helped keep the MSZ immune from such political conflicts. His command was unquestioned (except, again, on occasion during Olszewski's brief term of office). He was aided by good relations with Walesa; the two men seemed genuinely to respect one another. Skubiszewski also won the cooperation of the parliament. Despite the Sejm's fragmentation, changing composition, and generally disruptive behavior on domestic issues; only once did it reject a report from the foreign affairs minister.

Skubiszewski was one of the three defining personalities of the 1989-93 period of Solidarity governments. (Walesa and economic reform architect Leszek Balcerowicz were the other two.) His popularity stemmed from both his professional skill and erudition and his manner, which combined precision of thought and speech with an old-world grace and culture. As was also the case with Prime Minister Hanna Suchocka, Skubiszewski exemplified the traits that Poles associated with the Poznan region: diligence, orderliness, pragmatism, sobriety, and common sense. His personal asceticism—until his move to Warsaw, he lived in a single room apartment with a windowless kitchen and drove a Volkswagen "bug"—contributed to the image of selfless service to the state. His decision in May 1993 to heed the pleas of both Suchocka and Walesa and remain at his post, declining a prestigious nomination to the International Tribunal of Justice at the Hague (and with it a tax-free monthly salary of $12,000) enhanced this image.[38] This gesture acquired particular poignancy when Suchocka's government fell in a no-confidence vote only two weeks later. Throughout his tenure, Skubiszewski topped opinion polls on public trust in Polish politicians. Part of his appeal was certainly his seeming indifference to politics; his popularity, like that of Poland's civil rights spokesmen, stemmed from his ability to remain above the political fray.

Skubiszewski moved quickly to transform the foreign affairs ministry into as close to an apolitical institution as Poland could muster, although both the roundtable arrangement and a shortage of trained professionals delayed this process. As Skubiszewski said shortly after taking office in 1989, "It was only the appointment of Prime Minister Mazowiecki's government that separated the Foreign Ministry from the PZPR. I will not link the ministry with any party or political group. Foreign policy is a state policy and not that of a party, irrespective of its coloring. . . . [T]he influence of parties and political groups on the Foreign Ministry is possible only through the parliament."[39] Extricating the MSZ from the party's tentacles was no easy task, as the ministry had effectively functioned as a subunit of the Central Committee's foreign department.[40] Still, Skubiszewski moved to eliminate personnel who represented the party's past political or ideological domination while allowing diplomatic professionals inherited from the communist regime to stay on, especially if their specialization was secondary to Poland's foreign policy priorities. The new leadership emphasized "loyalty, qualifications, diligence" rather than affiliation. Deputy Foreign Minister Jan Majewski, whose ties with the MSZ dated back to the 1970s, kept his job, with responsibility for non-European countries, until early 1993.

Skubiszewski imported a new leadership to revamp the ministry. Jerzy Makarczyk, like Skubiszewski a respected professor of international law, was named deputy minister in 1989 and charged with reorganizing the MSZ. In June 1990 he was assigned to supervise all of the departments concerned with European affairs. (In 1992 he left the MSZ to take a seat on the European Human Rights Tribunal.) Two other outsiders, Aleksander Krzyminski and Antoni Kuklinski, took up posts as deputy ministers in September 1990, when two of the three remaining deputies from the PZPR were removed. Opposition activists such as Iwo Byczewski, Grzegorz Kostrzewa-Zorbas, and Andrzej Ananicz were brought in at lower levels in 1990 and 1991. Both Kostrzewa-Zorbas and Ananicz had been involved in underground publishing devoted to Poland's socialist neighbors in the 1980s, the former as editor-in-chief of *Nowa Koalicja,* the latter as founder and editor of *Oboz.*

Personnel turnover in the first months of Skubiszewski's tenure was dramatic, particularly in the diplomatic service, which the PZPR had used both to provide sinecures for loyal functionaries and as a waste bin for disgraced dignitaries. Ambassadors to key capitals (Washington, London, Bonn, Berlin, Rome, Prague, Budapest, Vienna, Madrid, and Bucharest) were recalled immediately after Mazowiecki's confirmation. By July 1990, 38 of Poland's ambassadors had returned to Warsaw.[41] Among the first recalled were General Wladyslaw Ciaston, the former secret police chief who was subsequently put on trial for ordering the murder of Father Jerzy Popieluszko, from his post as chargé d'affaires in Albania; General Jozef Baryla, a former Politburo member and deputy defense minister, from Syria; and a former deputy chief of the Central Union of Dairy Cooperatives, from Libya.[42] By early 1992, 62 of the 63 ambassadors who had been in office in October 1989 had been recalled.[43] In the entire 1989-93 period, 350 of 698 of the MSZ's Warsaw employees were removed, along with 90 percent of Poland's ambassadors and general consuls.[44] Replacements were drawn, as a rule, from the Solidarity camp, broadly defined. There were important exceptions, however. Former Politburo member and roundtable sponsor Stanislaw Ciosek was named ambassador to Moscow in 1989; he still held this post in early 1995.[45]

The most important fruit of the MSZ's initial reorganization was the creation of a new European department to supersede the old division into East and West. A new department for European institutions likewise reflected Skubiszewski's stress on Poland's goal of European integration. Military issues were downgraded from a full department to a unit limited to liaison with the defense ministry. The ministry faced major stumbling blocks in finding the staff to fill these new structures, however. First, there were legal obstacles to getting rid of unwanted employees; the law on ministerial employees made outright firings nearly impossible. The only substitute was to reorganize departments out of existence and offer employees early retirement; even then court challenges could be mounted. Second, the training and preparation of new diplomatic cadres required time and money, yet the pressure for new faces from both the Solidarity camp at home and émigré and Polonia circles abroad was intense. As Skubiszewski told the Sejm, "Neither Solidarity nor anyone else has an alternative corps for the foreign service." For this reason, "it is easier to dismiss than it is to appoint."[46] Third, the chronic shortage of government funds prevented the ministry from offering competitive wages to candidates with the desired skills, especially in foreign languages. In early 1994, the starting salary at the MSZ was $181 per month (well below the average industrial wage), while the minister himself collected only $672.[47]

Skubiszewski's transformation of the MSZ from an arm of the Communist Party into an apolitical state institution was not the subject of controversy during the four years of Solidarity governments. Since the triumph of the "postcommunist" forces in the 1993 elections, however, it has become the object of a more general attempt by the two victorious parties to redefine the initial Solidarity breakthrough and, by extension, to relativize communist rule. The fashion among adherents of the Democratic Left Alliance and, to a lesser extent, the Polish Peasant Party is to present the personnel changes of the 1989-93 period not as a reflection of a shift to democratic standards but rather as a simple case of replacing "your" people with "our" people for purely political reasons.[48] The "postcommunist" forces have lamented the Solidarity "republic of cronies"[49] they say was built up in 1989-93. This argument is being used to justify the new government's purge of Solidarity appointees and reinstatement of former party officials. With respect to the MSZ, this trend was reflected in the establishment, on 18 January 1994, of a special Sejm subcommittee to "assess the state of personnel" in the MSZ and the "methods of selecting foreign service employees." The rationale for the subcommittee was what members of the new two-party ruling coalition alleged was the "deprofessionalization" of the Polish diplomatic service between 1991 and 1993. Skubiszewski's successor, Andrzej Olechowski, expressed "astonishment and regret" at the subcommittee's formation and argued that it violated the separation of powers between the Sejm and the ministry. Walesa reacted with "surprise and incomprehension."[50] The opposition parties refused to participate in the subcommittee's deliberations, and an MSZ spokesman dubbed it a "McCarthy commission."[51]

In hearing testimony from disgruntled former employees of the MSZ, the subcommittee has focused on Skubiszewski's final attempt to clean house before leaving office. Skubiszewski signed notices of termination for 30 ministry employees on 17 September 1993, two days before the elections. These staffing cuts were necessitated by budget ceilings, the ministry said: the MSZ had 638 people on the payroll and funding for only 579. Twenty-six of those fired had their terminations reversed in appeals to the Main Administrative Court (NSA). In addition, in July 1993, the ministry formally liquidated the Polish Institute of International Affairs (PISM), the ministry's official research outfit, which had been dominated by academic apparatchiks, former communist diplomats, and secret police collaborators. The research unit was reconstituted within the MSZ as the Department of Strategic Studies, a maneuver apparently designed to enable the institute's director to choose only "untainted" scholars and experts for the new entity. Prominent among those excluded from the new department was Longin Pastusiak, a long-time communist apologist and expert on U.S. politics, who was elected to the Sejm on the SLD slate. The SLD considers Pastusiak one of its foreign policy aces. In fact, the parliamentary rumor mill described the formation of the special subcommittee as "Pastusiak's revenge" and predicted that PISM would be reestablished. The former MSZ employees heard by the subcommittee complained that Skubiszewski's appointees, or so-called "parachutists" from outside, had embarrassed Poland with their lack of training, and that cronyism and party affiliation rather than training or experience governed advancement in the foreign service.

Skubiszewski issued an angry retort. "Personnel changes stemmed from the fact of regaining independence," he said. "The Polish People's Republic administered foreign affairs but did not have its own policy. It belonged to the East bloc and was subordinated to Moscow in foreign affairs. Since 1989 we have conducted our own foreign policy, shaped by the country's *raison d'état*. This fundamental turning point had to have its effect on personnel changes—this is without question."[52] Skubiszewski warned that the subcommittee's approach suggested a craving to reverse the efforts undertaken to create a professional, apolitical civil service. Indeed, while Skubiszewski's appointments may have been unsuitable in individual cases, the coalition's reservations suggest a far more sweeping problem. The coalition parties are exceedingly suspicious of appointments made in the past four years and seem determined to put their people in every conceivable position of power, ignoring the distinction between a normal democratic change of government and the dismantling of communism. As in other areas of government, this view spells the return of officials who did the PZPR's bidding in the past, although the system of subordination to the party and Moscow appears to have been completely dismantled.

Taking over as one of the three "presidential" ministers in a cabinet dominated by parties in opposition to the president, Olechowski took initial steps to neutralize the threat of a reversion to the partisan control of the past. He has proposed a "modernization" of the foreign affairs ministry.[53] This plan, implemented on 1 July 1994, was to distinguish a set of "political" posts in the MSZ—the minister, deputy ministers, and the minister's personal advisory staff—that would be vacated with every change of government. The apolitical and professional "diplomatic corps" would remain unaffected, under the supervision of a nonparty "director general," who would also step in to run the ministry in interregnums. This revision seemed necessary to accommodate the demands of the ruling coalition for a supervisory role in each of the "presidential" ministries, without at the same time exposing the diplomatic service to new political pressures. Olechowski's proposed reform was expected to be a model for the defense and internal affairs ministries as well, but was never implemented.

CONSTITUTIONAL CONFUSION

The designation of defense, internal affairs, and foreign affairs as "presidential" ministries was the outcome of the showdown between Olszewski and Walesa in early 1992. The president's victory was codified in the "little constitution," a major constitutional amendment adopted to clarify the distribution of power within the executive branch and between the executive and the legislature. Designed under conditions of debilitating parliamentary fragmentation, when Walesa was seen as a stabilizing factor, the "little constitution" has failed to forestall new conflict between the president and the majority governing coalition formed in the wake of the 1993 elections. Despite the appointment of the president's candidate—Olechowski—to head the MSZ, foreign affairs may emerge as a battlefield for political influence, as defense and internal affairs did in the Olszewski period, as Poland attempts to decide whether it wants a presidential or a parliamentary system of government.

The constitutional problem dates back to the creation of the presidency as part of the roundtable bargain. Tailored to mirror the powers then enjoyed by Jaruzelski (as head of state and party leader), the presidency was oriented more toward blocking change than promoting it.[54] At the time, it seemed an extremely powerful institution, and the opposition bargained hard to limit the office with counterbalancing parliamentary controls. Opposition negotiators have since admitted that they deliberately designed the "presidential clauses" of the roundtable agreement to be as confusing as possible, with an eye to reducing Jaruzelski's room for maneuver.[55] As Walesa realized on inheriting the office in 1990, the hamstrung construction of the presidency did not provide ready tools to exert direct influence on the nation's affairs. The constitution implied sweeping powers, particularly in the areas of foreign policy, defense, and national security, but failed to specify the specific mechanisms necessary to exercise them in practice. In addition, the presidency failed to expand to reflect the elevation of the office implicit in the constitutional amendment of mid-1990 that mandated general presidential elections. Whereas Jaruzelski was selected by the parliament, in the tradition of ceremonial presidencies, Walesa won his mandate—and thus added prestige and authority—directly from the public.

In the roundtable version, in force from 1989 to 1992, the president is "the highest representative of the Polish state in internal and international relations." He is charged with ensuring "respect for the constitution; stands guard over the state's sovereignty, security, and territorial integrity"; and, in a shorthand for the Warsaw Pact, guarantees that "international political and military alliances are not violated." The president nominates the prime minister; who has the right to be consulted in the selection of the rest of the cabinet. He may convene and chair cabinet sessions devoted to "issues of extraordinary importance to the nation." He may submit draft legislation. He has veto power (the Sejm can override with a two-thirds majority). He can dissolve the parliament if it fails to form a government within three months; if it fails to pass a budget within three months; or "if it passes a law or adopts a resolution that prevents the president from performing his constitutional duties." He is commander in chief of the armed forces and chairs the National Defense Committee (KOK), constitutionally the "body properly responsible for matters of state defense and security." (KOK was the enigmatic body charged with setting security policies in the period following martial law; its relations to the defense and internal affairs ministries were left undefined.) In the case of an external threat to the country, the president can impose martial law and order a military mobilization. When domestic security is endangered or a natural catastrophe has occurred, he can impose a state of emergency, with the proviso that this last no longer than three months and is extended only once, with the Sejm's approval. Finally, the president ratifies international agreements (with the Sejm's approval, if they require substantial state spending), nominates the head of the National Bank, names judges, issues pardons, and awards citizenship.

In the period following the roundtable talks, legitimacy was as important as this catalogue of formal powers in setting institutional precedents. The

Mazowiecki government enjoyed a paradoxical freedom of movement because the "contractual" parliament acknowledged itself to be semilegitimate. The 1989 election mandate rested effectively with the Solidarity movement, rather than with the "65 percent-35 percent" Sejm. This recognition established a pragmatic (if not entirely logical or lasting) distinction: the "contractual" Sejm was adequate to process economic reform legislation and dismantle the most offending communist institutions, but it was generally considered to lack the legitimacy necessary to establish the constitutional foundations for the Third Republic. The same applied to Jaruzelski. As president, he seemed to agree that he owed his election to Solidarity's good will. He served out his abbreviated term of office with suitable humility, using his veto power only twice (once to ensure that the government reported regularly to the Sejm on land purchases made by foreigners; and once to send a pensions bill stripping long-time communist officials of their "dignitary" bonuses to the Constitutional Tribunal—which ruled the bill constitutional). He cooperated gracefully with Mazowiecki in foreign affairs. This behavior confounded the roundtable design and set the stage for a ceremonial presidency.

Enter Walesa. With the Solidarity leader's resounding victory in the 1990 elections, the focus of politics abruptly shifted to the president's office. For nearly a year, the presidency was the only Polish institution with full democratic legitimacy. Walesa was thus able to form a government (headed by Prime Minister Jan Krzysztof Bielecki) largely on his own authority, although this did not prevent the parliament from upending his legislative agenda. From the moment he declared his intention to run for office, Walesa made no secret of his preference for a political system centered in the presidency. Poland needed an "activist" president, he insisted, a "president with an ax" to chop through the communist underbrush. Walesa argued constantly that the prime minister should answer to the president rather than to the Sejm, in order to maintain stability in a period of inevitable economic upheaval. The Sejm's proper job was to process legislation and exercise constitutional control, Walesa argued, rather than to involve itself in the day-to-day functioning of the executive branch.

Walesa's presidential vision had both supporters and detractors. Positions on the issue tended to be fluid, however, as the Solidarity camp underwent its spasmodic process of division. The "center-right" groups that had supported Walesa's election campaign lobbied initially for a powerful "French-style presidency." Center Alliance leaders, who held the highest posts in the president's office until the end of 1991, argued for a "strong central decision-making apparatus" around the presidency that would control the police and the military.[56] In contrast, Mazowiecki's supporters, now organized in the Democratic Union, initially favored a purely parliamentary system, in large part out of fears that Walesa would prove an authoritarian and power-hungry president.

By mid-1992, these positions had reversed. During the course of 1991, the "center-right" forces grew disenchanted with Walesa, particularly because he was unwilling to give them full control over the government or to remove Balcerowicz. After the 1991 elections, however, the Center Alliance was able to forge a short-lived majority in favor of Olszewski as prime minister. This forced Walesa's hand; for lack of an alternative, the president was compelled to nominate Olszewski despite strong reservations about him. This move put two democratic institutions—the president and the now fully legitimate government—on a collision course. In the wake of Olszewski's ouster, the "center-right" parties emerged as Walesa's most vehement opponent. They condemned any attempt to expand the powers of the presidency without the prior removal of Walesa (whom they contended had sinister secret police connections and was spearheading a drive to "recommunize" the political system). In the meantime, the Democratic Union, never keen on the idea of a strong presidency, had come to a less categorical assessment of Walesa and was prepared to accept a mediating role for the president.

One of the defining factors of the 1989-93 period was Walesa's drive to remain the pivotal force in Polish politics. To this end, he strove to exercise all the powers, both explicit and implicit, designed for Jaruzelski, to establish further precedents extending these powers, and to campaign for the formal confirmation of a presidential system in the future constitution. Walesa's maximalist conception was a constant source of tension, even when the president was on good terms with the prime minister (as was the case with both Bielecki and Suchocka). Immediately after his election, for example, Walesa seemed poised to create a "supergovernment" by appointing "ministers of state" that were identified but not defined in the constitutional amendments creating the presidency. He also contemplated a pluralistic political council to function as a prosthesis for a legitimate parliament, only to abandon the idea when it met with strong criticism and limited support.[57] Finally, Walesa suggested that he would revamp the KOK, renaming it the National Security Council (RBN), to make it the central institution responsible for defining security policy and military reform. To this end, the president created a National Security Office (BBN) at Belweder to serve as the organizational backbone for the new council. Walesa caused Skubiszewski some initial anxiety by appointing a secretary of state for foreign policy: Janusz Ziolkowski, the Senate's Foreign Relations Committee chairman and a colleague of Skubiszewski's from Poznan University. At the time, Skubiszewski tactfully indicated that he would resign if the president's office interfered with his conduct of foreign policy. This did not, in fact, come to pass.

On occasion, however, presidential functionaries failed to cooperate with the government. The most striking example was a visit to the United States in July 1991 by Maciej Zalewski, a secretary of state at Belweder and secretary of the president's National Security Office.[58] The visit was made without prior consultation with the MSZ. During meetings with State Department, Pentagon, and CIA officials, Zalewski apparently hinted that Balcerowicz's ouster was imminent and discussed the Polish BBN's role in the event of a collapse of Poland's democratic structures. The visit was hotly debated in Poland; *Tygodnik Powszechny* worried in an editorial about the "dangerous dualism in Polish foreign policy."[59] Skubiszewski publicly criticized Zalewski for overstepping his authority and, clearly alarmed, twice discussed the matter with Walesa. Zalewski's maneuvering was attributed to the Center Alliance's ambition to present its policies as those of the president.

The full potential for institutional conflict emerged only after the 1991 elections, however, in the political war that erupted between Walesa on one side and Olszewski and his defense and interior ministers on the other. By this time, the Center Alliance had abandoned or been driven out of the president's office and had engineered the formation of a coalition whose aim was to enact the anticommunist "breakthrough" that Walesa had prevented after the 1990 presidential elections. The coalition government took shape over strenuous objections from Walesa, who did all he could to block its formation. In his inaugural address, Olszewski proclaimed "the beginning of the end of communism."[60] Skubiszewski initially declined to join the government, despite repeated requests from Olszewski. He relented only after a personal appeal from the president.[61] It soon became clear that the internal affairs minister and the defense minister, representing the "acceleration" option, had a different sense of the challenges facing Poland. Their statements were alarmist, evoking an atmosphere of threat and the danger of a communist resurgence. In his report on the state of Poland's security, for example, Internal Affairs Minister Antoni Macierewicz spoke of espionage, terrorism, and imminent threats to sovereignty.

The Olszewski government set out to curtail Walesa's influence over foreign and security policy; it stuck to the letter rather than the spirit of the roundtable constitution. Although Walesa had precedent on his side, Olszewski seemed to view all inherited constitutional practice as a postcommunist anomaly. Walesa fought back, attempting to maintain the presidency as the decision-making focus for defense and foreign policy.

This battle was fought out largely in the defense ministry, where Jan Parys—the first civilian to hold the post since the communist collapse—embarked on what he presented as an uncompromising effort to rid the military of communist and "pro Soviet" influences.[62] Without consulting Walesa, the defense minister began a dizzying series of personnel changes, both in the ministry and in the armed forces themselves, that removed officials who enjoyed the president's trust. Parys struck the first blow on 31 December 1991, when he ordered the forced retirement of Admiral Piotr Kolodziejczyk, who had served as defense minister from July 1990 until December 1991. The president had hoped to have Kolodziejczyk appointed armed forces Inspector General—a post that pending reform legislation envisioned as the nation's highest military office—both to reward his loyal service in Poland's transition to democracy and to help preserve the allegiance of a still predominantly postcommunist officer corps. Walesa's preference for Kolodziejczyk had been clear since mid 1991.

Olszewski supported Parys's decision, arguing that there was no appropriate position in the armed forces for someone of Kolodziejczyk's rank and suggesting that a naval officer was an inappropriate commander for a land-based military. The thrust of Olszewski's remarks was that Kolodziejczyk's communist past was the real problem (a graduate of the Voroshilov Military Academy, Kolodziejczyk had served as the head of the Polish Army's Main Political Administration in 1989). Parys also moved to scuttle plans for the reorganization of the army and defense ministry that the National Security Office had drafted in tandem with the Bielecki government.[63] Parys suggested that his actions signaled the "decommunization" of the armed forces. Walesa scoffed at this notion; Parys was merely replacing one set of former communist generals with another, he said.

The president's response was to pursue business as usual, working through his National Security Office. As was clear from the defense minister's later statements, Parys chose to interpret these activities as illicit, conspiratorial, and potentially leading to a coup d'état. The conflict reached its climax when, on 6 April, Parys read a prepared statement at a General Staff meeting in which he accused "certain politicians" of meeting with high ranking officers behind his back, in an attempt to lure them into partisan political intrigue through the offer of promotions. With television cameras rolling, Parys hinted that Poland faced the threat of a coup: "The army will not help anyone who wants to overthrow democracy . . . [or] take power by force," he warned.[64]

It later became apparent that the defense minister had succumbed to rhetorical excess. As a special Sejm investigative commission set up at the president's urging was later to ascertain, Parys was referring to a single meeting between Walesa's chief security official, Jerzy Milewski, and the Silesian military district commander, General Tadeusz Wilecki, which took place on 27 March. Neither Milewski nor Wilecki denied the meeting had taken place, and Wilecki confirmed that Milewski had informed him that Wilecki was the president's candidate to replace General Zdzislaw Stelmaszuk as General Staff chief. Was this an illicit move on the president's part? Only, it seemed, if one meant to deny the president a say in defense policy. The constitution stipulated at the time that the president name the General Staff chief via the defense minister's nomination, a formulation giving Parys the decisive role but implying a degree of consultation. Walesa himself noted caustically that, as commander in chief, he perhaps had the right to meet with the generals, while his spokesman asserted, "If the president, through his staff, requests a meeting [with an officer], this cannot be treated as a conspiracy."[65]

Rather than act to defuse the conflict, Parys and his supporters chose escalation.[66] Ordered on vacation but never disowned by Olszewski, the defense minister appeared at public gatherings to depict the president's office as a communistic, conspiratorial center determined to halt democratic reforms in the military, undermine ties with NATO, and defend the "pro-Russian status quo" in the armed forces. He accused the president of blocking "decommunization" and suggested that Walesa's name would figure on a "list of national infamy." At the same time, the progovernment daily *Nowy Swiat* launched an antipresidential offensive, insinuating, for example, that Walesa's office was contemplating the imposition of martial law. Center Alliance leader Jaroslaw Kaczynski asserted that actions of Walesa's most trusted political aide, the enigmatic Mieczyslaw Wachowski, "reek of foreign interference."[67] At about the same time, *Gazeta Wyborcza,* Poland's largest circulation daily, published a six-page compilation of statements by some of Walesa's closest former associates, in which the president was assigned faults ranging from ignorance and narcissism to power lust and authoritarianism.[68] While these charges were worrying, the Sejm took the president's side, dismissing as "groundless and damaging to the national interest" the defense minister's accusations. An unrepentant Parys was forced to resign on 18 May 1992.

The conflict took its toll on foreign policy as well, despite Skubiszewski's efforts to shield the MSZ from the effects of political conflict. Olszewski's "breakthrough" slogan was meant to apply to Poland's international position as well as its domestic politics. Parys and other members of Olszewski's cabinet were fairly open in classifying Russia as the chief potential threat to Poland; they lobbied aggressively for security guarantees from NATO. Parys dispatched his own representatives to Western capitals to press for swift admission to the alliance, despite NATO's evident unwillingness at that time to contemplate such a step. These efforts were undertaken without prior consultation with the MSZ. Under Skubiszewski's guidance, past governments had moved to build closer ties with NATO in a step by step, gradual fashion; now the Olszewski government created the impression that it was banging loudly on a closed door.

In addition, Parys seemed to fancy the idea of closer ties with Ukraine, with an eye to building a joint counterbalance to Russia. This aim ran counter to Skubiszewski's efforts to cultivate friendly ties with both Ukraine and Russia while assiduously avoiding even the hint of Polish partisanship in conflicts between the two. By suggesting government infighting on key security issues, Parys's actions appear to have left an unfavorable impression in the West.

The tension between president and prime minister reached its height during Walesa's visit to Moscow in May 1992. The government sent the president an urgent cryptogram instructing him not to sign the financial settlement regulating the Russian troop withdrawal unless a clause permitting the creation of private Polish-Russian joint ventures on former Soviet bases was removed. The government apparently believed such firms were a mechanism by which post-Soviet intelligence services could gain a foothold in Poland.[69] The clause in question had been discussed before Walesa's departure, but there was considerable institutional confusion over what course had in fact been agreed upon. After receiving the government's message, Walesa forced the reopening of negotiations; hard bargaining at the highest level and Yeltsin's personal intervention secured the removal of the offending clause. Immediately upon his return from Moscow, however, Walesa blasted the government for having dispatched the cryptogram. "The government's irresponsibility could have led to a complete breakdown in the talks," Walesa's office charged. The prime minister countered immediately with a statement insisting that Walesa had known of the government's reservations well before his departure for Moscow. Skubiszewski conceded this was in fact true but lamented "the unfortunate linkage of foreign policy issues with those of domestic politics" evident in the entire conflict.[70] Walesa used the cryptogram incident as the pretext for his final withdrawal of support for the government on 26 May.

PRESIDENTIAL PREROGATIVES: THE BATTLE CONTINUES

The total breakdown of cooperation between the president and the government in early 1992 prompted the Sejm to take action to eliminate the constitutional ambiguities surrounding the division of power. Despite a chorus of complaints from the forces that supported the ousted government, the "little constitution" adopted on 17 October 1992 made explicit the president's prerogatives in foreign and security policy.[71] In so doing, the parliament effectively confirmed, after the fact, the rationale the president had used in his battles with Parys and Olszewski. The Sejm did not take the extra step Walesa desired, however. Rather than adopt a full-fledged presidential system, it strove to erect a workable (and unambiguous) balance between government and president.

Unlike the roundtable amendments, the "little constitution" explicitly gives the president the right of general stewardship *(sprawuje ogolne kierownictwo)* over foreign policy and external and domestic security, while the government conducts *(prowadzi)* domestic and foreign policy and "ensures the external and internal security of the state." To reinforce the president's supervisory functions, the "little constitution" requires the prime minister to seek the president's opinion before choosing the foreign, defense, and internal affairs ministers. Walesa lobbied for veto power over these three nominations, but the Sejm balked at this proposal. The president retains the right to name the chief of the General Staff, but the "little constitution" expands his role by stipulating that he does this "in agreement with" rather than "on the nomination of" the defense minister.

On the other hand, the "little constitution" eliminated the formulation deeming KOK the body properly responsible for defense and security policy and defined the National Security Council as a purely advisory body whose structure was left entirely to the president's discretion. This thwarted the president's grander designs for the council. The "little constitution" imposed some new limitations on the presidency, as well. It deprived the president of the right to dissolve the parliament should it pass a law that prevents him from "performing his constitutional duties." It also took away his power to motion for the government's dismissal, the provision Walesa had used to oust Olszewski on 5 June 1992. But he did gain the power to authorize changes in the cabinet, on the prime minister's recommendation. Since the 1993 elections, Walesa has used this provision to block the nomination of a new finance minister and thereby exact concessions from the ruling coalition.

The "little constitution" was well suited to the arrangement that emerged after Olszewski's fall, when most of the Solidarity parties chose to forego ideological disputes and push on, under the guidance of Prime Minister Hanna Suchocka, with the more pragmatic tasks of economic reform. The Suchocka government was prepared to accept the president's guiding role in foreign and security policy. Cooperation in the executive branch was assisted, of course, by Skubiszewski's decision to serve in a fourth consecutive government. The appointment of Janusz Onyszkiewicz (a former deputy defense minister) as defense minister and Andrzej Milczanowski (the former head of the State Security Office) as internal affairs minister also helped restore calm, as both had Walesa's approval. Defense reform plans drafted before the Olszewski episode returned to the national agenda. This cooperation quickly bore fruit; on 11 November 1992, the KOK (chaired by Walesa, and consisting of the prime minister; the speakers of the Sejm and the Senate; the ministers of defense, foreign affairs, internal affairs, and finance; the chief of the General Staff; the head of the president's office; and the secretary of the National Security Office) approved the "Security Policy and Defense Strategy of the Republic of Poland."[72]

The incessant instability of Polish politics upended this relatively harmonious arrangement, however, as Solidarity's no-confidence vote brought down the Suchocka government in May 1993. The elections that followed set the stage for a new round of maneuvering to establish a revised balance of power among the power "triangle" of the parliament, the government, and the president. With the defeat of the Solidarity parties and the return of the "postcommunist" forces, new players took to the field. The rules set by the "little constitution" took on a new meaning in conditions in which the government enjoyed the support of a secure parliamentary majority and Walesa faced off against a parliament generally skeptical of his presidency. A triangular arrangement emerged. The two parties in the governing coalition—the Polish Peasant Party (PSL) and the Democratic Left Alliance (SLD)—formed something of an unholy alliance, coupled by the shared aim of exercising power but divided by numerous deep disagreements on economic and personnel policy. The new prime minister, PSL leader Waldemar Pawlak, sought an implicit understanding with the president in an attempt to build an effective counterweight to the SLD, the larger of the two coalition parties. Pawlak went beyond the constitutionally mandated "consulting" with the president on the three key ministries; he in fact allowed Walesa to select the candidates to fill the three posts. This concession not only won Walesa's assent but helped create a government divided into spheres of influence, with the SLD controlling the economic posts, the president in charge of the "strategic" ministries, and the PSL running public administration, agriculture, and everything else.

But the balance this created was more a tactical bargain than a lasting accord. All three parties seemed determined not only to bar the others from their own territory but also to expand their sphere of influence. The coalition parties were not content to leave the three "presidential" ministries under Walesa's exclusive jurisdiction; they pressed for the appointment of their own candidates as deputy ministers of defense, foreign affairs, and internal affairs. Walesa opposed these demands, arguing that coalition appointments would harmfully "politicize" the three strategic ministries. For his part, Walesa strove to create the impression that the three "presidential" ministries should answer directly to him, rather than to the prime minister or the parliament. For example, with Walesa's encouragement, the new defense minister—Piotr Kolodziejczyk, who returned to the post as a civilian—issued a public protest against the government's budget for 1994, on the grounds that the low level of defense spending threatened the maintenance of Poland's military capacity.

As the new parliament turns to the task of drafting a new constitution, this tug-of-war could have important implications. On the one hand, Walesa's attempt to isolate the three "presidential" ministries from particularistic party influence reflects a healthy desire to avoid the upheaval that has taken place in the state administration since the elections, in which more than half of Poland's 49 voivodship chiefs have been sacked and replaced for purely partisan reasons. It also suggests an attempt to defend policy continuity in three areas where stability is crucial. Olechowski, Walesa's choice to replace Skubiszewski, has pledged to pursue his predecessor's policies—although with a new stress on filling the treaties signed during Skubiszewski's term with economic content (to correct what leading SLD figures have criticized as Skubiszewski's "juridical tilt").[73] As Olechowski put it, "We will take the same road, just on the left-hand side."[74] Olechowski is a skillful negotiator, economist, and administrator, and his appointment thus promises the continued professional conduct of foreign relations. On the other hand, Walesa's attempt to bring the three ministries under his exclusive control runs the risk of thwarting parliamentary supervision and democratic accountability; in an extreme case, this could lead to the emergence of a state within a state. This issue has become more pressing as doubts have mounted about Walesa's attitude toward power. An unsavory aura has long surrounded the president's office, largely in connection with the mysterious past and strong-arm methods of Mieczyslaw Wachowski, the presidential chief of staff whom Walesa recently promoted to minister of state. Recent presidential decisions have reflected a certain arbitrariness and the naked pursuit of personal power.[75] These countervailing pressures suggest that final resolution of the issue of institutional control over foreign policy is not imminent.

"EUROPEANS" VS. "NATIONALISTS"

Foreign policy itself has remained largely unaffected by political conflict and institutional upheaval. Indeed, it is striking that even at the most unstable moment for the new Polish democracy, during the collapse of the Olszewski government, the parliament moved swiftly and with near unanimity to approve the country's association agreement with the European Community. In fact, Sejm and Senate debate on the EC pact took place under three different prime ministers. The Olszewski government introduced the motion in favor of ratification; the Sejm voted to approve the association agreement while Pawlak was making his first attempt to build a new cabinet in June 1992; and the Senate added its endorsement after the Suchocka government had taken office. The smooth passage of the agreement is all the more remarkable when one considers that relations with the EC were, relatively speaking, one of the more controversial Polish foreign policy issues in the Skubiszewski era.

Poland entered the "postcommunist" era without a defined party structure. The chief divide in politics initially cut between forces descended from the Solidarity tradition and forces with their roots in communism. From these beginnings, the creation of a functional political spectrum and workable political institutions was an agonizing process, as the Solidarity movement splintered into pro- and anti-Walesa wings and only then began to consolidate around coherent economic and ideological programs. The dualistic arrangement that defined politics in the 1980s gave way to extreme pluralism in the 1990s; at the height of fragmentation, in the wake of the 1991 "hyperproportional" parliamentary elections, 29 parties and groups had at least one seat in the Sejm. In the search to build distinct identities and carve out a distinct popular following, Poland's political parties used foreign policy issues as signposts in the debate on the shape of contemporary Polish society. These positions bore little or no reference to actual policy options. The few disputes that did arise on foreign policy generally reflected dissonant visions of the shape Polish society should take in new, democratic conditions.

"Poland's place in Europe" was the slogan that subsumed this debate. The positions staked out in this debate suggest what Poland's political spectrum might look like in "normal conditions," that is, in the absence of the deep fault lines that reflect the divide between communism and the opposition; between Walesa "accelerators" and Mazowiecki "evolutionists"; and between proponents and opponents of the "Balcerowicz plan." These uniquely Polish fault lines have made it difficult to categorize Polish parties in accordance with the spectrum along which European political life is arranged. In contrast, the Polish debate on the meaning of Europe expressed a more traditional—and more easily classifiable—range of ideological positions.

At the right end of the spectrum were Catholic conservatives, represented most prominently in political life by the Christian National Union (ZChN), who tended to favor the idea of a strong, centralized state built explicitly on Polish national identity and Christian social values. They spoke up for a prominent place for the Catholic Church in public life, patriotic education, national traditions, and a ban on abortion and were skeptical about national minority demands for broader cultural and educational rights. They bristled at any perceived threat to national sovereignty. With respect to European integration, they urged caution, on the grounds that Poland had as much to lose as to gain from "rejoining Europe." As the ZChN's Marek Jurek put it during a foreign policy debate in May 1992, "Poland does not have to fear remaining outside Europe, because Poland is in Europe. Unfortunately, we attribute to the concepts of Europe and Europeanism completely different meanings."[76] For the ZChN, contemporary Europe represented the twentieth-century dangers of materialism, atheism, and immorality to which Western civilization had succumbed. Poland's traditionally close ties to the Church had helped to preserve what lay at the roots of European culture, the ZChN argued. Poland thus had as much to offer Western Europe as it had to gain, and it should not feel compelled to assume the role of an inferior petitioner. Or, as the ZChN's Henryk Goryszewski argued, "Poland must find its place in the world of wolves, where wolves' laws apply, but in so doing, it must not betray the values that comprise its national identity."[77]

This perception of Europe helps explain the single parliamentary vote that went against Skubiszewski in his four years as foreign minister. In this case, the topic of debate was the creation of a "Carpathian Euroregion," a loose arrangement among local communities in Hungary, Poland, Slovakia, and Ukraine to develop cross-border cooperation that was formally established in Debrecen on 14 February 1993.[78] The government looked favorably on Euroregions as a means of assisting the economic and cultural development of border regions. Skubiszewski argued that such loose arrangements posed no threat to national sovereignty or territorial integrity, especially as the concept rested on the ironclad principle that regional, cross-border agreements could not conflict with the domestic legal order or international accords. The very idea of "Euroregions" prompted a fierce attack from the ZChN and other right-wing parties, however. One ZChN leader condemned the Carpathian Euroregion as "serving the idea of the partition of Poland, which has to be divided in order then to integrate it with Europe" and warned that there were "dark forces that have a plot to dismantle our borders."[79] Another Christian Democratic deputy criticized Euroregions as a "murky pan-European ideal" that contradicted the Church's supposed preference for the idea of a "Europe of fatherlands."[80] During the Senate debate on 5 March 1993, the Catholic deputy Ryszard Bender charged that Euroregions violated Poland *raison d'état*. "Euro-spirits are circling above Poland, but these are not the spirits of angels," he warned.[81] This barrage was by far the most hostile criticism ever directed at Skubiszewski. As emerged in later parliamentary debate, when detailed information on Euroregions was distributed and the modest nature of the undertaking was clear, the right wing parties were responding more to symbols and slogans than to the practical proposal at hand.

At the opposite end of the spectrum were the left-of-center, "pro-reform" parties, the Democratic Union and the Liberal Democratic Congress, which took a secular view of Polish society and culture and preferred to cultivate the ideal of a "citizens' state" rather than a "national state." Especially at the start of Poland's transition to democracy and the market, these parties tended to identify fairly uncritically with "European solutions" to domestic political and economic problems. The "European model" was used to buttress support for the government's economic transformation program; "European standards" were the guide for the conduct of domestic politics and international relations; and "European integration" was perceived as Poland's chief goal. This was the underlying philosophy of the first four Solidarity governments, and it seems to have served Poland well in providing a guidebook and a yardstick in the effort to realize postcommunist national aspirations.

While Poland's foreign policy priorities continued to meet with general public approval, disillusionment with the domestic bearers of this vision of "Poland's return to Europe" grew. The bulk of the problem, of course, was the sacrifice and upheaval entailed in the Balcerowicz plan. But it was also important that, in practice, Europe did not live up to the image extolled by Poland's "Europeans."

There were numerous examples. In the course of 1993, for example, the EC imposed numerous minor restrictions on Polish agricultural imports (on 19 July, for example, mandatory minimum prices were set for imported Polish cherries that exceeded current market prices in Europe; meat and livestock imports from Central and Eastern Europe were halted in April due to an outbreak of hoof and mouth disease in the Balkans). Such measures were perceived as concealed protectionism. Given that the EC was running a large and growing surplus in trade with Poland, such attempts to protect domestic markets seemed to reflect a petty policy of nickel-and-diming poorer neighbors. In addition, the products kept out of European markets involved only a small percentage of European imports but often reflected a sizable portion of Poland's exports. Polish governments were hard-pressed to convince their own peasant lobbies of the need to curtail agricultural subsidies and open borders to foreign competition when European countries were balking at dismantling farm supports and eliminating trade barriers. The sight of French farmers and fishermen smashing cargoes from the East did not promote self-restraint in Poland. Indeed, there were a number of poignant occasions on which Polish leaders felt compelled to remind European officials of the true meaning of "Europe." In a major policy speech to the Sejm on 29 April 1993, for example, Skubiszewski called upon the EC to "remain faithful to the ideals of its founders and not transform itself into a fortress closed off to the rest of Europe."[82]

The outcome of the 1993 elections was—at least in part—a reflection of public disillusionment with the European ideal. This was a chord sounded by the president, who told a visiting World Bank delegation that "society did not vote against reform . . . it voted against the West's lack of solidarity with us, which promised help and cooperation and now imposes restrictions on our goods."[83] Walesa's charge was echoed by Suchocka,[84] Balcerowicz,[85] and many others in the losing camp. As with the general debate on Poland and Europe, however, this disillusionment did not affect Poland's policy on European integration—joining the European Union still remained Poland's number-one foreign policy goal, along with membership in NATO—but it may have undermined the effectiveness of "European" arguments in domestic politics and, particularly, economics. This outcome would be in keeping with the experience of the Skubiszewski years, in which a broad consensus on foreign policy priorities coexisted with nearly total disagreement on all issues in domestic politics.

THE SKUBISZEWSKI ERA AND BEYOND

The elections of 1993 were a watershed in Polish public life. Skubiszewski's removal was only one of many consequences of the shift in power from the broad Solidarity camp to the postcommunist forces. The ultimate meaning of this transfer of power—a democratic change of government or a partial reversion to past practices—remains unclear. In the meantime, the creation of a two-party coalition based on the successor to the Communist Party and the descendant of that party's rural ally has reopened the question of the wisdom of the roundtable philosophy, particularly the assumption that one could draw, as Mazowiecki did rhetorically in his inaugural address, a "thick line" *(gruba kreska)*[86] separating the past from the present.

In foreign policy as in domestic politics, the isolation of Poland's democratic experiment mandated self-limitation. As this isolation ended and the former external constraints collapsed, domestic political conflict centered on the issue of if, when, and how to abandon the roundtable compromise. This debate took place inside the Solidarity camp; at the time, there was little sense that the postcommunist forces would survive, let alone flourish. The roundtable approach prolonged the process of making inherited structures fully democratic; this delay blurred Mazowiecki's "thick line," leaving a number of issues—especially the constitution and the division of powers among the parliament, the president, and the government—seemingly in a state of perpetual transition. In the 1989-93 period, Poland managed to put these hybrid structures to good use, erecting a genuine—if turbulent—democracy and laying the foundations for a market economy. As the initial compromise faded into the past, however, the pace of the eradication of the institutional vestiges of communism became bogged down. The postcommunist comeback in the 1993 elections may work to embalm Polish institutions in their current, hybrid form.

The achievements of the four-year period of Solidarity governments are thus crucial to Poland's future development. To what extent did the democratic opposition put its opportunity—vast but unexpectedly brief—to use? Since the election defeat, this has itself become the topic of much soul-searching.[87] In politics, the picture is fairly grim. Despite a shared vision of the goals to which Poland should aspire, division, infighting, and relentless degrading of rivals were the rule within the Solidarity camp. The venom spilt in these conflicts not only weakened the Solidarity parties internally but also made the former communists appear calm and cultured by comparison. In economics, the picture is somewhat rosier; the four governments managed to attain a sort of "stability in instability," as each new prime minister, however reluctantly, embraced the logic of the Balcerowicz plan. The atmosphere of a perpetual election campaign that characterized the four year period took its toll here as well, however, as vital economic decisions were delayed or distorted in the populist free-for-all.

Stability reigned alone in foreign policy. This achievement was Skubiszewski's formidable contribution to Poland's transition; it also reflected the sanctity of foreign policy for a newly independent nation. During his four years in office, Skubiszewski was able to implant his foreign policy principles into Polish political life. These principles were at once sovereign and pragmatic, reflecting both Poland's aspirations and the limitations of its geographical position and economic weakness. In the rare political debates that took place on foreign policy, objective constraints were at times mistaken for roundtable self limitation (on the occasion of the Olszewski government's "agents" disclosures they were even construed as traitorous sabotage). Critics were most justified in faulting Skubiszewski for moving too slowly on the withdrawal of Soviet troops; but even here, the government's delay was as much a deliberate strategic choice as a roundtable concession. Fortunately, the troops issue was rendered moot by the successful conclusion of the withdrawal, while the larger—and indeed perpetual—Polish dilemma of how to cope with a potentially threatening Russian neighbor remains constant.

Poland cannot resolve this dilemma on its own; the solution lies with the larger European and international community. This explains why the "return to Europe"—Poland's twin goals of NATO and EU membership—has acquired crucial importance in Polish foreign policy. Here much does depend on the Poles themselves. The continued conduct of an independent foreign policy rests on Poland's ability to maintain the Skubiszewski consensus regardless of shifting political configurations. As the domestic debate on "Poland's place in Europe" suggests, however, Europe has its own part to play in preserving this consensus. Poland's stable integration into Europe depends not only on continued Polish success as what Olechowski has called a "regional exporter of stability"[88] but also on Europe's own commitment to live up to "European" standards.

Notes

1. Polska Agencja Prasowa (hereafter PAP), 27 October 1993.
2. See Anna Sabbat-Swidlicka, "Friendship Declarations Signed with Ukraine and Russia," *Report on Eastern Europe* (2 November 1990).
3. Poland signed a new bilateral treaty with Germany on 17 June 1991; with Ukraine on 18 May 1992; with Russia on 22 May 1992; with Belarus on 23 June 1992; with Latvia on 1 July 1992; and with Estonia on 2 July 1992. After arduous, protracted negotiations focusing on national minority rights and the assessment of historical conflicts between the two countries, a bilateral treaty with Lithuania was initialed by the two foreign ministers in Warsaw on 18 March 1994. It was signed by the two presidents on 26 April 1994.
4. PAP, 18 April 1994.
5. On the Polish elections of 1989, see Zoltan D. Barany and Louisa Vinton, "Breakthrough to Democracy: Elections in Poland and Hungary," *Studies in Comparative Communism* 23, no. 2 (Summer 1990): 191-212.
6. Radio Warsaw, 5 June 1989.
7. *Gazeta Wyborcza,* 26 July 1989.
8. See Michael Shafir, "East European Reactions to Polish Developments," RAD Background Report 197, *Radio Free Europe Research* (hereafter RFER) (16 October 1989).
9. This Romanian message was conveyed to the Polish ambassador in Bucharest at midnight on 19 August 1989 and was dispatched to the other Warsaw Pact countries as well. The PZPR responded on 21 August with an unpublished statement that rejected the Romanian party's views and stressed that the political changes underway in Poland did not threaten the country's loyal participation in the CMEA or the Warsaw Pact. This exchange was not made public until *Gazeta Wyborcza* broke the story on 29 September 1989.
10. For the new government's initial foreign policy statements, see Polish Situation Report (SR) 15, RFER, 12 October 1989, item 2; and Polish SR 16, RFER, 14 November 1989, item 2.
11. *Rzeczpospolita,* 13 September 1989.

12. During a meeting of the Citizens' Parliamentary Caucus on 23 August 1989. Quoted in *Gazeta Wyborcza*, 24 August 1989.

13. Waldemar Kuczynski, *Zwierzenia zausznika* (Warsaw: Polska Oficyna Wydawnicza "BGW," n.d. [1991?]), p. 47.

14. On Jaruzelski's Consultative Council, see Polish SR 19, RFER, 16 December 1986, item 2; Polish SR 15, RFER, 4 November 1987, item 4.

15. Kuczynski, *Zwierzenia zausznika*, 47.

16. On this issue, see Louisa Vinton, "The Politics of Property: Divesting the Polish Communist Party of Its Assets," *Report on Eastern Europe*, 17 (27 April 1990).

17. Walesa first used this expression in May 1990. See, for example, Walesa's press conference in Puck on 10 May 1990, as reported in "A Peaceful War of Each Against All," *Gazeta Wyborcza*, 11 May 1990; and Walesa's address to the Citizens' Committee on 13 May, *Gazeta Wyborcza*, 14 May 1990.

18. Center Alliance leader Jaroslaw Kaczynski, in an interview with *Slowo Powszechne*, 20-22 August 1990.

19. On the Polish troop withdrawal negotiations, see Douglas L. Clarke, "Soviet Troop Withdrawals from Eastern Europe," *Report on Eastern Europe* (30 March 1990); Douglas L. Clarke, "Poland and the Soviet Troops in Germany," *Report on Eastern Europe* (25 January 1991); Louisa Vinton, "Soviet Union Begins Withdrawing Troops—But on its Own Terms," *Report on Eastern Europe* (26 April 1991); Jan B. de Weydenthal, "Polish-Russian Relations Disturbed by Troop Dispute" *RFE/RL Research Report* (13 March 1992), Jan B. de Weydenthal, "Poland Free of Russian Combat Troops," *RFE/RL Research Report* no. 45 (13 November 1992).

20. Malgorzata Niezabitowska, at a press conference on 15 March 1990, quoted by Polish Television, 15 March 1990.

21. A Soviet government statement published in *Izvestia*, 11 February 1990, quoted in Clarke, "Soviet Troop Withdrawals."

22. Radio Warsaw, 21 February 1990.

23. Janusz Reiter, "Po co te wojska," *Gazeta Wyborcza*, 14 February 1990.

24. Radio Warsaw, 26 April 1990.

25. *Rzeczpospolita*, 9-10 September 1990.

26. *Frankfurter Rundschau*, 30 January 1991.

27. For a firsthand account of the withdrawal talks, see *Pozegnanie z armia,* a book-length interview with General Zdzislaw Ostrowski, the Polish government's plenipotentiary for Soviet forces from October 1990 to the present (Warsaw: Czytelnik, 1992). See also the interview with Grzegorz Kostrzewa-Zorbas, deputy director of the European Department at the MSZ from 1 June 1990 to November 1991 and chief Polish negotiator in the troop withdrawal talks from November

1990 until June 1991, in *Lewy czerwcowy*, ed. Jacek Kurski and Piotr Semka, (Warsaw: Editions Spotkania, 1992), pp. 147-188. Ostrowski argues that Kostrzewa-Zorbas's appointment was an error by the Polish side, because his abrasive style and constant stress on Polish sovereignty antagonized the Soviet side. Kostrzewa-Zorbas, for his part, charges that the government did not press its case hard enough; he blames Walesa for accepting what he calls the "Finlandization" of Poland.

28. See, for example, *Gazeta Wyborcza*, 16 January 1991; *Polityka*, 13 April 1991.

29. Jaroslaw Kurski, *Wodz* (Warsaw: Pomost, 1991), p. 94.

30. Associated Press, 15 February 1990.

31. See the interview in *Gazeta Wyborcza*, 24 January 1991.

32. Ibid.

33. See Louisa Vinton, "Poland," *Report on Eastern Europe* (30 August 1991).

34. On this session, see *Report on Eastern Europe* (29 August 1991); *Trybuna*, 29 August 1991; Elzbieta Isakiewicz, "Dygot przed wschodem," *Tygodnik Solidarnosc*, 6 September 1991. For Najder's arguments, see his article, "Spor o polska polityke wschodnia," *Rzeczpospolita*, 1 October 1991.

35. Quoted in *Gazeta Wyborcza*, 29 August 1991. Walesa's words were "*nasze zyczenie, a nie mozliwosci sprawcze.*"

36. In an interview with *Polityka*, 17 October 1992.

37. See Louisa Vinton, "Olszewski's Ouster Leaves Poland Polarized," *RFE/RL Research Report*, no. 25 (19 June 1992); Vinton, "Poland's Government Crisis: An End in Sight?" *RFE/RL Research Report*, no. 30 (24 July 1992); and Vinton, "Poland's Governing Coalition: Will the Truce Hold?" *RFE/RL Research Report*, no. 31 (31 July 1992).

38. *Rzeczpospolita*, 11 May 1993. Skubiszewski discusses this decision at some length in an interview with *Zycie Warszawy*, 15 June 1993.

39. PAP (in English), 16 November 1989.

40. See Stanislaw Marek Krolak, "Spadek PRL-u," *Tygodnik Gdanski*, 18 March 1990. Of Poland's 73 ambassadors at the end of 1989, 71 were PZPR members (most were former party activists from the Central Committee, party youth organizations, or the internal affairs ministry) and 2 were from the United Peasant Party.

41. Wlodzimierz Krzyzanowski, "Czar Dyplomaty," *Przeglad Tygodniowy*, 8 July 1990.

42. *Gazeta Wyborcza*, 13 February 1990.

43. According to Elzbieta Gutkowska, Director of the MSZ's Personnel Department, at a press conference reported by PAP, 14 February 1992.

44. *Rzeczpospolita*, 21 January 1994.

45. See the interview with Ciosek in *Przeglad Tygodniowy*, 23 January 1994.

46. *Rzeczpospolita,* 18 January 1990.

47. Krzysztof Mroziewicz and Witold Pawlowski, "Dyplomatyka i glowy," *Polityka,* 16 April 1994. See also Elzbieta Pawelek, "Jasnie pan konsul," *Zycie Warszawy,* 2-3 January 1993.

48. Typical of this approach is Mroziewicz and Pawlowski, "Dyplomatyka i glowy."

49. SLD leader Aleksander Kwasniewski used this expression in his first major address to the Sejm after the creation of the new government, on 9 November 1993. See *Rzeczpospolita,* 10-11 November 1993.

50. *Trybuna,* 20 January 1994.

51. *Rzeczpospolita,* 21 January 1994. See also *Rzeczposlita,* 7 March 1994; *Sztandar Mlodych,* 18 January 1994; *Gazeta Wyborcza,* 24 February 1994; and *Slowo,* 9 March 1994.

52. *Gazeta Wyborcza,* 24 February 1994.

53. *Gazeta Wyborcza,* 7 April 1994. The plan was drafted by Jerzy Kozminski (an MSZ secretary of state appointed by Olechowski who has since taken up the position of ambassador to the United States). Kozminski helped design the "Balcerowicz plan" and was later an assistant to Prime Minister Hanna Suchocka.

54. The presidency was created in legislation approved by the Sejm on 7 April 1989. For the text of the amendment, see *Rzeczpospolita,* 10 April 1989. See also Anna Sabbat-Swidlicka, "The Powers of the Presidency," *Report on Eastern Europe,* no. 44 (2 November 1990).

55. Marcin Krol, interviewed by *Tygodnik Powszechny,* 10 May 1992.

56. PAP, 30 June 1991.

57. See Louisa Vinton, "The Walesa Presidency Takes Shape," *Report on Eastern Europe,* no. 7 (15 February 1991).

58. On the Zalewski visit, see *Zycie Warszawy,* 16 July and 22 July 1991; *The Voice* (Warsaw: 21 July and 4 August 1991); *Gazeta Wyborcza,* 24 July 1991; *Tygodnik Solidarnosc,* 2 August 1991; *Rzeczpospolita,* 24 July 1991.

59. Roman Graczyk, "Ludzie prezydenta" *Tygodnik Powszechny,* 28 July 1991.

60. PAP, 21 December 1991.

61. Skubiszewski told an interviewer that he regretted having decided to join the Olszewski government. See *Zycie Warszawy,* 15 June 1993.

62. For Parys's views, see the interview in Kurski and Semka, eds., *Lewy czerwcowy,* pp. 57-96.

63. See Jan B. de Weydenthal, Poland: Building a National Security System," *Report on Eastern Europe,* no. 24 (14 June 1991); "Political Problems Affect Security Work in Poland," *RFE/RL Research Report,* no. 16 (17 April 1992); and "Poland Prepares a New Military Doctrine," *RFE/RL Research Report,* no. 33 (21 August 1992).

64. *Polska Zbrojna,* 7 April 1992.

65. *Zycie Warszawy,* 9 April 1992.

66. For a blow-by-blow account, see "Military and Security Notes," *RFE/RL Research Report,* no. 3 (17 January 1992); no. 9 (28 February 1992); no. 18 (1 May 1992); and no. 20 (15 May 1992).

67. In an interview with *Tygodnik Solidarnosc,* 24 April 1992.

68. *Gazeta Wyborcza,* 22 April 1992.

69. See the interview with Grzegorz Kostrzewa-Zorbas in Kurski and Semka, eds., *Lewy czerwcowy,* p. 174.

70. See Jan B. de Weydenthal, "Poland and Russia Open a New Chapter in Their Relations," *RFE/RL Research Report,* no. 25 (19 June 1992).

71. See Louisa Vinton, "Poland's 'Little Constitution' Clarifies Walesa's Powers," *RFE/RL Research Report,* no. 35 (4 September 1992). For the text of the "little constitution," see *Dziennik Ustaw,* no. 84, 23 November 1992. In book form, see Maria Kruk, ed., *Mala konstytucja z komentarzem* (Warsaw: Wydawnictwo AWA, 1992). For an English translation, see JPRS-EER-93-009-S, 28 January 1993, pp. 29-35.

72. For the text, see PAP, 11 November 1992. For an English-language version, see *European Security* 2, no. 2 (Summer 1993): 320-340. See also Jan B. de Weydenthal, "Poland's Security Policy," *RFE/RL Research Report,* no. 14 (2 April 1993).

73. SLD foreign policy expert Tadeusz Iwinski, in an interview with *Glos Poranny,* 28 October 1993.

74. PAP, 17 November 1993.

75. See Louisa Vinton, Walesa and the Collaboration Issue," *RFE/RL Research Report,* no. 6 (5 February 1993); Anna Sabbat-Swidlicka, "Questions about the Polish Security Police," *RFE/RL Research Report,* no. 39 (1 October 1993); and Anna Sabbat-Swidlicka, Walesa's Conflicts and Ambitions," *RFE/RL Research Report,* no. 14 (8 April 1994).

76. PAP, 8 May 1992.

77. Quoted in *Rzeczpospolita,* 22 May 1992.

78. See Jan B. de Weydenthal, "Controversy in Poland over 'Euroregions,'" *RFE/RL Research Report,* no. 16 (16 April 1993); Witold Pawlowski, "Unia oplotkow," *Polityka,* 27 February 1993; and Jerzy Kleer and Adam Krzeminski, "W sosie wlasnym czy obcym," *Polityka,* 29 May 1993. For accounts of the Sejm debate, see *Rzeczpospolita,* 22 February and 4 March 1993.

79. Jan Lopuszanski, quoted in *Rzeczpospolita,* 22 February 1993.

80. Piotr Walerych, quoted in *Polityka,* 27 February 1993.

81. PAP, 5 March 1993.

82. PAP, 26 April 1993.

83. PAP, 11 October 1993.

84. Daniel Michaels, "Defeated Polish Leader Blasts Protectionism," *Wall Street Journal*, 11 October 1993.

85. "Why the Leftists Won the Polish Election," *Wall Street Journal*, 28 September 1993.

86. Mazowiecki's exact words were *"Przeszlosc odkreslamy gruba linia."* For the text, see *Gazeta Wyborcza*, 25-27 August 1989. The expression *gruba kreska* became a shorthand for the policy of prosecuting the former authorities only for crimes that could be fully documented and were violations of the legal order at the time they were committed. This is not what Mazowiecki meant in using the expression in the first place, but the expression reflected the policies his government was to follow in practice.

87. See, for example, Jacek Zakowski, "Cos w Polsce peklo, cos sie skonczylo," *Gazeta Wyborcza*, 16-17 April 1994, and numerous responses in subsequent issues.

88. Olechowski presented an outline of Eastern policy to the Senate's Foreign Relations Commission on 17 February 1994. His remarks were published in *Rzeczpospolita*, 18 February 1994.

3

Safeguarding the Third Republic: Security Policy and Military Reform

Andrew A. Michta

Paradoxically, civil war in Russia as well as the past political deadlock in that country were most beneficial for us, while the current strengthening of the army and the imperial tendencies that can be easily discerned in Moscow today are truly detrimental to our position. The West now takes into consideration first and foremost the viewpoint of Russian generals. At the same time, Poland is now under Russian pressure not to do anything that might run counter [to] the Russian national interest as it is defined by the groups tied to the military. The freedom to maneuver in our foreign policy has been dramatically circumscribed, while the policy itself has yet to be articulated.

—Jerzy Marek Nowakowski,
in an interview for *Slowo,* 12 October 1993

You look up to us like some sort of an oracle, like a child expecting the impossible.

—an American diplomat commenting
on Poland's aspirations to join NATO,
quoted in *Wprost,* 23 January 1994

WAITING FOR NATO

Since the formal dissolution of the Warsaw Pact in 1991 Poland has existed in a security vacuum created in East-Central Europe by the implosion of the Soviet empire and by the reunification of Germany within the existing framework of NATO and the European Union. These two events have revolutionized Europe's geopolitics. For Poland, Bonn's continued commitment to the transatlantic institutions has created an opportunity to build a new relationship with Germany as a conduit to the West; conversely, the continued crisis within the former Soviet Union has transformed Poland's hegemon into the potentially most dangerous element of instability in European politics.

Poland had existed as an independent state for only 20 of the two hundred years before 1989. The emergence of the Third Republic is thus only the second chance Poland has had in the past two centuries to formulate a security policy free of outside domination. Once again, Polish security policy has endeavored to come to grips with the historical problem of being a medium-sized and relatively weak nation facing much stronger and potentially dangerous neighbors.

Polish security policy since 1989 has evolved amid continued uncertainty about Poland's place in Europe, accompanied by a sense of insecurity vis-à-vis its former Russian hegemon. Warsaw has recognized that the current conditions in the East are transitory, while NATO continues to search for a new security role for itself. For four years Polish security policy has set as its objective an unequivocal and speedy incorporation of the country in the existing Western security system. In that light, Warsaw has defined the goal of NATO membership as a vital national security interest. At the same time, Poland has tried to avoid antagonizing Russia, while arguing that continued reform in the East has been fundamental to the creation of a lasting cooperative security system in Central Europe.

During his visit to Washington in December 1993, Polish foreign minister Andrzej Olechowski outlined the guiding principles that have informed (and continue to inform) Warsaw's thinking on national security.[1] To begin with, Poland considers continued American engagement in Europe, including military presence, essential to Poland's long-term security, because it mitigates against the resurgence of Russo-German competition in the region. Warsaw considers American engagement in NATO as well as Poland's eventual inclusion in the alliance a sine qua non of its continued independence. The Polish government realizes as well that the current security vacuum in East-Central Europe is a temporary phenomenon resulting on the one hand from the protracted crisis in Russia and on the other hand from Germany's absorption with domestic problems caused by the reunification. In Olechowski's view, the perpetuation of the current situation, whereby Poland remains in a "no-man's land" between the East and the West, is ultimately dangerous not only to Poland but also to the region as a whole because it prevents Warsaw from playing a larger stabilizing role in eastern and central Europe. Therefore, as the Polish foreign minister argued in Washington, the West's refusal to let Poland be anchored in the European Union, the Western European Union, and NATO "will turn Poland into a nucleus of instability and conflict."

Notwithstanding Poland's declared support for the idea of pan-Europeanism and for the CSCE process, Warsaw has had a limited ability to affect the direction of change in the European security system. Therefore, in practical terms, the Poles have sought to expand the existing Western security institutions to bring East-Central Europe into the transatlantic alliance. In 1990 and 1991 this policy was buttressed by a series of successful diplomatic initiatives in the West, especially the dramatic improvement in Polish-German relations symbolized by a new border treaty and a treaty on good neighborly relations. The prospect of a genuine Polish-German partnership, similar to that between France and Germany since World War II, has become a reasonable policy objective as well as raised expectations in Warsaw that Bonn would serve as champion of Poland's inclusion in NATO. Another encouraging development came in August 1993 when Russia briefly appeared willing to acquiesce in Poland's inclusion in NATO, as expressed by Russian president Boris Yeltsin during his visit to Warsaw. Even though Moscow quickly retracted the offer, Warsaw has remained unequivocal in its support for continued reform in Russia and for democratic forces in the East. Poland has also steered clear of the Russian-Ukrainian conflict, despite pressure from Kiev to bring the security policies of Poland and Ukraine closer together. In sum, while Poland has continued to work toward its goal of NATO membership, it has made a concerted effort not to give the Russians a reason to view its security policy objectives as a threat.

The rapid succession of events in late 1993, including the October military confrontation in Moscow between Boris Yeltsin and his parliamentary opposition and the December election that brought the neo-imperialist forces to the fore, has resulted in a deteriorating security situation along Poland's eastern border. Russia's military agreements with Belarus and its unyielding pressure on Ukraine raised the possibility that Moscow would restore its control over the two "near-abroad" republics. Warsaw expressed its growing concern that Russia's progress toward democracy might have already slowed down irreversibly, raising once more the specter of Russian imperialism as a powerful force in European politics. As a result, in late 1993 Poland redoubled its efforts to be included in NATO, or at least to obtain a clear set of conditions and a timetable from the West for the eventual membership in the alliance.

The most dramatic blow to Poland's NATO policy came in January 1994, as Brussels acceded to Moscow's pressure not to extend the alliance eastward. The lack of options in the face of the American rejection of the Visegrad Group's application for NATO membership left Warsaw no choice but to accept President Bill Clinton's "Partnership for Peace" (PFP) formula, notwithstanding Warsaw's bitter disappointment with NATO's unwillingness to open itself up to new members. The Polish government chose to put the best possible spin on the American snub, calling the PFP a "road map leading to NATO membership." NATO's uncertainty about its future notwithstanding, Poland has remained committed to the goals of gaining full membership in the alliance.

THE MILITARY DOCTRINE

In November 1992 President Lech Walesa signed a government white paper outlining the country's new security policy. The document had been drafted by a committee set up by Walesa within the National Security Office (Biuro Bezpieczenstwa Narodowego or BBN) and led by the chief of the BBN, Jerzy Milewski. Prior to its adoption, the new defense doctrine was discussed at two sessions of the National Defense Committee (Komitet Obrony Kraju or KOK), in February 1992 and July 1992.

Poland's defense strategy, outlined in the *Defense Doctrine, 1993-2000* [2] has three general objectives: (1) to maintain and to expand the country's existing defense infrastructure; (2) to ensure the defense readiness of society; and (3) to prepare the armed forces for defensive operations in case of aggression against Polish territory.[3] The new doctrine stresses Poland's commitment to Western European institutions and identifies Poland's future membership in NATO and the Western European Union (WEU) as the key "strategic goal." In the interim, it affirms the country's readiness to cooperate within the Visegrad Group with its regional partners (the Czech Republic, Slovakia, and Hungary). It treats the

Visegrad Group not as a military alliance, but rather as a means for reducing instability in the region. Likewise, stability in the East is to be enhanced by Poland's bilateral treaties with Russia, Belarus, and Ukraine.

According to the new doctrine, the Polish armed forces' principal goal is to defend the security and the territorial integrity of the Polish state. The Polish army is to be prepared to deal effectively with local and limited regional conflicts. However, in case of a general war, the army's task will be to offer the longest possible resistance to the attacker in order to "gain time for other countries and international organizations to react." While the army remains predominantly conscription-based, Warsaw's long-term objective is to increase its professional component.

The Polish defense doctrine identifies no specific threat to the country, nor does it speak of a particular state that might harbor hostile intentions toward Poland. It calls for the redeployment of the existing units to provide for a balanced coverage of the country's territory. For the first time in half a century the Polish army is not charged with protecting the state's political system. It is defined as a military force whose sole task is the protection of the territorial integrity and sovereignty of the state.[4]

THE NATIONAL ARMED FORCES

The military reform undertaken after the collapse of communism and the disintegration of the Warsaw Pact has led to the redrafting of Poland's military districts. In place of the three military districts of the communist era (the Pomeranian District, the Silesian District, and the Warsaw District), Poland today plans to deploy its forces in four districts: (1) the Pomeranian Military District (Pomorski Okreg Wojskowy), with the headquarters in Bydgoszcz; (2) the Silesian Military District (Slaski Okreg Wojskowy), with the headquarters in Wroclaw; (3) the Warsaw Military District (Warszawski Okreg Wojskowy), with the headquarters in Warsaw; and (4) the Cracow Military District (Krakowski Okreg Wojskowy), with the headquarters in Cracow (Map 3.1). The redeployment of units is to be completed by the year 2000, with 40 percent of the forces stationed in the western part of the country, 30 percent in the central region, and 30 percent in the eastern region.

The "Little Constitution" states that the president of Poland is the commander in chief of the armed forces.[5] Since the selection of the defense minister requires presidential approval, the issue of civilian oversight over the military has become a source of friction between the president and the

Map 3.1
THE NEW POLISH MILITARY DISTRICTS

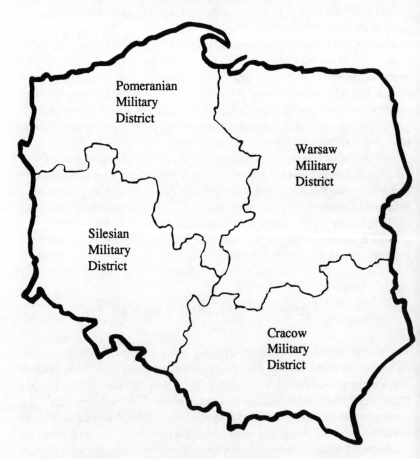

Pomeranian Military District

Warsaw Military District

Silesian Military District

Cracow Military District

Source: Sily Zbrojne Rzeczpospolitej Polskiej—1992: Wybor Materialow dla Prasy (Warsaw: Ministerstwo Obrony Narodowej, Biuro Rzecznika Prasowego, December 1992), p. 16

parliament. The central command structure of the armed forces is built around the General Staff, whose chief is appointed by the president on the recommendation of the minister of defense. In case of war, the parliament (Sejm) or the president if the parliament is not in session, appoints the Supreme Commander of the Armed Forces, who is directly subordinated to the president.

The new command structure currently being adopted by the Polish armed forces will result in a fundamental change in the role played by the General Staff. The power to control the day-to-day operations of the Polish armed forces will be concentrated in the hands of the Chief of the General Staff, who will be responsible for the overall readiness, training, and general mobilization plans.

Once the reorganization has been completed, the Chief of the General Staff will be assisted by five deputies, one each for strategic defense planning, the ground forces, the air and air defense forces, the navy, and logistics. The new General Staff, which will be much smaller than its communist predecessor, is to be reconstituted in the case of war into the principal coordination center for each armed service. The commander of the ground forces will preside over the forces recast into brigades and corps, which will enjoy greater mobility and flexibility than the pre-existing divisional structure. In the formula used by the Polish army during the communist period, the three military districts were to be transformed into armies in wartime, with the Pomeranian and Silesian districts becoming the first echelon forces and the Warsaw district constituting the second echelon. Under the current system, the four military districts provide for the even coverage of the country's territory. The newly established Cracow Military District is intended to fill the gap in the country's eastern defenses. Still, considering the limited resources allocated for defense, the development of the Cracow district's military infrastructure will take time, as will the redeployment of units envisioned by the military reform.[6]

The Polish armed forces rely on the draft for its principal manpower needs, while the officer corps and a portion of the noncommissioned officer corps are staffed with professional military. The armed forces are divided into the ground forces, the air and air defense forces, and the navy. The units of all three services are allocated either to the so-called Operational Army, which constitutes the core of the armed forces, or to the Territorial Defense Units, whose role is to support the Operational Army and to defend their assigned regions.

The ground forces are the backbone of the Polish army. Their core consists of 12 mechanized infantry divisions, an airborne brigade, a coastal defense brigade, and mountain brigade. In 1992 the army had 2,850 tanks of the relatively modern T-72 type, as well as the obsolete T-55AM and T-55 models, but this number was slated for reduction to meet the CFE Treaty limits. The army is supported by the rocket and artillery forces (2,496 artillery pieces in total in 1992), as well as the engineering, chemical defense, communications, reconnaissance, and supply units.

Compared to the two other services, the air and air defense forces are kept at the highest level of readiness in peacetime. Poland maintains three air defense corps, headquartered in Warsaw, Bydgoszcz, and Wroclaw. The air corps is headquartered in Poznan. The three air defense corps jointly cover the entire territory of the country, while the air corps, consisting of fighter bomber and reconnaissance aircraft, as well as communications and support elements, operates as an autonomous unit. In 1992 the air force had 460 aircraft, including the MiG 29, the MiG 23, and the MiG 21 fighters, the MiG 21R reconnaissance aircraft, and the Su 22M4 and the Su 20 fighter bombers, plus 30 Mi 24 attack helicopters. The numbers of fixed-wing aircraft were subsequently revised downward, although Poland is allowed by the CFE Treaty to increase its number of helicopters.

The Polish navy is predominantly a coastal defense force assigned to patrol and defend the Baltic Sea coast. It consists of two coastal defense fleets plus a small operational fleet that includes one destroyer and several submarines. The navy relies on two air force regiments and a helicopter squadron for air support. In total, in 1992 the Polish navy had 67 vessels, including one destroyer, several submarines, and a number of antisubmarine ships and mine sweepers.

The Polish armed forces will continue to downsize, as their numerical size and equipment levels are constrained by the CFE 1 Treaty, which set limits on the number of tanks at 1,730, infantry fighting vehicles and armored personnel carriers at 2,150, artillery pieces with a caliber of 100mm and above at 1,610, combat aircraft at 460, and helicopters at 130. The numerical size of the Polish armed forces is limited by the CFE Treaty to 234,000 troops; this limit will go into effect on 17 November 1995. The reduction in the size of the army and the redeployment of the units is reflected in the declining size of the defense budget, which dropped from 2.4 percent of the GDP in 1990 to 1.9 percent in 1993. This decline has significantly affected the ability of the Polish defense industry to function and to continue meeting the army's basic needs.

DEFENSE SPENDING AND THE DEFENSE INDUSTRY

The current military reform program, the "Plan for the Development of the Armed Forces of the Polish Republic in 1993-95" (*Plan Rozwoju Sil Zbrojnych RP w latach 1993-95*) outlines weapons and equipment procurement through the year 2010.[7] As a result of the growing concern over the resurgence of Russian imperialism and the continued instability in the East, the Polish government has tried since 1994 to arrest the decline of the country's defense potential. Prime Minister Waldemar Pawlak announced in November 1993 that the target for military spending in the future would rise to 3 percent of the GDP.[8] This represented an amplification of the early, more guarded commitment made in his opening address to the parliament to "halt the decline of expenditures for the military and gradually to modernize the army."[9] Still, the renewed assertions by the Polish government that it remained committed to maintaining self-sufficiency in basic weaponry and equipment has to be judged against the harsh reality of budgetary constraints. Save for a national emergency, it is unlikely that the budgetary allocations for defense will increase substantially any time soon. In 1992 the government estimated that between 1986 and 1993, the budget of the Ministry of Defense would decline overall by over 60 percent (Table 3.1). This has resulted in an increase in the percentage of the defense budget allocated for personnel costs (from 54 percent in 1989 to 66 percent in 1993) and a commensurate decrease in the percentage spent for new military hardware (from 23 percent in 1989 to only 3 percent in 1993).[10]

The pattern of Poland's defense spending over the last eight years, especially when considered in light of the overall performance of the economy (1993 was the first year of Poland's economic growth) strongly suggests that the country will be unable to modernize its armed forces without a significant increase in budgetary allocations or foreign assistance. The 1.9 percent of the GDP allocated for defense in 1993 also raises the question of how Poland will bring its army up to the NATO standard if and when it is granted membership in the alliance.

The continued reductions in defense spending have devastated the Polish defense manufacturing base. The core of the Polish defense industry consists of 90 plants, of which 63 are subordinated to the Ministry of Industry and Trade (Ministerstwo Przemyslu i Handlu; MPiH), 19 to the Ministry of Defense, and eight to other ministries. The progressive marketization of the Polish economy has deprived the defense industry of its former privileged position and has forced the plants to operate according to the rules applied in the private sector.[11] The result has been the weakening of Poland's ability to sustain the basic defense industries and a virtual freeze in advanced R&D.

The government responded to the profound crisis in the defense industry by effectively taking over the key defense plants. The 1992 program for the restructuring of the defense industry has placed under direct state control 28 plants from the MPiH, plus 11 repair and maintenance plants originally established by the Ministry of Defense. Ten defense plants deemed critical to the country's defense potential (Table 3.2) have been transformed into corporations with the State Treasury as their sole stockholder.

In light of the deteriorating situation in the East, the strengthening of Poland's indigenous defense potential became in 1994 an important policy objective of the government. However, even if resources were made available through government borrowing the armed forces would not show substantial improvement in equipment right away. Overall, the Polish army remains poorly equipped. For example, 1,000 of the CFE mandated ceiling of 1,730 Polish tanks are of the obsolete T-55A and T-55AM type, while none of the approximately 800 T-72-type tanks (considered average by world standards) has reactive armor, a modern fire control system, or thermal sights. In fact, only the ten T-72 "Twardy"-type tanks purchased in 1993 can be considered close to the world standard.

Likewise, the Polish army's infantry fighting vehicles lack sophisticated fire control and thermal sights. Most of the Polish army five rocket and artillery units need to be supplied with modern ammunition, while the air force has only one squadron of modern MiG-29 aircraft and four Su-22 regiments, with the majority of the equipment still consisting of the obsolete MiG-21 aircraft. Finally, out of the 130 helicopters that Poland is allowed by the CFE, only 30 (the Mi-24s) can be considered modern.[12]

PARTNERSHIP FOR PEACE

In February 1994 Prime Minister Waldemar Pawlak signed in Brussels the documents making Poland formally a participant in NATO's "Partnership for Peace" program. The Polish government, which prior to the January 1994 NATO summit had called for full membership in NATO and had rejected interim solutions, by the spring of 1994 began to explore aggressively the limitations of the PFP formula. On 25 April 1994, Poland's defense minister, Piotr Kolodziejczyk, submitted to Brussels an 11-page "presentation document" outlining his country's plans for military cooperation with NATO within the framework of the Partnership for Peace program. At the same time, Warsaw reaffirmed that it considered the PFP as only an interim step toward full NATO membership. In the words of Jerzy Milewski, chief of the National Security Office (BBN), Poland "considers the Partnership for Peace as a method for accelerating the attainment of that objective."[13] As outlined by Milewski, Warsaw anticipates a three-stage integration process, beginning with Poland's political integration with NATO, to be followed by joint Polish-NATO military planning, to be concluded by Poland's full military integration with NATO. The Polish "presentation document" (Poland was the first country to

TABLE 3.1

Polish Defense Spending as the Percentage of the GDP and the Government Budget

Years	Defense Spending as the Percentage of	
	GDP	Government Budget
1986	3.2	8.3
1987	3.0	8.5
1988	2.6	7.7
1989	1.9	6.4
1990	2.4[*]	7.6[*]
1991	2.0	7.5
1992	2.2	6.6
1993	1.9[**]	6.0[**]

[*]This increase over 1989 is due to the sharp decline in the GDP.
[**]These figures do not take into account expenditures on social security.
Source: *Sily zbrojne Rzeczpospolitej Polskiej, 1992* (Warsaw: Ministerstwo Obrony Narodowej, Biuro Rzecznika Prasowego, December 1992), p. 35.

TABLE 3.2

Key Defense Plants and Production

Plant and Location	Production	Percentage of Production Related to Defense in 1991 (%)
Zaklady Metalowe "Lucznik"; Radom	small arms	15.6
Zaklady Mechaniczne "Tarnow"; Tarnow	anti-aircraft cannon; small arms	34.7
Zaklady Metalowe "Mesko"; Skarzysko-Kamienna	ammunition; anti-tank missiles	46.8
Zaklady Tworzyw Sztucznych "Pionki"; Pronit	explosives	16.0
Zaklady Metalowe "Dezamet"; Nowa Deba	bombs	52.5
Zaklady Sprzetu Precyzyjnego "Niewiadow"; Niewiadow	munitions; mines	1.9
Fabryka Wyrobow Tloczonych "Presta"; Bolechowo	artillery shells; bomb and rocket shells	60.2
Centrum Naukowo-Produkcyjne Elektorniki Profesjonalnej "Radwar"; Warsaw	monitoring and detection systems; command systems	84.0
Przemyslowe Centrum Optyki; Warsaw	range finders; fire control systems	90.0
Zaklady Elektroniczne "Warel"; Warsaw	radio equipment	81.1

Source: *Raport o stanie bezpieczenstwa panstwa: aspekty zewnetrzne* (Warsaw: Polski Instytut Spraw Miedzynarodowych, 1993), p. 127.

submit such plans) outlines 19 military exercises in which Poland wants to participate and pledges Warsaw's commitment to consolidating democratic control over the armed forces.[14] In keeping with Poland's goal of NATO membership, the document calls for "technical, procedural an structural moderization of the armed forces in accordance with NATO standards.[15]

However, the participation in the Partnership for Peace constitutes a fiscal dilemma for the Polish Ministry of Defense, because the added cost of the program has not been included in the country's military budget. The Poles have requested financial assistance from the United States to underwrite bilateral cooperation projects.[16]

While the political dimension of the PFP remains paramount, Poland's participation in the program has an economic aspect as well. The protracted crisis of the Polish defense industry can be alleviated if the PFP opens up new opportunities for cooperation between the Polish defense industry and the defense industries of NATO member countries. The Polish army hopes that the PFP will give Poland access to advanced Western military technologies, accelerate the modernization of the domestic defense industry, help utilize the West's expertise in converting selected military plants to civilian production, and, most important, accelerate the process of changing Polish defense production to meet NATO standards, the requisite step for the Polish army's full integration with the alliance.[17]

In the spring of 1994, the Poles became increasingly uneasy about Moscow's pressure on NATO to grant Russia a special status within the PFP in recognition of its great power position in Europe. Russian defense minister Pavel Grachev's suggestion that the granting of the "special status" might be the necessary precondition for Russia signing on to the program was interpreted in Warsaw as an attempt to prevent NATO's expansion to the East. Polish foreign minister Andrzej Olechowski expressed the growing Polish fears over Russia's demands in his address to the North Atlantic Cooperation Council (NACC) meeting in Istanbul on 10 June 1994. Upon his return to Warsaw, Olechowski remarked that while Poland "recognized the need for a strong partnership between NATO and Russia, it would be a paradox of history . . . if this new partnership were to lead to the marginalization of smaller countries." Olechowski was particularly upset over Russia's success in blocking the inclusion in the NACC statement of a clause saying that active participation in the Partnership For Peace would help lead to future NATO membership; he called it a sign that "Russia has not fully accepted a Polish role in the PFP and the Western European Union."[18]

It appears that despite its early opposition to the PFP, Warsaw has decided to explore aggressively the limits of the program, not because it considers the formula the desirable framework for integration with Western security structures, but rather because it has realized that the alternative is to abandon the NATO policy altogether. In the end, the PFP's value to Polish security will depend on the extent to which the program will serve to integrate Poland with NATO.

A REALITY CHECK:
NATIONAL SECURITY POLICY TODAY AND TOMORROW

The national security position of Poland today is without a doubt the best it has been in three hundred years. For the first time, neither of Poland's two powerful neighbors constitutes a direct threat to its security. Likewise, Poland does not face irredentist claims on its territory. Although the assertions by the leader of Russia's Liberal-Democratic Party, Vladimir Zhirinovskiy, that Russia should restore its empire at the expense of neighboring states has certainly been disconcerting to the Poles, so far the threat to Poland's security position in the East has not been immediate. While it is true that the results of the parliamentary election in Russia in October 1993 strengthened the hands of the communist and fascist forces in Russia and led to the hardening of Moscow's foreign-policy line, that change has yet to reach a point where it would threaten directly Poland's recently regained sovereignty.

For the first time in its history Poland borders on a democratic German state anchored in the Western economic and security system. Despite the occasional friction between Warsaw and Bonn over migration to Germany from or through Poland, the two countries have built a strong working relationship based on a clear perception of the mutuality of national security interests. For Poland, Germany is the window to Western Europe and the best hope for full integration with the West; for Germany, a stable democratic Poland on its immediate eastern periphery is a vital security asset.

In addition to considerable progress in the areas of economic reform and political transformation, Poland today has another unique advantage that dramatically improves its overall security position in the region: It is for the first time in its history not only a sovereign state but also an ethnically homogenous one. Poland today has no significant ethnic minority on its territory whose treatment by the government could strain relations with the country's neighbors. Even if occasionally there appears the question of minority rights for ethnic Germans in Silesia or ethnic Ukrainians or Lithuanians in the East, these are marginal issues whose scope cannot fundamentally alter the overall good relations between Poland and its immediate neighbors.

The central question for the future direction of Polish national security policy is whether the current overall favorable security situation of the Third Republic can be maintained in the long run, and if not, what actions the government should take to ensure that a deteriorating environment in the East would not once again reduce Poland to the status of a Russian client or, worse yet, make it a pawn in the Russo-German competition.

The Polish national security consensus, as well as the military reform drafted by the postcommunist government and already partially implemented constitute a coherent package. However, the actual prospects for their implementation depend on the political constraints of post–Cold War Europe and the tough economic realities facing Poland today. The key obstacle to the implementation of the comprehensive national security strategy, outlined by Foreign Minister Olechowski during his 1993 visit to Washington, remains the overall absence of a clear strategic vision on the part of the United States and its principal NATO allies toward the former Soviet bloc, save for the demonstrated willingness by the Clinton administration to give its relationship with Russia priority over its relationship with the other states in the region. Implicitly the American policy grants Moscow a strategic prerogative in eastern and central Europe—a development that Poland cannot contemplate with equanimity.

In the area of military reform, the constraints facing the Polish planners are equally severe. The declining military budget and the reduced procurement levels have already resulted in the bankruptcy of 30 percent of the Polish armaments factories. Some of the largest former suppliers of the Polish army face the prospect of terminating all military contracts; for example, in 1993 the Huta Stalowa Wola works, one of the largest military suppliers under the communist regime, sold only 3 percent of its output to the army.[19] Direct government intervention has proved necessary to ensure that the army has domestic sources of vital supplies and ammunition in the future; it remains to be seen whether this attempt to save the domestic defense industry will succeed.

The problem of the continued cutbacks in the defense budget gained new urgency in 1994 after the resurgence of Russian imperialism. In response to the new situation, in November and December 1993, the Ministry of Defense was allocated an additional 650 billion zloty from the Ministry of Finance's budgetary reserves to improve the combat readiness of the armed forces. The supplementary spending was coordinated by a plan drafted by the chief of the National Security Office (BBN), Jerzy Milewski. An additional 350 billion zloty was allocated to the Ministry of Internal Affairs.[20]

The procurement crisis in the Polish armed forces is likely to continue, notwithstanding the new monies authorized by the government in the winter of 1993. Absent substantial additional outlays on defense, the 1994 defense budget will allow the army to purchase only ten modernized tanks (the Twardy type), eight trainer aircraft, and a dozen helicopters.[21] Between 1990 and 1993 the difficult economic conditions in Poland made it impossible to entertain the idea of increases in military spending of the size required to complete successfully the military reform process. Furthermore, Warsaw's growing concern over the survival of the country's indigenous defense industry may, paradoxically, prove a significant factor mitigating against the modernization and re-equipment of the Polish armed forces with up-to-date Western hardware. According to Polish defense minister Admiral Piotr Kolodziejczyk, 75 percent of all budgetary allocations for purchases of military equipment in 1994 will be spent on contracts awarded to Polish manufacturers.[22] Therefore, Poland's ability to buy modern Western equipment is likely to remain limited in the foreseeable future, even though the country has developed technical military cooperation with France and Sweden and intends to strengthen its cooperation with Germany.

The Polish government's disappointment associated with NATO's resolution to postpone any decision on Poland's membership in the alliance, and to offer the former Soviet bloc the "Partnership for Peace" formula instead, has proved instrumental in broadening the Polish debate on the future shape of national security policy. The lesson of the January 1994 Prague summit proved especially bitter for President Walesa, who had assumed the leading role in pressuring the United States to transform the PFP into a genuine formula for opening NATO eastward. In March 1994, during an official visit to France, Polish defense minister Piotr Kolodziejczyk expressed the growing concern that Poland's membership in NATO may prove in the end an elusive goal and noted that Poland "has a much greater chance to become integrated with the Western European Union than to join NATO."[23] Subsequently, in the spring of 1994 nine former Soviet satellites, including Poland, signed an agreement with the WEU granting them associate partnership status with the organization.[24]

It may very well be that the January 1994 NATO summit also ended all plans for future security cooperation within the Visegrad Group, as only Slovakia supported Walesa's position actively. Slovak president Kovac called for the immediate, full, political membership in NATO for the group, to be accompanied by real security guarantees. In contrast, the Czech Republic effectively disavowed the future viability of Visegrad, while Hungary proved remarkably restrained in criticizing the PFP. In the end, Warsaw's determination to transform the issue of NATO membership for the Visegrad Group into a litmus test of the West's intentions resulted in a negative message from the West. The issue of the Visegrad Group's dubious long-term viability was highlighted by the meeting of the Group's defense ministers on the eve of the January NATO summit. As if to underscore Prague's lack of faith in the Visegrad process, the Czech Republic dispatched to the meeting not its defense minister but a deputy defense minister. His message to the Poles, Slovaks, and Hungarians was that "if the inclusion of all four states in NATO is questionable, the [Visegrad Group] states ought to act individually"[25]—a clear indication that Prague intended to distance itself from the other members.

In 1994 Warsaw's disappointment at NATO's refusal to extend an offer of membership to the Visegrad Group prompted a discussion in the government and the media on the priorities of Polish security policy. The debate was accompanied by the growing awareness of the "renaissance of the imperial idea"[26] in Russia, with its potentially dangerous consequences for Polish security. A number of Polish politicians and academics argued that Polish Eastern policy as a whole required a redirection to build a working partnership with Russia, to encourage the consolidation of Ukraine and (to the degree that it might still be possible) of Belarus as independent states. Calls for a more balanced relationship with Russia to complement Poland's unequivocal pro-Western orientation of the last three years of independence included a proposal to form an equivalent to the "Partnership for Peace" in Poland's relations with Russia, Lithuania, and Ukraine. This was seen as essential to long term Polish national security interests.[27] Trade and economic cooperation with the East were singled out as a means to begin developing the new policy.

Advocates of change in Polish security policy, which since 1989 emphasized complete integration with the West, have called for a new concept of "bipolar integration," which would complement Poland's opening to the West with an opening toward Russia and the Soviet successor states.[28] This new security arrangement would rest on a strong economic partnership with Russia, including a free trade zone with the East to supplement Poland's efforts to enter the European Union. The idea of basing Polish security on "bipolar integration" was in effect a modification of the formula advanced by the founding father of the Second Republic, Marshal Jozef Pilsudski, whose recipe for Poland's national survival was to navigate between Western Europe and Russia. However, the 1994 evolution of Pilsudski's vision would replace the aloofness of the prewar period with a form of "friendly neutrality,"[29] whereby Poland could develop progressively closer ties with both the East and the West without becoming a hostage to the policies of either. Still, whatever the merit of the "bipolar integration" proposal, the ultimate feasibility of this vision depends on the evolution of Russian domestic politics rather than on Polish diplomatic initiatives. Therefore, the NATO option has remained paramount in Poland's national security policy.

Today Poland continues to strive for membership in NATO. Both President Lech Walesa and Prime Minister Waldemar Pawlak reaffirmed after the January 1994 NATO summit that they would not be seeking alternative military alliances to NATO, including bilateral security arrangements.[30] The "Partnership for Peace" formula offered to the former Warsaw Pact states is a disappointment; Walesa called it "too small a step in the right direction."[31] However, Foreign Minister Andrzej Olechowski's assessment that "in terms of the standards of democracy and the development of the military sector Poland is in no worse condition than, for example, Greece at the time of its admission to NATO,"[32] while basically correct, brushes aside the fundamental difference between the Europe of the Cold War era and the Europe of today.

The renewed emphasis on a more effective Eastern policy as a precondition for Poland's security has become a greater part of the Polish debate on security and foreign policies. As articulated by the chairman of the Sejm Commission on Foreign Relations, Bronislaw Geremek, "Poland should seek in Russia a friendly partner, not an adversary."[33] Warsaw has also lowered somewhat its earlier expectations that NATO would soon make itself open to new members in central and eastern Europe. The Poles seem to have recognized that even if NATO were to decide in the future to extend its security guarantees to Poland, such a move would have to be preceded by an extensive public debate in the United States, which by Foreign Minister Olechowski's own admission "has yet to begin."[34]

The Polish security policy formula pursued by the four post-Solidarity governments rested on the premise that NATO membership for the Visegrad Group would be a precondition for broadening the area of stability in Europe. At the same time, the policy never presented the NATO option as a means of insulating Poland from Russia. This view is still present, as reflected in Foreign Minister Olechowski's assertion that "Poland's position in the West will depend on Poland's position in the East,"[35] that is, that in order to maintain its independence and to protect its security interests, Poland must also have a strong economic and political relationship with Russia built on the principle of genuine partnership.

In 1994 Warsaw remained seriously concerned about the potential for instability in the East. The fear that in the end the West may opt to stay out of East-Central Europe altogether prompted President Lech Walesa in January 1994 to warn of the threat of resurgent neocommunism facilitated by the West's acceptance of Russian influence in the East.[36] The mood of uncertainty in Warsaw was exacerbated by Yeltsin's 1994 hardened foreign-policy stance, which was underscored by a speech to Russian ambassadors to the CIS delivered by Foreign Minister Andrey Kozyrev on 19 January 1994. Kozyrev argued that Russia "should not withdraw from those regions which have been the sphere of Russian interests for centuries." These assertions of a Russian sphere of influence in eastern Europe were another signal to Warsaw that Moscow might entertain renewed hegemonic aspirations toward Poland.[37] The Poles are concerned that should Russia revert to totalitarianism, a continued Russian-American security partnership would in fact be detrimental to regional as well as Polish security.

In order to help transform Russia from a latent threat to a stabilizing factor, Poland has advocated a policy that would eventually make Russia a part of the existing economic institutions, including bringing Russia in as a permanent member of the G-7 group of leading economic powers. Poland has also advocated the establishment of a broad agreement with the European Union to develop a free trade zone linking Russia and the West, with the long-term objective of full economic integration of Russia with the European Union. Poland has been a leading advocate of Western economic assistance to Russia and to other Soviet successor states in order to stabilize their economies and lessen the potential burden on Russia. Warsaw has asked for Western help to rejuvenate regional trade and its infrastructure and to establish regional trade institutions in the former Soviet bloc. In addition, Poland has been a strong advocate of using UN forces (in addition to the Russian army) for peacekeeping operations in the former Soviet Union. Warsaw's support of reform in Russia was based on the realization that the worst-case scenario from the vantage point of Poland's security interests would be its continued exclusion from the Western-led security system accompanied by a deteriorating relationship with Russia. That concern became particularly visible in Poland after the 1993 announcement of the new Russian defense doctrine.[38]

By 1994 the initial expectations that regional cooperation, such as the Visegrad Group, would quickly pave the way for Poland's inclusion in the Western security system were dashed, while the "Partnership for Peace" formula sent a clear message to Warsaw that the United States and its allies were not yet willing to extend NATO eastward. For Poland the new situation has called for careful and balanced foreign and security policies. While the goal of "rejoining the West" remains paramount, Warsaw needs to rethink the conditions on which it would be welcome in the West. In the post–Cold War era there is little interest in the West in incurring additional security commitments in eastern and central Europe which might lead to a confrontation with Russia.

If Poland is to count on being included in NATO in the future, it has to be perceived first and foremost not as a liability but as an asset to the alliance. It is also debatable to what extent Poland would benefit from being once again a frontier state of the West. If in the end the neoimperialists dominate in Russia,

Poland may have no choice but to accept this role as a price of being included in the Western system; however, it should by no means consider becoming a "frontier state" as the best solution to its security dilemma.

The continued sovereignty and security of the Polish state must rest on a realistic assessment of the existing geopolitical situation in the region as well as on a global view of American interests and commitments. While Poland's membership in NATO is clearly a desirable outcome, for now it is a long-term option. It is a matter for serious debate whether Poland would be better off in terms of its national security if the membership in NATO were bought at the price of unyielding Russian hostility. In the final analysis, the terms on which Poland might be included in NATO will have to be negotiated by the United States and Russia, and the outcome will owe more to the skill and vision of American diplomacy than to anything Poland might directly contribute to it. If anything, this is the lesson from the snub Lech Walesa received from the American side when he launched his campaign to pressure Washington into action.

Today the old adage of the Polish security dilemma, demanding that the country "navigate between Germany and Russia" still holds, but with a positive twist. At present Poland has nothing to fear from Bonn, while its concerns about a Russian threat are still largely hypothetical. This constitutes a unique window of opportunity for Poland to develop a relationship with Russia that would at least begin to approach its excellent working relationship with Germany. Trade and cultural ties would go a long way in establishing a modicum of trust between Warsaw and Moscow. Should neo-imperialists dominate Russia, Poland also has a lot to gain from maintaining good relations with its non-Russian Eastern neighbors: Lithuania, Belarus, and especially Ukraine. Regardless of their inherent limitations, Polish diplomatic efforts to support the continued independence and sovereignty of Soviet successor states in eastern Europe are a safeguard against the resurgence of Russian domination.

In early 1994 Warsaw's gravest fear was that NATO's policy would effectively allow the existing divisions of Europe to become petrified, which might eventually result in the restoration of an imperial and undemocratic Russia as the hegemonic power in the region. The return of Russian imperial influence in East-Central Europe, combined with the West's simultaneous desertion of the region, would leave Poland no alternative but to build a regional coalition in a desperate effort to counterbalance Russia and to compensate for the absence of a Western security umbrella. Such a drive for an autonomous defensive alliance in the region, with Ukraine for example, would set Poland on the course of direct and unpredictable confrontation with Russia.

As articulated by Foreign Minister Andrzej Olechowski in the winter of 1993, the overriding Polish security objective is to foster a new "Euroatlantic

contract" that would extend NATO first to the Visegrad Group and subsequently to other states that have made progress toward democracy and market
capitalism. This new security arrangement would also require closer cooperation
between NATO and Russia as a precondition of further democratization in the
East and an eventual strategic partnership between Russia and the West. It is
revealing of Poland's security concerns that Olechowski singled out Ukraine as
the state whose ties to NATO in the future European security system ought to
approximate those of Russia. By 1994, the apparent consensus in Moscow on
an assertive foreign policy directed at restoring Russia's great power position in
Europe, and especially the West's willingness (at least for now) to acquiesce in
those aspirations, has deferred Olechowski's vision of a "Euroatlantic contract"
until some unspecified point in time.

In broad terms, the security dilemma facing Poland since regaining its
independence in 1989 is similar to that facing East Central Europe as a whole.
The states in the region lack both the economic and population resources to
"self-insure" against potential pressures by outside powers. Under these circumstances the primary policy objective facing Poland is to accelerate the country's
modernization to begin compensating for a half-century of retarded economic
growth. Here a more balanced West-East approach may prove effective. In light
of the progressive closing off of the European Union to new entrants from the
East, Poland may find it difficult to make sustained economic progress without
relying to a greater degree on the potentially vast Eastern market. It is also
questionable whether Poland's wholesale accession to the regulatory EU rules
and controls, while politically important, is something that the country can
ultimately afford, for it will add to the already formidable obstacles to economic
modernization.

As 1994 unfolded, Poland stood on the threshold of important decisions in
its relations with the East as it also considered the implication for its relations with
the West of the "Partnership for Peace" formula and the prospects for NATO
membership. While the words of the Polish ambassador to Moscow, Stanislaw
Ciosek, that in Poland's relations with Russia the time has come to "switch from
the cushioning mechanism in the relationship to . . . cooperative mechanisms,"[39]
are overly optimistic, Poland needs to explore to the fullest extent possible the limits
of its cooperative relationship with Russia. In January 1994, the Polish ambassador
to Brussels and the representative to NATO, Andrzej Krzeczunowicz, warned that
Russian policy toward eastern and central Europe amounted to a "Russian version
of the policy of containment,'" and that "today the Russians are attempting to
contain NATO along the Oder river because they find such status quo acceptable."[40] It is essential to Polish national security that the Russian version of
"containment" not become the new norm in European politics. If, however, the

resurgence of an imperial and menacing Russia becomes the reality of the post–Cold War era, Poland must ensure that the new East-West frontier does not run along the Oder-Neisse line separating Germany and Poland, but rather along the Bug River on Poland's eastern border.

Notes

1. The following discussion is based on the transcript of Olechowski's address delivered at the Center for Strategic and International Studies in Washington on December 1993, and subsequently released by the Polish Embassy.

2. The following is based on the official *Podstawowe zalozenia strategii Rzeczypospolitej Polskiej na lata 1993-2000,* released by the Polish Ministry of Defense in November 1992.

3. *Sily zbrojne Rzeczpospolitej Polskiej, 1992* (Warsaw: Ministerstwo Obrony Narodowej, Biuro Rzecznika Prasowego, December 1992), p. 8.

4. The discussion of the organizational structure of the Polish armed forces is based on *Sily zbrojne Rzeczpospolitej Polskiej—1992: Wybor Materialow dla Prasy* (Warsaw: Ministerstwo Obrony Narodowej, Grudzien, 1992).

5. *Mala Konstytucja z komentarzem* (Warszawa: Wydawnictwo AWA, 1992), Article 35.

6. Maria Wagrowska, "Byc daleko od polityki: Rozmowa z Piotrem Kolodziejczykiem, ministrem obrony narodowej," *Rzeczpospolita,* 26 January 1994.

7. Coloniel Stanislaw Lukaszewski and Major Mariusz Jedrzejko, "Obrona i bezpieczenstwo kraju nie sa wylacznie sprawa armii: Odprawa kierowniczej kadry Sil Zrojnych RP," *Polska Zbrojna,* 9 November 1993.

8. Ibid.

9. "Expose Waldemara Pawlaka," *Rzeczpospolita,* 9 November 1993.

10. *Sily zbrojne Rzeczpospolitej Polskiej, 1992,* p. 30.

11. Raport o stanie bezpieczenstwa panstwa: aspekty zeqnetrzne (Warsaw: Panstwowy Instytut Spraw Miedzynarodowych, 1993), p. 124.

12. Ibid., pp. 110-111.

13. Interview with Jerzy J. Milewski in Janusz B. Grochowski, "Gramy powaznie," *Polska Zbrojna,* 5 May 1994.

14. "Poland Presents Partnership Outline," *RFE/RL Military Notes,* 29 April 1994.

15. Polish "Presentation Document," Partnership for Peace (excerpts), p. 1.

16. Interview with Jerzy J. Milewski in "Gramy powaznie."

17. Pawel, Wieczorek, "Czy bedziemy kooperowac z krajami NATO w przemysle obronnym?" *Polska Zbronjan,* 3 March 1994.

18. "Russia's Stance on NATO Worries Poland," *RFE/RL Military Notes,* 17 June 1994.
19. "Ostatni Dzwonek," *Polska Zbrojna,* 21-23 January 1994.
20. "Bilion na bezpieczenstwo," *Polska Zbrojna,* 18 January 1994.
21. "Budget i obronnosc kraju," *Zycie Warszawy,* 17 January 1994.
22. "Admiral nie opuszcza mostka," *Nowa Europa,* 24 January 1994.
23. Jacek Czernecki, "Rozmowa min. P. Kolodziejczyka we Francji: Polska w europejskim systemie bezpieczenstwa," *Polska Zbrojna,* 3 March 1994.
24. "Do NATO przez UZE," *Zycie Warszawy,* 10 May 1994.
25. "Cel jeden, drogi rozne: Ministrowie obrony Grupy Wyszehradzkiej," *Rzeczpospolita,* 8–9 January 1994.
26. The term coined by Jerzy Marek Nowakowski in "W poszukiwaniu nowej koncepcji: Polityka wschodnia Polski—Perspektywa XXI wieku," *Rzeczpospolita,* 14 January 1994.
27. Ibid.
28. Marian Pilka, "Dwubiegunowa integracja," *Rzeczpospolita,* 21 January 1994.
29. The term coined in 1994 by Adam Bien, the last surviving minister of the wartime Polish government-in-exile. See: "Polska byle jaka," *Tygodnik Solidarnosc,* 21 January 1994.
30. Malgorzata Subotic, "Zbyt krotki krok we wlasciwym kierunku: Prezydent i rzad o NATO," *Rzeczpospolita,* 11 January 1994.
31. Ibid.
32. Ibid.
33. Janusz Gizinski and Maria Graczyk, "Racja stanu: Rozmowa z prof. Bronislawem Geremkiem, przewodniczacym Komisji Spraw Zagranicznych Sejmu RP," *Wprost,* 9 January 1994.
34. Krystyna Szelestowska and Dariusz Szymczycha, "Warszawa—miedzy Moskwa i Waszyngtonem," *Trybuna,* 31 December 1993–2 January 1994.
35. Ibid.
36. "Walesa Says NATO Risks New Communist Threat," *International Herald Tribune,* 4 January 1994, p. 1.
37. "Kozyrev Puts Eastern Europe into Sphere of Interest," *RFE/RL Daily Report,* 15 February 1994.
38. This was suggested in an interview with Jerzy Milewski, State Secretary for National Security. See Janusz B. Grochowski, "Zdecyduje polityka, nie doktryna" *Polska Zbrojna,* 8 November 1993.
39. "Zdobyc Rosje portfelem," *Przeglad Tygodniowy,* 23 January 1994.
40. Witold Kalinowski, "Najmocniejsza Gwarancja: Wywiad tygodnia z Andrzejem Krzechunowiczem, ambasadorem RP w Brukseli, przedstawicielem rzadu polskiego przy NATO," *Tygodnik Solidarnosc,* 21 January 1994.

4

Warsaw's Ostpolitik: A New Encounter with Positivism

Ilya Prizel

Poland has a thousand-year-old history, but does not have a "yesterday" to which to refer.

> —Juliusz Mieroszewski,
> "The Political Thoughts of Kultura," in *Kultura Essays*

Before our very eyes Communism, the curse of the twentieth century, is dying, and with it the Soviet empire, the curse of my nation, but I cannot be happy. I am scared.

> —Adam Michnik, "Na skraju czarnej dziury,"
> *Gazeta Wyborcza,* 23 December 1991

The collapse of communism revolutionized the geopolitical position of Poland. All of its neighbors mutated beyond recognition: Germany re-united, once again becoming a colossus in the heart of the continent; Czechoslovakia's contentious experiment with binationalism ended in a "velvet divorce"; and the Soviet empire ceased to exist in December of 1991 without a whimper.

Yet despite the tempest in East-Central Europe and the almost chronically unstable governments in Warsaw, Poland's foreign policy has remained one of the most consistent features of postcommunist Europe. While Poles have yet to agree about the optimum method for re-creating a market economy in their country, or what role foreign capital should play in the economy, or what role is appropriate for the Catholic Church in a democratic Poland, Polish foreign policy has enjoyed remarkable consensus and stability.

Although no one could predict the time and the manner of the collapse of communism and the Soviet empire, since 1947 Polish intellectuals clustered around the émigré journal *Kultura* had been refining an appropriate geopolitical model for Poland. While these analysts frequently differed on many issues over the four decades that *Kultura* published as a dissident publication, if there was ever a consistent view among its authors, it was that Poland's return to normalcy would be contingent on its ability to end its six-century-old struggle with its eastern neighbors.

In 1966 the eminent historian Juliusz Mieroszewski, in one of the most systematic studies of Poland's predicament, made several iconoclastic observations that challenged many fundamental assumptions of Poland's thinking during much of the twentieth century.[1] Mieroszewski noted that the territorial changes imposed on Poland after World War II were not only irreversible but, as Czeslaw Milosz noted, also the culmination of the final disappearance of the commonwealth with Lithuania, which began following the defeat of the Polish uprising of 1863. Furthermore, Mieroszewski conceded that "an independent Poland is necessary for us [the Poles] but not for Europe." Therefore, if Poland was to regain its independence, it would have to completely restructure its self-image and its role within the international community.

Poland will fail to assume an important role in Europe, Mieroszewski continued, if it attempts to be a latter-day *antemurale Christianitatis,* trying to defend Europe from Russia, since in the final analysis Russia is far more important for the West than Poland will ever be. Instead Poland should exploit its position of being both a Latin Catholic and a Slavic state, thereby providing a bridge between Russia and the West. Poland could continue an anti-Russian posture only if Poland became a multinational state again, a proposition that has been rejected by both the Poles and their immediate eastern neighbors. Poland must come to terms with the fact that Russia, regardless of whether it succeeds or fails to retain its empire, will remain by far the most powerful state in Europe. Instead of continuing its failed centuries-long quest to liquidate Russia as a great power, Poland should devote its energies to "Europeanizing"

Russia. Only such a process will enable Poland to escape the fate of either becoming a Russian satellite or facing a Rapallo-like condominium between Moscow and Berlin.

"Poland must win a peace with Russia because it cannot win a war," Mieroszewski argued. Poland cannot insist on both its pre-1939 frontiers in the east and the Oder-Neisse border in the west. Poland must accept the loss of the eastern borderlands (Kresy) as the price for normal relations with Ukraine, Belarus, and Lithuania. In comparing Nikita Khrushchev to Klemens von Metternich as a conservative leader who was "terrified by the spring of nations," Mieroszewski made the prophetic observation that no empire could forever resist the pressures of nationalism:

> Neither the Soviet Union nor the most liberal and enlightened colonial policy of the Western states will manage the nationality problem; they will not manage to persuade people on five continents that only certain nations have the right to independence . . . the Soviet empire will be no different and ultimately break up as well.[2]

Although Mieroszewski remained skeptical as to whether there could be a short-term reconciliation between Poland and Germany, he felt that the developments in Russia would ultimately shape the future of Poland and Europe:

> The liquidation of the "cold war" on our continent, including Russia in a broader European system, normalizing Polish-Russia relations—all of this depends on the decolonialization of the Soviet Union . . . Russia is in a significantly better position than France and England, because she has greater possibilities for making partners out of her satellites. As a consequence, decolonialization would make Russia stronger not weaker.[3]

Mieroszewski noted that even if the Cold War ended and communism collapsed, Russia and Poland would retain a historic link as postcommunist states trying to find a place in the international arena. As Poland's ultimate security and freedom are tied to its ability to come to terms with its eastern neighbors, the Poles have to abandon the attitude of hate-*cum*-contempt toward the Russians that for so long was a part of Poland's national ethos.

Works of intellectuals such as Mieroszewski, published in the Paris-based *Kultura* and the London-based *Aneks,* laid a solid foundation upon which Poland could build a postcommunist structure. When communism finally collapsed, Poland, unlike many of its neighbors, thus had a well-defined paradigm in place, one that has generally been competently executed by Foreign Minister Krzysztof Skubiszewski.

From the very start Poland's policy planners set four fundamental goals for their country. First, Poland would need some guarantee of long-term independence, a goal, most Poles agreed, that at best could be attained only if the Soviet Union democratized and decentralized, or at least dissolved. Second, in order to free itself from the hegemony of Moscow, Poland would need to bring about a reconciliation with Germany, a process that would necessitate dealing with the controversial issue of the German minority in Poland. Third, in order to escape the role of the perennial weak leg of the Berlin-Warsaw-Moscow triangle, Poland would need to join the North Atlantic Treaty Organization (NATO) at the earliest possible moment to use U.S. presence in Europe against Poland's most powerful neighbors. And fourth, in order to assure long-term economic prosperity, Poland would need to integrate into Western Europe, a process that could be attained only if Poland carried through internal economic reforms and avoided acrimonious relationships with its neighbors (unlike during the interwar period).

To accomplish these goals, the Skubiszewski team realized, Poland would have to avoid two potentially fatal pitfalls. First, Poland had to break with its tradition of cataloging the historic wrongs inflicted upon it by its neighbors, which invariably dragged Poland into a diplomacy of bombastic symbolism. And second, despite the limelight that Poland might currently enjoy, Poles could not forget that theirs is a mid-sized European state with limited resources; under no circumstance could Poland act beyond its actual capabilities.[4]

EASTERN POLICY REVISITED

Although Poland's relationship with Germany has been affected by the historic baggage of their millennium-long struggle, this relationship is qualitatively different from Poland's relationship with Russia. Despite cycles of war and bloodletting, the fact remains that there have been long periods of Polish-German collaboration, cultural sharing, and peaceful relations. Even during Poland's primacy in the sixteenth and seventeenth centuries, when large Polish-speaking areas remained under Prussian domination, the ethnic Germans who formed the burgher class in Polish cities coexisted with the Poles without much tension on either side. The Poles may fear the more numerous and better organized Germans, but they have never questioned the fact that they share a civilization with their western neighbors; for that matter they have defined the ultimate standing of their state solely in terms of its relationship with Germany.

It was due to its expansion in the east that Poland acquired its status as Europe's premier military power, and to its confrontation with the Muslim Tatars and Byzantine East Slavs that Poland acquired its identity as the bastion of Christianity as well as a great power. It was on the vast expanses of the eastern region that a disproportionate number of Poland's wealthy, landed elites lived, and it was Poland's relationship with the East that played a pivotal role in shaping its national ethos. What makes the relationship with the East extraordinarily complicated is not only Poland's profound attachment to the Kresy but also the bitter memory of Russian domination in the nineteenth century and again in 1945-89, a domination that generally exceeded in brutality that of Prussia and Austria (a fact that the Poles find hard to bear in light of their prevailing sense of cultural superiority over and contempt toward Russians). Reflecting on this pervading Polish perception, Czeslaw Milosz observed: "Russia was something *outside,* beyond the orbit of the civilized world. Consequently their [the Poles'] defeat at the hands of Russia shocked them."[5] Thus while accord with Germany could be reduced to the issues of borders and security, an agreement with its eastern neighbors demanded from Poland a redefinition of six hundred years of national identity.

Polish intellectuals, trying to devise a policy for Poland in a postcommunist world, recognized that Poland's attitude toward the East would have to undergo profound revision. For Poland to become a truly normal and independent country, the following developments would have to take place: (1) Poland would have to abandon all claims to the Kresy and accept its current eastern frontiers as permanent; (2) Poland would have to recognize the national aspirations of the people of Lithuania, Belarus, and Ukraine and support their independence from both Moscow and Warsaw, abandoning the notion that the Ukrainian and Belarusan people are merely an "ethnographic mass" devoid of indigenous culture; and (3) Poles would have to separate in their minds the Russian state from the Soviet Union and, despite their loathing for communism and "inferior" Russian culture, offer Poland as a bridge and a catalyst for Russia's Europeanization instead of acting as *antemurale Christianitatis* against "Asiatic" Russia.

Although the theoretical precepts advocated by Poland's intellectuals since 1947 were largely internalized by Poland's postcommunist elite, their implementation proved to be far more complex. The reasons for this difficulty were threefold. First, the essential factor in attaining these goals was the profound transformation of the Soviet Union—a process in which Poland could play at best a marginal role. Second, with the German frontier issue remaining unsettled, Poland's postcommunist government felt no less dependent on the Soviet Union's defensive shield than did its communist predecessors and consequently was constrained both in terms of its ability to support democratization within the Soviet Union and in terms of its ability to deepen relations with its immediate neighbors (Ukraine, Belarus, and Lithuania). Finally, despite the overwhelming support for a historic reconciliation with Ukraine and Lithuania, parts of the Polish polity found it hard to resign themselves to the loss of Lwow and Wilno (Lviv and Vilnius); nor could the collective memory shaped by strife with the Ukrainians easily free itself from a latent fear of an independent Ukraine.

Responding to the conflicting pressures exerted on Poland's postcommunist regime, Warsaw's foreign policy consisted of a two-track approach. In the West, while striving toward a historic reconciliation with Germany, Warsaw simultaneously continued to request that Soviet troops remain on Polish soil until the relations with Germany normalized. In the East, while it made no secret of its sympathies for the aspirations of the Baltic peoples and the Ukrainians, Warsaw was willing to deepen links with its eastern neighbors only to the degree that such action did not compromise its relationship with Moscow.

With the European architecture undergoing an extraordinarily rapid metamorphosis characterized by the imminent reunification of Germany and growing disintegration of the Soviet Union, Poland's immediate dilemma was how to respond to the rapidly altering situation in the East. While there was a consensus that the disintegration of the Soviet Union might well be in Poland's long-term interest, few in Poland were prepared for the swift change. In one of the first academic analyses of Poland's relationship with the East, Agnieszka Magdziak-Miszewska and Jerzy Marek Nowakowski, director of the Institute of Foreign Affairs attached to the Polish Senate, wrote in late 1990 that although the breakup of the Soviet Union might well be under way, it would be a mistake for Poles to indulge in a "senile policy" *(zdziecinnienie starcze)* that relived an interwar reality that had long ceased to exist. Poland had to cease treating all Soviet citizens as a monolith and avoid all appearance of paternalism. The Soviet Union might well break up, but the new states emerging on Russia's fringe would remain economically and militarily dependent on Moscow. Thus the authors urged the Polish government to conduct a multidimensional foreign policy, to reach out to Gorbachev, Yeltsin, and other republican leaders. Poland's road to normalcy, as well as its acceptance by the West, was contingent upon a good relationship with Russia.[6]

With the prospect of a united Germany casting a shadow on Poland, Warsaw attempted to counterbalance the situation by advocating the integration of the Soviet Union (as a unit) into the architecture of Europe, stressing that the key to Poland's long-term security was the victory of the "Westernizers" in Russia, with the aspiration of the peoples of the borderlands remaining secondary.[7] In fact as late as 1990, Poland, nervous about German intentions, continued to advocate the maintenance of the Warsaw Pact (albeit in a new form). It was only in the autumn of 1990, following the successful resolution of the German border issue, that Poland reversed its position and began advocating the dissolution of the Warsaw Pact.[8]

Rhetoric notwithstanding, this stance in effect confined Poland to a passive position. Skubiszewski's two-track policy, in which Poland continued to defer to the increasingly feeble Kremlin while simultaneously professing support for the aspirations of the Baltics and Ukraine, was not meant to last. On the one hand, the perceived need for the presence of Soviet troops in Poland disappeared soon after the German government accepted the Oder-Neisse line and signed a friendship treaty with Poland. In fact, within a very short period of time the continued Soviet military presence on Polish soil, instead of giving a sense of security, was perceived by most Poles as anachronistic at best and humiliating at worst. Furthermore, Poland's measured policy toward its immediate eastern neighbors was coming under increased public scrutiny, especially following the massacre of Lithuanian civilians at the television tower in Vilnius in January 1991. Nevertheless, Poles remained split over whether the breakup of the Soviet Union would actually serve Poland's interests: some groups saw an independent Ukraine as a guarantor of genuine Polish sovereignty, while others saw a potential threat to Poland's security.[9]

Because of these constraints and ambiguities it is not surprising that Poland's initial two-track policy did little to inspire Baltic and Ukrainian nationalists' craving for independence or to please a vast majority of Poland's electorate. In September 1990 the Polish Senate held hearings on Poland's Eastern policy and criticized the government's lack of links to the individual republics of the Soviet Union. Yet the Sejm refused to fully support the independence aspirations of the Soviet republics along the Polish border, thereby limiting its commitment to the hope that the Soviet Union would evolve as a "genuine confederacy."[10]

By the time Lech Walesa declared his candidacy for president and challenged his hand-picked prime minister, Tadeusz Mazowiecki, the entire question of Poland's Eastern policy had become a hotly contested electoral issue. Once elected and advised by Zdzislaw Najder,[11] who advocated a far more activist policy along Poland's eastern rim, President Walesa did not wait long to signal a fundamental change, starting with his inaugural speech. Walesa startled his audience by extending his greetings to Poland's eastern neighbors— Lithuania, Byelorussia, and Ukraine—and ignoring the Soviet Union altogether. President Walesa's seemingly open challenge to the integrity of the

Soviet Union drew an angry response from the Soviet media, with several Soviet newspapers reminding Walesa that Ukraine was a part of the Soviet Union. Yet, despite Moscow's obvious displeasure, Poland's new government continued to pursue enthusiastically the cause of Byelorussian, Ukrainian, and Russian independence, as witnessed by a dramatic increase in mutual exchanges and visits between Poland and the three countries. Even before the collapse of the Soviet Union, the Polish government appropriated to itself the role of Europeanizing these emerging republics and bringing them into the fold, seeing it as an opportunity to bolster Poland's international presence. Najder's view that Poland's attitude toward Ukraine would help Poland to Europeanize itself, thereby bolstering its position within the international system, was reinforced by the nearly universal belief that Ukraine, unlike Russia, would embark on a relatively quick and painless transformation to democracy and a market economy, and that without Ukraine Russia would cease to be a superpower.[12]

If one was to compare the posture of postcommunist Poland with that of interwar Poland, one would see that a fundamental change had occurred in Poland's self-perception in the late 1980s. Whereas prewar Poland saw its source of legitimacy in its reclaiming of the Jagiellonian tradition, which demanded expansion to the east, postcommunist Poland saw its legitimacy deriving from the transformation of Poland into a normal European state. If prewar Poland saw its importance to Europe based on Poland's ability to be a rampart against Russia, the new Polish elites recognized that Poland's integration into the West was contingent on Russia's Europeanization and on Poland's ability to sustain normal relations with the East.

While Poland attempted to retain a cordial relationship with the Soviet Union, the last year of the Soviet state was marked with controversies with Poland. On the symbolic level, the Poles were infuriated by the Kremlin's stonewalling posture when it came to addressing the issue of the NKVD's 1940 massacre of thousands of Polish officers in the Katyn and Mednoye forests. Moscow was irked by what it perceived as Polish obstruction of the movement of Soviet troops across Polish territory as they were leaving Germany. The Kremlin's adoption of the so-called Kvitsinsky Doctrine, which insisted that Poland follow Romania's lead and commit itself to not joining any alliance that Moscow perceived as anti-Soviet, was firmly rejected by Warsaw as an affront to Polish independence, as a doctrine that relegated Poland once again to the status of a buffer state.[13] The relationship was further embittered by what was perceived in Moscow as an ungrateful Polish insistence on the rapid withdrawal of Soviet troops and by Warsaw's ire over Moscow's high-handed negotiation style along with demands for excessive financial compensation for alleged improvements by the departing Soviet troops.

The collapse of the Soviet Union in August 1991 provided both Poland and its eastern neighbors with an opportunity for a final reconciliation. Poland was the first country outside the Commonwealth of Independent States (CIS) to recognize independent Ukraine, Belarus, and Russia. Believing that there could be no stability in Eastern Europe without reconciliation with its eastern neighbors,[14] Poland managed to sign friendship treaties with all of its neighbors, thereby achieving stability along Polish frontiers for the first time in a millennium. Although the disintegration of the Soviet Union went beyond the hopes of the Polish Senate, which as late as September 1990 hoped for the emergence of a confederacy to replace the highly centralized Soviet Union, Poland's Eastern policy remained ambivalent, contradictory, and a hostage to Poland's traditional preoccupation with the two most powerful states in the region: Germany and Russia. Clearly, the independence of the Baltics, Belarus, and, most important, Ukraine had finally given Poland the assurance that it would not be doomed to being an immediate neighbor of the Russian-dominated juggernaut. Furthermore, the emergence of new buffer states between Poland and Russia seemed to improve dramatically Poland's prospects of joining NATO and the European Community (EC).

Yet despite the dramatic improvement in Poland's geopolitical situation and genuine desire to re-create a cultural as well as an economic partnership with its new neighbors, the Polish Eastern policy was more a study in constraints than one of bold initiative. Miroslaw Glogowski, writing within weeks after the disintegration of the Soviet Union, observed that in the new geopolitical environment, Russia might well become Poland's vital partner in maintaining the status quo in Central Europe. Seeing a Russia that shared virtually no border with Poland, Glogowski believed that there was a far greater probability of territorial tensions between Poland and Germany, Ukraine, Belarus, or Lithuania than with Russia. Furthermore, Glogowski stressed, the newly independent states of the commonwealth would always view Poland as a "second-best alternative" behind the West and Russia. Thus the Baltic states would opt for Scandinavia over Poland, and Ukraine would always have a preference for Germany. Under such circumstances, Poland must retain a close link with Moscow to avoid regional isolation.[15]

Unlike Jozef Pilsudski's interwar Poland, which relegated the power of Soviet Russia to that of a "cadaver," Poland's postcommunist elites firmly believed that despite the collapse of the Soviet Union, Russia would remain a great power with whom Poland must come to terms. Pilsudski saw Poland as the premier power that would supplement Russia's regional preponderance. President Lech Walesa, on the other hand, described the current Polish-Russian balance in the following manner: "Yeltsin and I are like drivers on a strange road at night, without road markings. The difference between us is that I am driving a baby Fiat and he a huge juggernaut."[16] As a result, Poland's Eastern policy reflected its new self-image of a mid-sized European state in search of anchorage within the West European context.

Being the driver of a "baby Fiat," Poland took its Eastern policy along a careful route. The cardinal assumption (of all postcommunist Polish governments) was that Russia, despite the loss of its empire and the *smutnoyie vermye* ("times of trouble") befalling its political structure, remained a great power that would overcome its political crisis and again cast its shadow across Europe. The second postulate of the Polish foreign ministry was that although Poland had benefited from the breakup of the Soviet Union, it had to remain cognizant of the fact that the new states of Ukraine and Belarus would remain an area of profound Russian interest. Therefore, while Warsaw was anxious to bolster its relations with these states—and, indeed, renew long-interrupted cultural and political links with Kiev and Minsk—it was willing to do so only as long as it did not compromise the all-important link with Moscow. Finally, Poland's ultimate goal, the hope of joining the EC and NATO, could be accomplished only if Polish membership did not saddle NATO with tensions between Poland and the CIS members.[17]

Given these assumptions and constraints, and the clear preference for a Western orientation, Poland's postcommunist governments expended their utmost to normalize relations with Russia. Within months of the collapse of the Soviet Union, Poland had negotiated terms with Russia for the removal of ex-Soviet troops from its soil. The terms of the agreement were not without controversy: Poland agreed to drop all financial claims resulting from the ecological damage inflicted on Poland by Soviet troops, and former Soviet bases were to be turned into joint Polish-Russian stock companies, an arrangement that many Poles perceived as permitting a vestige of colonial Russian presence. Furthermore, wide sectors of the Polish polity were dismayed that the Polish-Russian Treaty of Friendship and Good Neighborly Cooperation made no mention of the murders at Katyn. Walesa had to be satisfied with a joint declaration stating that both Poles and Russians were victims of Stalinism. Prior to his departure to Moscow, he admitted: "The treaty is not future oriented and you can see the old epoch in it."[18] Despite continued dissatisfaction on several key issues, Walesa asserted that he supported this imperfect accord because he felt it was an essential step "to break with the past."[19]

It is interesting to note that while President Walesa's office remained far more skeptical about Russia's intentions than the Foreign Ministry, and thus far more eager to embrace "NATO-bis" or another subregional organization that might enhance Poland's security, Walesa's national security adviser, Jerzy

Milewski, said that Poles "should not forget Russia. . . . Whether we want it or not, Russia has not ceased to be a big power, and is treated as one by the United States, Western Europe, the whole world."[20] This view was echoed by Prime Minister Hanna Suchocka, who noted: "All long-term planning must, however, be based on the assumption that Russia—regardless of the scope of its current problems—will also in the future be a great country coshaping [along with Germany] the situation in our region."[21]

With the belief that Poland can integrate itself into Western Europe only by becoming a catalyst to Europeanizing Russia, Poland's political mainstream continued to support the policy of rapprochement with Moscow, consciously avoiding linking the current Russian government with Stalinist crimes. Similarly, in economic terms, while Poland managed to reorient most of its trade to the West, Russia remained Poland's main source of oil and gas and a substantial buyer of Polish textiles, coal, grain, and pharmaceuticals—sectors of the Polish economy that do not appear to be capable of competition with the West. The growing economic interdependence between Russia and Poland revived in both countries a mutually reinforcing lobby of directors of state-owned enterprises who pressed for a deepening of the relationship. In an analysis of the Russo-Polish economic relationship, Marek Henzler observed that while Poland, with a great degree of effort, could free itself from dependence on Russian oil and gas, Poland would remain dependent on the Russian market for a long time to come.[22] In fact, although the Suchocka-Skubiszewski team continued to strive for a balanced relationship with both East and West, leftist members of the Sejm were expressing concern that Poland's Western orientation ignored the fact that the West's policy remained pro-Russia, and, therefore, Poland must retain close links with the East if it is not to fall out of the loop.[23]

Recognizing that Poland must establish cordial relations with Russia, most of the Polish elite nevertheless feared that the Russian democratic experiment might fail and that Russia might revert to its historic imperialist pattern. While some rightists, such as Leszek Moczulski's Confederation for an Independent Poland (KPN), believed that the only way for Poland to secure its integrity was to create a Polish-led bloc of states between the Baltic and Black seas, the majority of Poles rejected the idea of Miedzymorze as being a dangerous throwback to Poland's interwar doctrine, which yielded the tragic results of reducing Poland to a buffer between the great powers.

Consequently, one of the most consistent goals of consecutive Polish governments has been to join NATO at the earliest possible date. This desire was heightened when Russia published its defense doctrine classifying Poland as a potential threat to Russia's security and squarely placing Poland within Russia's sphere of interest.[24]

Boris Yeltsin's withdrawal of Russian objection to Polish membership in NATO, announced during his trip to Poland, elated most Poles and induced Skubiszewski to renew Poland's demands to admit the country into NATO expeditiously. This concession by the Russian president, however, triggered a barrage of criticism across the political spectrum in Russia,[25] forcing Yeltsin to reverse himself, profoundly undermining his own credibility and underlining to the Poles the endemic instability of Russia. Yeltsin's confrontation with Parliament, which he managed to resolve only by calling in the army, convinced the Polish government that with Yeltsin beholden to the armed forces, Moscow was bound to pursue an increasingly imperial foreign policy that would inevitably impact on Poland. Paradoxically, throughout the turbulence in Russia, which started in September 1993 when President Yeltsin dissolved Parliament and crested in the December general elections when Vladimir Zhirinovskiy's pseudofascist Liberal Democratic Party garnered nearly a quarter of the vote, Poland's Russian policy remained remarkably consistent. At the same time, the rise in the tide of Russian nationalism made Poland's clamor for admission into NATO all the more persistent.

When Poland's new government, dominated by former communists, took office in September 1993, it continued to insist that building a more profound understanding with Russia was a priority. Poland's new foreign minister, Andrzej Olechowski, although a presidential appointee, noted during his debut in front of the foreign affairs committee of the Sejm that he was committed to enshrining greater "cordiality" in Poland's relations with Moscow and warned that Poland's "relations with Russia and Germany should be at least as good as those between the countries themselves."[26] Olechowski added that there could be no European security system without the participation of Russia.

Moscow's renewed veto of Polish membership in NATO provoked an indignant response across the Polish political spectrum, with most Polish politicians insisting that Poland would continue to lobby for membership in NATO regardless of Russia's objections. The Polish government, however, took a much more introspective attitude. Social Democratic leader Aleksander Kwasniewski, whose party is the senior partner in the ruling coalition, commented that while he found Yeltsin's position "incomprehensible," Poland, in order to have an effective security system, would need "a clearly defined vision of cooperation with Russia, so as to rule out the threat that Russia might be our enemy."[27] The violent October events in Moscow frightened Poland's population, doubling to 31 percent the proportion of Poles expressing fear of Russia.[28] The fear that Russia is reverting to a more stridently nationalist mode in which Yeltsin's role will be greatly circumscribed was shared by some of Poland's best-known political analysts. Jadwiga Staniszkis observed that Russia's foreign policy would inevitably become more "collective"—a situation in which Yeltsin's moderate preferences would be of diminishing importance. Jerzy Marek Nowakowski went further, asserting that given Yeltsin's new weakness, Poland would have to face a set of dynamics with "Europe connecting to Russia."[29]

Yeltsin's weakness has already adversely affected Poland's position vis-à-vis the West, according to Nowakowski:

> Regardless of whether Yeltsin is a "collective" leader or figurehead, the West will move to accommodate Yeltsin. The Germans already proved it to us [the Poles] when they changed overnight their position regarding Poland's membership in NATO. Russian reservations are for them the fundamental issue, in the same way as it is for the Americans. In this situation cooperation with Poland will decrease in the eyes of the West.[30]

Since Yeltsin was bound to practice what Professor Vladimir Zubok called the "tyranny of the weak,"[31] blackmailing the West into supporting Russia by threatening anarchy, Poland's options, according to Nowakowski, were limited. While Poland should continue to insist on a stronger partnership with the West, this partnership can be attained only if Poland does not attempt to engage in building a cordon sanitaire around Russia.

Poland's political leaders were facing a dilemma in dealing with Moscow's pragmatic attitude. Karol Modzelewski of the Labor Union (UP) warned the Poles that "one should not tease the Russian national pride by getting engaged in their internal affairs. Anyway, the army will not forget Poland's little pleasure which it got during the withdrawal of Soviet troops." Modzelewski reminded his countrymen that "Poland will have to live with the understanding that it is not a superpower. Poland will have to make efforts to maintain good relations with the East."[32]

Although the electoral results in Russia—where nationalists and communists showed surprising strength—did prompt Poland to dispatch Foreign Minister Olechowski to Washington to intensify Poland's lobbying for membership in NATO, the more important issue had become the democratization of Russia as the ultimate path to world stability. Speaking in Washington, Olechowski observed: "Unless Russia is a democratic country with a market economy, no U.S. strategic partnership with her will be truly advantageous to world security." Olechowski urged the United States to "lead the world in an effort to help Russia to build its democratic identity and presence in the world." To attain that goal, the Polish minister urged a permanent membership for Russia in the Group of Seven, greater economic aid, and access to Western markets.[33] Olechowski stated that while Poland was unconditionally tying its future to NATO, the Atlantic alliance would have to build a strategic relationship with Russia. In fact, although the Poles were angered by NATO's decision not to admit the Visegrad Group (the Czech and Slovak republics, Hungary, and Poland) into NATO, the anger appeared to be primarily directed at the West rather than at Russia. This bitterness was pointedly reflected in Kazimierz Pytko's editorial in *Zycie Warszawy* under the title "When Saxophone Players Rule."[34]

Clear signals from NATO that Poland would not be readily brought under its protective umbrella, and increasing political and economic atrophy within the European Union (EU), occurring against the backdrop of a resurgent Russia, induced a serious debate over the direction of Poland's foreign policy and Poland's ultimate role within the international system.

President Clinton's "Partnership for Peace" proposal embittered President Walesa and many Poles, who saw in that rejection yet another repeat of the Yalta experience. Sober Polish analysts, however, viewed the event as the final blow that would force Poland to finally come to terms with reality. The current limbo in Poland's geostrategic position evoked a broad array of responses. Krzysztof Krawczyk, writing in the prestigious *Polityka,* asserted that Poles were always unrealistic about their importance to the West, and that the only way Warsaw would ever get the West's attention was if it established a "central bloc" consisting of Ukraine and the Visegrad Group. Given the current weakness of Central Europe, American policymakers are keen to "steer Zhirinovskiy's anger somewhere else than toward Alaska," and Poland, therefore, will have to take charge of its own security.[35] Jerzy Nowakowski criticized the political elite's unrealistic assumption that Russian political passivity would be a long-lasting phenomenon, leading it to proceed with a policy toward the West that was increasingly oblivious to the Kremlin's sensibilities. Nowakowski argued that it was this intellectual vacuum in Warsaw's dealing with the Kremlin that led to the clash between resurgent Russian imperialism and Poland's Western policy. Nowakowski concluded that while "Partnership for Peace" might not have met the aspirations of many Poles, it did promote Warsaw's integration into the West while continuing to enhance cooperation with Russia.[36] Going further than Nowakowski in his criticism of Poland's diplomatic doctrine, Marian Pilka of the Christian National Union (ZChN) stressed that Poland's weakness was a direct product of the country's economic weakness, a weakness that would not be remedied by membership in the EU, since there Poland would always be a poor appendage. Russia, according to Pilka, threatened by an increasingly dynamic China, has no imperial ambitions in Poland and, in fact, sees it as a vital opening to the West. Poland, therefore, must follow a policy of parallelism between the EU and Moscow. Only by a consistent implementation of such a dual policy will Poland regain its economic vitality and avoid, once again, the status of a satellite.[37]

The relationship between Moscow and Warsaw remains strained. Russian foreign minister Andrei Kozyrev's visit to Kraków in February 1994 only accentuated the differences between the two countries, with Poland's potential membership in NATO being the main source of contention. The meeting between Kozyrev and Olechowski was overtly chilly, and the sole formal agreement between the two parties dealt with the issue of the maintenance of World War II cemeteries. Olechowski, however, insisted that an effective system of European security must include Russia, irrespective of whether NATO existed or not.[38]

The burden of history has not fully lifted from Polish-Russian relations. Although Russia's hegemonic history and potential future behavior continue to cast a shadow on Warsaw, postcommunist Poland has remained remarkably consistent in its policy toward Russia, attempting to be a catalyst in the integration of Russia into the international system and reversing centuries of diplomatic tradition.

RELATIONS WITH UKRAINE AND BELARUS

The final disintegration of the Soviet Union in December 1991 fulfilled a dream long cherished by much of Poland's elite. For the first time in four centuries Poland did not have an aggressive neighbor to the east. The rebirth of independent Ukraine, Belarus, and Lithuania overnight transformed Poland from an East European buffer state separating the Soviet Union from the heart of Europe to a Central European state in the orbit of Germany and Scandinavia.

Besides affording Poland greater political and military security, the collapse of the former Soviet Union brought about other changes as well. While there was virtually universal agreement that Poland must not alter its post-1945 frontiers and a recognition that the peoples to the east are not a mere ethnographic mass or Russified Poles,[39] the emergence of these newly independent countries allowed Poland to reestablish its centuries-old cultural links with the region. Although Warsaw had become a "window on the West" to millions of Ukrainians and Byelorussians, and an economic as well as a political model, Poland's relationship with the countries of the Kresy could not fully escape either the burden of history or the geopolitical realities of the post–Cold War world order. On the one hand, significant parts of the collective memory, especially in Lithuania and western Ukraine, were haunted by the historic encounters of these peoples with the Poles, particularly during the interwar period. On the other hand, Poland's policy, especially toward Ukraine and Belarus, despite heartfelt sympathy for their newly won independence, continued to be constrained by Warsaw's far more important relationship with Moscow.

Nowhere were these contradictory pressures and constraints more visible than in the Polish-Ukrainian relationship. Ukraine's sheer determination to separate from Russia put Poland's diplomacy to the hardest test.

The collapse of the communist regime in Poland filled Ukrainian nationalists with great hope that postcommunist Poland would champion Ukrainian independence. Given the fact that Prime Minister Tadeusz Mazowiecki was a longtime Catholic dissident as well as the hand-picked nominee of Lech Walesa, the expectation of Polish support was not unreasonable. Indeed, Poland's initial moves toward its eastern neighbors were encouraging. The 1989 declaration of the Polish Sejm that it had no territorial claims on any of its eastern neighbors helped to alleviate Ukraine's lingering suspicion of Poland. Cardinal Jozef Glemp's energetic effort to revive the Uniate Church in Belarus and Ukraine impressed many in the East as a genuine Polish effort to become the conduit for Ukraine and Belarus to Europe.

The initial policy of Poland's first postcommunist government, however, was bound to disappoint its eastern neighbors. Facing imminent German reunification and stubborn resistance from Chancellor Helmut Kohl to an a priori German recognition of the Oder-Neisse as Germany's eastern border, the Mazowiecki government not only did not join Hungary and Czechoslovakia in demanding the withdrawal of Soviet troops, but actually requested their continued presence on Polish soil. Under these circumstances, Poland's ability to conduct a policy offensive to the Kremlin was very much circumscribed. While this position was understandable, given the constraints placed on Poland, an important precedent was set, indicating that Poland's Eastern policy, sympathies notwithstanding, would remain subordinate to its relationship with Germany and the Soviet Union (later Russia). In addition to the restraints imposed on the Polish government by the primacy of the Russian connection, an additional reason for Poland to temper its support for Ukrainian and Byelorussian independence was the lack of clarity about how deep the aspirations toward full independence ran in those countries. Not only did the communist governments of these two republics continue to take evasive positions on this issue, but the situation was further complicated by the fact that in both Ukraine and Byelorussia the populations voted in Gorbachev's March 1991 referendum in convincing majorities (70 percent in Ukraine) to preserve a "reformed union."[40]

Despite overt sympathy, Poland's policy toward Ukraine did not crystallize until May 1992, when Warsaw declared a foreign policy based on the belief that there could be no stability in Eastern Europe without a Polish-Ukrainian reconciliation[41] and managed to sign friendship treaties with most of its neighbors.

Despite the dramatic improvement in Poland's geopolitical situation and Poland's genuine desire to re-create a cultural as well as an economic partnership with its new neighbors, the Polish Eastern policy was more a study in constraints than one of bold initiative. Initially, Polish analysts saw Poland's role as a "bridge" between Ukraine and Europe, whereas Kiev saw in Poland an escape hatch from Russian domination.[42] Although Poland was the first independent country to recognize Ukraine's independence, the relationship soon reached a certain plateau and has only rarely developed beyond broad declarations of principle. Poland and Ukraine did sign several economic protocols and an agreement of joint defense purposes and agreed to establish a "Euroregion" along their mutual frontier and a consultative body at the executive level. The Polish attitude toward Ukraine, however, failed to attain the depth of commitment that many Ukrainians hoped to reach and, in fact, continued on a two-track policy conditioned by Warsaw's relationship with Moscow.

There are several factors that continue to inhibit the deepening of Poland's links with its eastern neighbor. First, despite the absence of any major issue to divide Poland from Ukraine and the presence of a strong symbiotic relationship between the two states, the heavy baggage of ethnonationalist history has continued to haunt Polish-Ukrainian relations. The reemergence of the catacomb Uniate Church created severe property clashes with Poland's Roman Catholic Church. The clash was especially bitter and at times violent in the dispute over the Carmelite Cathedral of St. Theresa in Przemysl, which originally belonged to the Uniate Church. Some Polish nationalists were dismayed by the claims of the Ukrainian State Independence Organization (a self-proclaimed successor organization to the interwar Organization of Ukrainian Nationalists) that Ukraine was entitled to territories currently part of Poland, Russia, Moldova, and Belarus.[43] While there is overwhelming support in Poland for the Polish-Ukrainian accord, with the current Polish-Ukrainian border enshrined, some splinter irredentist groups continue to question the current arrangements, reviving old fears and distrust. The Polish Society of Friends of Lwow, for one, challenged President Walesa's right to abdicate Poland's claim to Lviv. In an open letter to Walesa, the president of the society wrote: "You are the first politician in our thousand year old history who as head of state officially abandoned claims by the Polish nation to parts of the Fatherland and to 'the most Faithful City' without consultation with the nation and against the raison d'être."[44] The Polish sense of historic slight was further aggravated during Prime Minister's Suchocka's visit to Ukraine in January 1993. The speaker of the Ukrainian parliament, while insisting on additional information about operation Wisla, which resulted in the forced dispersement of thousands of Polish Ukrainians from their ancestral lands in 1947, refused to address the "ethnic cleansing" carried out by some Ukrainian nationalists in Galicia and Volhynia during World War II.[45] Ukraine's position prompted Poland's Christian National Union to demand that Poland freeze its relations with Ukraine until Kiev revealed all the data about the massacre of Poles in Volhynia and formally apologized to the Poles.[46]

Ukraine's insistence on an army of 400,000, as well as the ambiguity of its position on nuclear weapons, alarmed the Polish population. In a public opinion poll conducted in Poland in June 1992, 53 percent of those responding chose Ukraine as the country posing the greatest threat to Poland.[47] In fact it would appear that Poland's relationship with Ukraine is affected to a very large degree by the very different collective memories of Polish society. The Polish elite see the disintegration of the Soviet Union as an opportunity to reestablish a cultural commonwealth and to replace Russia as the cultural center of the region. Many Poles, however, instead of focusing on the sixteenth-century commonwealth as "usable history," can only see the twentieth century's bloody history. Despite two years of good neighborliness between Poland and Ukraine, 65 percent of Poles are antipathetic toward the Ukrainians, according to a public opinion poll conducted by the prestigious CBOS organization in September 1993.[48] In Ukraine, paradoxically, Poland is one of the most admired countries.

Nevertheless, distrust has been fueled by activities of right-wing organizations with irredentist agendas in the East. Ukraine's Orthodox Church (both the Kiev and Moscow patriarchates) was angered by what it perceived as Polish Primate Jozef Glemp's missionary zeal in Byzantine lands, which caused an angry exchange between Moscow's patriarch Alexiy II and Cardinal Glemp and forced the papal nuncio to Ukraine, Archbishop Antonio Franco, to renounce officially any ambition to convert Orthodox Christians to Roman Catholicism.[49] While both the Orthodox Church and the Vatican attempted to cool tempers, and Cardinal Glemp made a reconciliation trip to Moscow during the summer of 1992, both sides agreed that under current circumstances it would be inappropriate for the Polish pope to visit the CIS.[50]

The relationship between the Greek Catholic (Uniate) Church of Ukraine and the Vatican has also deteriorated as a result of the policies of the Vatican as well as of the Polish Catholic Church in the East. The 1991 decision of the Council of the Ukrainian Catholic Church (Uniate) to standardize the Ukrainian Uniate ritual along the standards of the 1720s (the high point of Latinization of that church) was received by many Ukrainians as an effort by a Polish pope to Latinize and hence Polonize the church, which is Ukraine's most authentic national institution. The tensions were further aggravated by Pope John Paul II's instruction to Metropolitan Sterniuk of Lviv forbidding the ordination of married priests—even for service in his own archeparchy—an order that, if carried out, would lead to a sharp decline in the number of young Ukrainian priests and thus force greater reliance on Polish Latin priests. Furthermore, some Ukrainian Greek Catholics responded with dismay to the Vatican's decision to create a Latin-Catholic bishopric in Kiev, abiding by the Russian Orthodox Church's proscription against Uniate expansion outside western Ukraine.

Ukrainians perceived these actions by the Polish cardinal and Polish pope as examples of Polish cultural irredentism. In fact, the question of Polish cultural presence in the Kresy borderlands is far more contentious than generally assumed. Even publications such as *Kultura* and *Tygodnik Powszechny,* which consistently called for a reconciliation with Ukraine on the basis of the current border between the two countries, made this reconciliation virtually conditional on the guarantee of minority rights of ethnic Poles in the eastern border states as well as on the perpetuation of strong cultural links with Poland. Moreover, both the Catholic Church and the Polonia Society spent substantial resources to revive Polish culture east of Poland's borders. The Ukrainian government has pursued an admirably enlightened policy toward its minorities. Nevertheless, mounting resentment and fear in western Ukraine that Poland's cultural presence is a harbinger of political intervention were enough to force Prime Minister Suchocka to cancel her Lviv meeting with representatives of the Polish community.

Although both Poles and Ukrainians attribute a great deal of importance to improving relations, particularly among the Polish and Ukrainian intellectuals, who share a strong mutual sympathy and admiration, there are few constituencies to support that relationship. Popular opinion in Poland and to a lesser degree in Ukraine continues to manifest unease about the reconciliation, making that relationship politically difficult to sustain. The popular Polish ambiguity toward close relations with Ukraine is by no means limited to mass opinion, however. While the elite politically is far more sympathetic to Ukraine, views of how intimate to become with Ukraine continue to be divided.

On the extremes, the Polish elite perceives Ukraine either as a great opportunity or as a mortal threat to Polish interests. At one extreme there is a school of Polish thought represented by Poland's former defense minister, Jan Parys; the leader of the Confederation for an Independent Poland, Leszek Moczulski;[51] and, to a much lesser degree, President Walesa. These men believe that the only viable security, as well as economic structure, for the region is in what Moczulski calls Miedzymorze ("between the sea"; the countries between the Baltic and Black seas),[52] and in a Polish-Ukrainian alliance that would "save European civilization from Russia."[53] The other extreme position, articulated by Tomasz Gabis and Zdzislaw Winnicki of the rightist RealPolitik, is that Poland's ultimate natural ally is Russia, while the existence of an independent Ukraine only serves sinister German interests and compromises the interest of the Polish minority in the East.[54] The mainstream of the Polish political elite tends to fall between these two positions.

Poland's intimacy with the border states continues to be a vexing issue. Basically three inhibiting factors limit Poland's commitment to Ukraine and, to a lesser degree, Belarus: the unease generated by the history of relations between the Poles and their eastern neighbors; the impact of these links on Poland's relationship with Russia; and Poland's desire to "return to Europe."

Poland does not want to be caught in the middle of a quarrel between Russia and Ukraine. Foreign Minister Krzysztof Skubiszewski, in an interview in *Polityka,* stated bluntly: "Russia has remained a major power, despite its current limitations and problems, and it is going to reinforce this position. . . . Poland does not want to side with either party in the Russo-Ukrainian conflict."[55] Ukraine's self-declared role as Europe's bastion against Asiatic Russia does not parallel Poland's views on Russia's role in Europe. There is an element of anxiety in Poland that a complete Russian disengagement from Europe may lead to a German-centered configuration, a situation that many Poles still find troubling, as manifested in Poland's adamancy about any change in the status of the Kaliningrad district. A further factor inhibiting closer Polish-Ukrainian security ties is the anxiety voiced repeatedly by Polish officials and academics: a military Polish-Ukrainian alliance consisting of over 80 million people and possibly nuclear weapons would be perceived by both Russia and Germany as a security threat, inducing the rebirth of a Russo-German axis, the ultimate nightmare to Polish policymakers. In explaining Polish foreign policy doctrine to the Sejm, Skubiszewski observed that Poland's first priority should be to avoid a repetition of the Molotov-Ribbentrop pact.[56]

The Russian factor aside, Poland's policy toward Ukraine and Belarus is constrained by Poland's declared policy of returning to the West. While Polish officials continue to insist that Poland has a historic right to be admitted into the European Union and NATO, they realize that the ultimate criterion for Poland's admission will be the degree to which Poland reforms its own economy and presents itself as a stable European state. So long as Ukraine's economic reforms continue to backslide and Ukraine remains at odds with the international community over the nuclear issue and its continuing tensions with Russia, Poland will remain reluctant to identify itself with Ukraine. If initially some Polish analysts believed that Poland could help Europeanize its eastern neighbors, the political developments in the former Soviet Union were such that any involvement with the new border states could compromise Poland's fundamental interests.

Finally, there is a strong economic factor that limits the level of engagement of Poland with its eastern border states. First, despite chronic political instability in Poland, the desire to redirect that country's trade from the East to the West has remained a consistent policy. In fact by 1992 over 70 percent of Poland's trade was with the West, with the perception being that trade with the East would only retard Poland's pace of modernization. Polish trade with Russia and Belarus has revived, with Russia supplying Poland with energy and minerals in exchange for Polish food and consumer goods, thereby providing welcome relief for Poland's battered and uncompetitive industries and agriculture. But in the case of Ukraine, official trade with Poland steeply declined. With hundreds of thousands of Ukrainians working in Poland and many more involved in barter and informal trade, however, the economic interchange between these countries is certainly far larger than official figures would indicate. Nevertheless, Ukraine's inability to revive its potentially powerful economy clearly affects the depth of Polish engagement with that country. The Polish sociologist Jadwiga Staniszkis, in an interview with the author, noted that the emergence of vigorous trade with Russia, accompanied by a decline in trade with Ukraine, created in Poland a strong pro-Russian lobby that is willing to advocate a foreign policy detrimental to a Polish-Ukrainian alliance. This lack of an economic basis for improving Polish-Ukrainian relations was lamented by Skubiszewski, who noted that for a continuous deepening in Polish-Ukrainian relations "there is a need for a breakthrough in the [bilateral] economic relations."[57]

Given the marked symbiosis between Poland and its eastern borderlands and the inherent limitations to a mutually beneficial relationship with both Ukraine and Belarus, the policy dilemma for Poland is how to support the sovereignty and independence of Ukraine and Belarus without complicating Poland's relationship with either Russia or the West. Poland's delicate position is further complicated by the fact that Poland is perceived as a vital partner in extricating Ukraine and Belarus (although to a far lesser degree) from Russian domination.

For Ukraine, whose national agenda is integration into Europe and differentiation from Russia, Poland is the natural gateway. Upon gaining its independence, Ukraine made strenuous efforts to bolster its ties with Poland, seeing a close relationship with Poland as a means to free Ukraine from its client status vis-à-vis Moscow and as an anchor within the international system. In one of his first trips outside the CIS, Ukrainian president Leonid Kravchuk, while in Warsaw, declared: "The degree of cooperation with Poland will be

higher than with any other country of the CIS, including Russia."[58] Yet
Ukraine's initial enthusiasm has been met with only a tepid response from
Poland. The Polish government, still negotiating the terms of Russian troop
withdrawal and striving to integrate Poland into the West, has shown little
interest in moving Polish-Ukrainian relations beyond symbolic gestures. Two
days after Kravchuk's departure, Walesa traveled to Moscow, where he declared
that he "would like Poland and Russia to be the pillars in Eastern Europe.
Poland is ready for and wants to, but it takes two to tango."[59] To the dismay
of the Ukrainians, Walesa failed to include Ukraine in that configuration. This
precedent of ultimately accommodating Moscow even when Ukrainian interests were affected was repeated when Poland offered to build a gas pipeline from
Russia to Germany across Belarus and Poland, bypassing the "capricious" states
of Ukraine and Lithuania.[60] This move provoked Ukraine's prime minister,
Leonid Kuchma, into accusing Poland of conducting an anti-Ukrainian policy,[61] evoking among some Ukrainians the specter of the treaties of Andrusovo
(1667) and Riga (1921), when Poland, confronted with Russian might, twice
opted to accommodate Russia at the expense of Ukraine.

In reality, however, during the first year of Ukraine's independence,
Polish attitudes toward Ukraine fell into two camps. The foreign ministry
tended to favor taking a remote position toward Ukraine, arguing that an open
alliance with Ukraine would adversely affect Poland's relationship with Russia,
especially at a time when Poland had yet to see the total departure of Russian
troops from its soil. Furthermore, Polish politicians noted that in economic
terms trade with Russia was far more important than trade with Ukraine.
Relative to Poland's relationship with the West, there was concern that given
Ukraine's inability to start reforming its economy and its growing friction with
the West over the issue of nuclear weapons, an overt identification with Ukraine
would compromise Poland's efforts to join the West, as well as complicate its
delicate relationship with Russia.

The other camp, which included Jan Parys, Leszek Moczulski, and Lech
Walesa, favored Miedzymorze as a means to ensure security between the Baltic
and Black seas. There is a fundamental difference between the positions of
Moczulski and Walesa, however. Whereas Moczulski sees in an alignment
between Poland, Ukraine, Belarus, the Baltic states, Hungary, and the Czech
and Slovak republics an effort to create a "third force" in Europe between Russia
and NATO, President Walesa sees this kind of alignment as a "halfway house"
that would enhance these countries' prospects of entering NATO. Walesa's
proposition has received the enthusiastic support of Ukrainian president
Kravchuk and Deputy foreign minister Borys Tarasiuk and some qualified
support from the Hungarian prime minister, Jozsef Antall.

Yet despite such support, the idea of a regional defense alignment in Central Europe has encountered fierce resistance from several quarters. The United States, fearing that such an alignment would be construed by Moscow as an attempt to isolate Russia from the European mainstream, openly discouraged it.[62] Furthermore, the notion of NATO II or a Black Sea–Baltic alliance encountered serious resistance from Poland's foreign and defense ministries, both of which viewed membership in NATO as a means to leverage Poland's position vis-à-vis Russia and Germany. The feeling in these ministries is that any regional alliance not only would ruin Poland's prospects of being admitted into NATO, but would actually condemn Poland to revert again to a gray zone between Russia and the West. Polish officials are aware that participation in an alliance that is construed as anti-Russian would doom Poland's prospects of joining NATO. As Defense Minister Janusz Onyszkiewicz observed: "A Poland at odds with Russia will not be an attractive partner for NATO."[63]

Despite continued rhetoric about Poland's commitment to Ukraine, Poland's treatment of the country as secondary to its relationship with Russia and the West has also forced Ukraine to reconsider its Polish policy. In May 1992 President Kravchuk spoke of Poland's supplementing Russia as Ukraine's most important partner, but by December 1992 Ukraine's ambassador to Warsaw stated: "[W]e are not going to build our relationship [with Poland] at the expense of others, and these relations should not effect the relationship between Ukraine and Russia."[64]

Perhaps the strongest indication of the deepening chill in relations between Kiev and Warsaw was the reception accorded Premier Suchocka when she visited Kiev in January 1993. Not only did President Kravchuk, who was on a state visit to Israel, fail to meet her, but the Ukrainian media, which remain largely state-controlled, virtually ignored her visit. Suchocka stressed Poland's concern for Ukraine's integrity and independence, noting that "Poland and Ukraine are interested in stabilizing the CIS, with Ukraine preserving full freedom."[65] Jan Rokita, Poland's cabinet secretary, went further, stating: "The price of this stability under no circumstance can be a weakening of state sovereignty of Ukraine or Ukraine becoming fully dependent on any other state or the hegemony by one of the members of the Commonwealth of Independent States."[66] Prime Minister Kuchma, however, replied that "our [Polish-Ukrainian] partnership, under no conditions, should harm the third party [Russia]." Reflecting on Ukraine's growing economic dependence on Russia, Kuchma said, "Nobody in Europe is waiting for Ukraine."[67]

While there is anxiety in Warsaw that Ukraine may feel increasingly isolated and, thus, either turn inward or follow Belarus's lead back into the Russian fold, the dominant view in Warsaw remains that though Poland has a practical motive as well as a moral obligation to help bring Ukraine into the international main-stream, Poland is willing to do so only to the extent that it will not complicate its links with either the EC or Russia. For this reason, when President Kravchuk asked his Polish counterpart in May 1993 about the formation of a Black Sea–Baltic bloc, President Walesa agreed, "without enthusiasm," to study the proposal.[68] In a sense, from Poland's perspective, Ukraine, by virtue of its independence, has accomplished the most important goal—separating itself from Russia; beyond that, Poland's limited resources dictate a limited engagement with its eastern neighbor.

The tragic history of Polish-Ukrainian interaction continues to cast a long shadow over the relationship, and, indeed, no meeting between the two parties passes without allusion to that lurid past. However, a new phase has begun. While the two nations are pursuing different strategies in their efforts to reenter the international mainstream, for the first time in six hundred years neither party sees the success of one as the negation of the success of the other. This sentiment was best captured by President Walesa during arrival ceremonies while on a state visit to Ukraine:

> We must remember that we are to build the future. The past should be
> corrected in textbooks, but in the future we are sentenced to one another.
> *Whenever we differed, a third party took advantage of us.*[69]

President Walesa's sentiments indeed reflect a historic reality: as Polish-Ukrainian agendas diverge, outside powers increasingly manipulate this divergence for their own purposes. Perhaps the clearest example was demonstrated by Boris Yeltsin, who, during his visit to Warsaw in August 1993, stated that Russia would no longer stand in the way of Poland's joining NATO. The Russian president's declaration produced a flurry of activity on the Polish side, which attempted to accelerate Poland's entry into NATO while simultaneously distancing Poland even further from Ukraine.[70] This divergence of Polish and Ukrainian interests (along with Ukraine's faltering economy) was exploited by Yeltsin, who, during the September summit meeting with President Kravchuk, extracted from Ukraine a promise to "sell" its share in the Black Sea fleet as well as to turn over to Russia its nuclear warheads. While most Ukrainian commentators conceded that Kravchuk's negotiating position was severely weakened by that country's anemic economy, lack of diplomatic support from the outside (especially from Poland) was an additional factor in weakening Ukraine's position vis-à-vis Russia.

The immediate prospects for a Polish-Ukrainian alliance do not appear to be encouraging. Yeltsin, beholden to his generals for their support in putting down the "White House" uprising, has assumed a far more assertive foreign policy posture, withdrawing Russia's "permission" for Poland to join NATO, threatening to veto sanctions against Libya, and demanding far greater deference to Russia's interests from members of the CIS. Russia's publication of its new defense doctrine further indicates a hardening of its hegemonic position within the parameters of the former Soviet Union. Although Yeltsin's debt to his armed forces clearly contributed to a return to a more assertive posture, the overall hardening of Russia's position vis-à-vis Eastern Europe was nonetheless clearly detectable even before Yeltsin's confrontation with Parliament. Even Alexei Pushkov, the deputy editor of the liberal daily *Moscow News,* noted that the inclusion of Poland in NATO was "playing with fire," reminding his readers that "political democracy will not free Russia from its geopolitical interests and possible contradictions with Western states."[71] This Russian hardening alone is sufficient to discourage Poland from pursuing an overly intimate policy toward Ukraine.

The electorial change in Poland, where former communists have regained power, while not altering the substance of Poland's foreign policy, will clearly have an impact on its priorities. Having been elected with the support of Poland's farmers and workers from large declining industries, the new government is very much aware that Russia remains by far the largest economic outlet to the constituency that elected it. Hence the new government should do all it can to foster the link with Russia. In terms of a security doctrine, while the new government continues to articulate interest in joining NATO, the sense of urgency seems to be gone. Poland's new defense minister, Admiral Piotr Kolodziejczyk, is known for his skepticism about Polish membership in NATO.[72] Poland, which sought membership in NATO as a means to create a link to the United States and improve its position vis-à-vis Russia and Germany, is bound to feel all the more vulnerable, given the proposals of U.S. defense secretary Les Aspin at the Travemunde meeting in October 1993 to rule out early expansion of the alliance. Both Poland and Ukraine are in the process of once again redefining their place in the European architecture; after a brief period in the international limelight both are readjusting to their respective roles as mid-sized states within an increasingly atavistic international system.

While Polish officials continue to attribute importance to Ukraine's independence, and indeed are anxious to see the Ukrainian state become a stable, democratic player in European politics, Poland itself is finally coming to terms with the fact that despite its long-held belief that it has by birthright a place in the West, one result of the end of the Cold War has been the collapse of the West as a coherent entity.[73] Therefore Poland once again finds itself on Europe's fault line. Poland's leaders recognize that it will not be able to become a normal country without permanently reconciling with Ukraine and putting behind it the centuries-old feud between these peoples. Furthermore, Poland's political elite thoroughly understands that Poland's independence can be fully guaranteed only in the absence of a reconstitution of a Russian-dominated empire, thus making Ukraine a vital element in assuring Polish sovereignty. In a sense, Poland's Eastern policy has come full circle, from a limited two-track policy in the waning days of the Soviet Union to one of a short-lived embrace of Ukraine as a possible ally that would enhance Poland's own integration into the West and remove Warsaw from the shadow of the Russian giant, to a renewed circumscribed policy as Ukraine's reforms falter and Russian assertiveness grows.

Poland's commitment to Ukraine's sovereignty, derived from both moral conviction and self-interest, will assure its support for Ukraine's integration in the family of nations. Poland's policy toward Ukraine, however, will always be limited by its perceived impact on relations with Russia and the West.

A closer Polish-Ukrainian relationship could be induced by two possible scenarios. The first would result from a transformation of the Russo-Ukrainian relationship, in which an abatement of tension between these two former Soviet republics would enable Ukraine to develop normal relations with other neighbors. While Yeltsin's victory has probably reduced the tension between the two Slavic giants, the drift in Russia toward greater assertiveness vis-à-vis the "near abroad" seems to be gathering momentum despite the democratization of Russia's politics. The possibility of a deepening Polish-Ukrainian relationship under the benign gaze of the Kremlin seems rather unlikely.

A second scenario that might induce a Warsaw-Kiev axis is the reversion by Russia to aggressive patterns of behavior. A Russia that is recognized as a threat by the West might well compel the West to admit Poland and perhaps even Ukraine into NATO as a latter-day *antemurale Christianitatis* once again. For this scenario to occur, the perception of the Russian threat would have to be alarming enough to bring about a concerted Western (particularly American) reaction. While the first scenario is more likely than the second, it should be kept in mind that to bring about a concerted Western reaction, Russia would have to present a threat of truly global proportions. In the absence of this dramatic change, Poland's foreign policy toward Ukraine will continue to be one of carefully restrained support for Ukrainian independence and statehood within the limits of Russian tolerance.

RELATIONS WITH LITHUANIA

Although Lithuania does not cast its shadow on Poland in the manner of either Russia or Germany, Poland's relationship with that small country has a profound impact on Poland's national identity and self-definition. The relationship is complicated by the fact that the two countries were part of the same state for nearly four hundred years, an experience that is engraved very differently in the collective memories of the Poles and the Lithuanians. To the Poles, the "Commonwealth of Two Nations" is the high point of Polish history, a period when Poland was among the largest states in Europe, experiencing prosperity and setting Europe's standards of democracy and tolerance. Not only did a disproportionate share of Poland's interwar political leaders, including Pilsudski, hail from Lithuania, but to successive generations of Poland's leading men of letters Lithuania was an undisputable part of Poland's national patrimony and a source of inspiration. Poland's national poet, Adam Mickiewicz, in his epic *Pan Tadeusz*, encapsulates Polish attachment to Lithuania with the words *"Litwo! Ojczyzno moja"* ("Lithuania my Fatherland!").

Poland's nostalgia for Lithuania continued well into the twentieth century. Tadeusz Konwicki, who is Lithuanian born and one of Poland's most influential contemporary authors, in a fictionalized autobiography, describes Lithuania as the cradle of what made Poland a reality.[74] Similarly, Czeslaw Milosz, in his evocative *Szukanie ojczyzny* (Search for a Fatherland), sees Lithuania, with its mélange of peoples, languages, and cultures, as a magnificent monument to the commonwealth.[75]

If Poland's collective memory harks to the Polish-Lithuanian commonwealth (Rzeczpospolita Obojga Narodow) as the high point of Polish civilization, Lithuanian nationalist intellectuals focus on the fact that a commonwealth with Poland resulted in the Polonization of Lithuania's nobility and a cultural denuding of Lithuania. Instead of focusing on the more distant past, Lithuanian collective memory is preoccupied with the 1920 forced annexation of Vilnius by Polish general Lucjan Zeligowski and the 1938 ultimatum issued by Poland that coerced Lithuania into recognizing Polish sovereignty over Lithuania's historic capital. Furthermore, while Poland's search for a usable past entails the commonwealth as a means of reasserting its role in European civilization, Lithuania, anxious to develop a distinct identity, is keen on obliterating all remnants of that relationship.[76]

When Lithuania took bold steps to reassert its independence, the reactions of the Polish government and the Polish public were of great enthusiasm. Yet Warsaw, not anxious to provoke the Kremlin, pursued a cautious policy of not allowing its sympathies to upset its relationship with the Soviet Union. Despite the inherent danger, however, numerous Polish parliamentarians and other public figures traveled to Vilnius to offer moral support to the defiant Lithuanians. When Lithuania declared independence in March 1990, both chambers of the Polish parliament passed resolutions endorsing Lithuania's right to self-determination.[77]

Although since the 1940s Poland's intellectuals have advocated the recognition of Lithuania's current borders, and the Poles have shown heartfelt enthusiasm for Lithuania's struggles, the weight of history continues to frustrate efforts to establish normal relations between the two countries. Even as *Kultura* endorsed Lithuania's right to independence within its current configuration, Polish visionaries assumed that once Poland abandoned all territorial claims toward its eastern neighbors, these states would tolerate and indeed encourage the cultural rights of Polish minorities outside Poland. Such was not the case. What was perceived in Poland as the normal European exercise of cultural affinity toward people of the same ethnic stock across a political border appeared to Lithuanians as a harbinger of irredentist territorial expansion to be followed by potential territorial claims. Thus, from the beginning, relations between Warsaw and Vilnius were poisoned by Poland's overt concern for the cultural rights of some 250,000 Poles in Lithuania and Lithuania's jealous defense of perceived slights to its independence. After two years of full Lithuanian independence, relations between the two countries have yet to recover.

The pretext for antagonism between Warsaw and Vilnius was the Lithuanian government's decision to dissolve the local councils in Polish-populated areas and impose direct rule (based on accusations of pro-Russian sympathies). Poland promptly demanded the reestablishment of the councils. The acrimony worsened with Lithuania's ban against the use of the Polish names of Lithuanian towns in the Polish-Ukrainian press and Polish accusations that the ban was a deviation from European standards of democracy. Furthermore, Warsaw alleged that the privatization program in Lithuania discriminated against Poles. The burden of a difficult historic relationship was further manifested in the Lithuanian government's refusal to register Armja Krajowa, the social club of the veterans of the Polish resistance to Nazi occupation. Lithuania alleged that the Polish partisans were an anti-state organization, since they fought for Polish independence and thus opposed Lithuanian territorial integrity. This action by Lithuania engendered Polish accusations of Lithuanian collaboration with the Nazis during World War II.

Although in January 1992, Poland's foreign minister, Krzysztof Skubiszewski, and Lithuania's, Algirdas Saudargas, issued a joint communiqué confirming a commitment to existing borders between their two countries and the maintenance of European standards of minority rights, the issues dividing the two countries were far from resolved. Poland's demand for a Polish-language university in Lithuania provoked the chairman of the Lithuanian Supreme Council, Vytautus Landsbergis, into accusing the Poles of being "nationalist and expansionist"[78] and other Lithuanian officials into claiming that there were no Poles in Lithuania but "Polonized Lithuanians." Poland's decision to redeploy some of its troops from western Poland to the east, and the statement by Poland's ambassador Jan Widacki that "the Poles in Lithuania never left Poland, but rather Poland left this place," triggered indignant accusations in Vilnius that Poland was engaging in an irredentist campaign against Lithuania.

Until April of 1994, Lithuania remained the sole neighbor with whom Warsaw had failed to conclude a treaty of friendship. The issue was reported to be held up over Lithuanian demands for, and Warsaw's refusal of, a Polish apology for the annexation of Vilnius in 1920. In reality it was the inability of both polities to free themselves from their collective memories that continued to hinder full reconciliation.

CONCLUSION

Continued friction with Lithuania notwithstanding, Poland has redefined its fundamental orientation in the geopolitical structure of Europe and in international affairs in the main. While this self-redefinition was in part imposed by the post–World War II settlement, it was substantially the result of a long and painful debate, starting within the émigré publication *Kultura* and continued throughout Poland itself in earnest since the mid-1950s. The last vestiges of an *imperial mission* in the East, or the role of a great power within the European concert, were permanently abandoned in favor of an image of a mid-sized European state whose interests and even self-preservation could be attained only through continuous accommodation with its immediate neighbors and a relentless positivist effort to enhance the economic viability and national institutions of Poland.

This notion of fundamental change in Poland's orientation was perceptively encapsulated by Adam Krzeminski and Wieslaw Wladyka, who argued that perhaps Poland's greatest historic weakness was the elite's obsession with independence, over the need to build an "organically evolved nation." The profound lack of *podmiotowosc* (productive purposefulness) begot many of the tragedies that beset Poland. Yet contemporary Poland is fundamentally different from its historic predecessors:

> There is, however, a major difference between today's Poland and those of the interwar period or the Commonwealth of Two Nations. Both of the predecessors were endangered from the East and the West, while Poland at the same time was striving to be a regional superpower. Today's Poland is not endangered by Germany or Russia, and the borders are

recognized by all parties. Walesa's Poland does not pretend to be a superpower; we do not long for a "from sea to sea" Poland, and we do not want to be anybody's policemen; nor do we want to "save" anyone. The appreciation of our own predicament is far less pathetic than before 1939, and on this score we are far more "European" than ever before.[79]

Post–World War II history fundamentally reshaped Poland's perception of its place within the international community. The West's indifference to the Warsaw uprising in 1944, the West's support of Willy Brandt's *Ostpolitik*, which seemed to condemn Poland permanently to Soviet domination,[80] and finally the European Union's snail-paced economic opening, along with a cold shoulder from NATO, forced Poles to seriously reconsider the direction their country was taking. Poland's unshakable belief that it was an integral part of the West was fundamentally shaken. Even in the cultural sphere, Czeslaw Milosz advocated the creation of "Middle Europe," not as a political bloc, but rather as a cultural space to avoid yet another bout of subservience to the West.

Contemporary Poland faces monumental foreign policy challenges: the paralysis within NATO over the Balkan crisis, President Clinton's Harding-like preoccupation with a return to normalcy in U.S. domestic politics, and deepening economic and political disorientation within the European Union. The Polish elite now recognizes that its dream of a return to Europe will not become reality for a long time to come. A Russia seemingly determined to reimpose its hegemony within the former Soviet Union and reclaim its status as a great power is maneuvering against a background of Western psychological lethargy. Despite these difficulties, a non-Promethean Poland, cognizant of its attractiveness to its eastern neighbors as a Western model, and aware of its limited role within the international community and of its modest economic base, will manage to revive its symbiotic economic relationship with the former Soviet Union. Poland will continue to modernize its economy and to guard its independence jealously. Without admitting to it, Poland may well emulate Finland's foreign policy, which is based on the recognition that the reality of being a neighbor of an awkward and restless Russia is inescapable.

Commenting on Poland's historic dilemmas, Adam Bien, a minister in the former Polish government-in-exile in London, expressed doubt in the political will of NATO to admit Poland and, more importantly, in the durability of the U.S. presence in Europe. He observed that Poland was a state that threatens no one; however, by joining an alliance with either one of its powerful neighbors, Poland would be the ultimate loser: "The first neighbor will take us for granted since he received us for nothing, while the other neighbor will see us as an enemy." Thus the overriding premise of Polish foreign policy ought to be the maintenance of a neutral policy with an overriding positivist interest in the continued modernization of Poland's economy and society.[81] While few Poles are willing to embrace neutralization, the energies of today's Poles are directed at Poland's economic revival, rather than Promethean diplomacy.

Notes

1. For the English-language version, see Juliusz Mieroszewski, "The Political Thoughts of Kultura," in *Kultura Essays,* ed. Leopold Tyrmand (New York: Free Press, 1970).

2. Ibid., p. 321.

3. Ibid., p. 267.

4. Antoni A. Piotrowski, "Wokol polityki zagranicznej," *Politka Polska,* March–April 1991.

5. Czeslaw Milosz, *Native Realm: A Search for Self-Definition* (Berkeley: University of California Press, 1981), p. 130 (emphasis in the original).

6. Agnieszka Magdziak-Miszewska and Jerzy Marek Nowakowski, "Droga do Rosji," *Polityka Polska,* November 1990, pp. 10-17.

7. See Ronald Asmus and Thomas Szayna, *Polish National Security Thinking in a Changing Europe* (Santa Monica, CA: Rand/UCLA Center for Soviet Studies, 1991), p. 22.

8. Ibid.

9. See Stephen R. Burant, "International Relations in a Regional Context: Poland and Its Eastern Neighbors—Lithuania, Belarus, Ukraine," *Europe-Asia Studies* 45, no. 3 (1990): pp. 395-418.

10. Polska Agencja Prasowa (PAP), 5 September 1990.

11. For Najder's views, see "Spor o polska polityke wschodnia," *Rzeczpospolita,* 1 November 1991.

12. See Andrzej Romanowski, *Tygodnik Powszechny,* 15 December 1991.

13. See Adam Michnik, "What Next Russia?" *Gazeta Wyborcza,* 20 February 1990, as reported in FBIS EEU-90-035, 21 February 1990.

14. See *Gazeta Wyborcza,* 19 May 1992.

15. Miroslaw Glogowski, "Klopota na wschodzie," *Prawo I Zycie,* 7 September 1991.

16. Nick Thorpe, "Why the Poles (and Others) Are Pulling for Yeltsin," *Gazette* (Montreal), 30 April 1993.

17. See Skubiszewski's report to the Sejm's Foreign Affairs Committee, PAP, 18 November 1992.

18. PAP, 22 May 1992.

19. Ibid.

20. *Gazetta Wyborcza,* 22 September 1992.

21. Hanna Suchocka, "We count on understanding not only of unity of aims but also of unity of interests," speech at Lublin Catholic University, 18 October 1992.

22. Marek Henzler, "Na czarna godzine" (For the black hour), *Polityka,* 16 October 1993.

23. See interview with Jozef Oleksy, *Przeglad Tygodniowy,* no. 5 (7 February 1993).

24. See Stephen Foye, "The Army Gets a Doctrine: Updating Russian Civil-Military Relations," *RFE/RL Research Reports,* 19 November 1993, pp. 44-50.

25. It was not only General Pavel Grachev and the military that objected to the inclusion of Poland in NATO. For a liberal critique, see Alexei Pushkov, "Do Not Make an Enemy," *Moscow News,* 22 September 1993.

26. *Rzeczpospolita,* 10-11 November 1993, p. 2.

27. Anna Wielopolska and Zbigniew Lentowicz, "Politics of Yeltsin's Statement," *Rzeczpospolita,* 2-3 October 1993.

28. *Rzeczpospolita,* 2 December 1993, p. 23.

29. Piotr Jendroszczyk interview with Jerzy Marek Nowakowski, "Przylaczenie Europy do Rosji," *Slowo,* 12 October 1993.

30. Ibid.

31. Vladimir Zubok, "Tyranny of the Weak: Russia's New Foreign Policy," *World Policy Journal* 9, no. 2 (Spring 1992): 191-218.

32. *Rzeczpospolita,* 5 October 1993.

33. Andrzej Olechowski, "Seven Statements on Poland's Security," address at the Center for Strategic and International Studies, Washington, D.C., 14 December 1993.

34. *Zycie Warszawy,* 28 October 1993.

35. Krzysztof M. Krawczyk, "Partnerstwo niepokoju," *Polityka,* 29 January 1994.

36. Jerzy Marek Nowakowski, "W poszukiwaniu nowej koncepcji," *Rzeczpospolita,* 14 January 1994.

37. Marian Pilka, "Dwubiegunowa integracja," *Rzeczpospolita,* 21 January 1994.

38. PAP, 23 February 1994.

39. For an excellent discussion of the traditional Polish attitude toward Ukrainian statehood, see T. Mackiw, "Problem ukrainskiej panstwowosci w publicystyce Polskiej" (The problem of Ukrainian statehood in Polish journalism), *Kultura,* May 1987, pp. 93-99.

40. See Burant, "International Relations in a Regional Context."

41. *Gazeta Wyborcza,* 19 May 1992.

42. See Wojciech Pieciak and Andrzej Romanowski's interview with Ruch leader Ivan Drach, "Nasza droga wiedzie przez Polske," *Tygodnik Powszechny*, 13 October 1993.

43. See Janusz Bugajski, *Nations in Turmoil: Conflict and Cooperation in Eastern Europe* (Boulder, CO: Westview Press, 1993), p. 43.

44. J. Kresowiakow, "Nie mozna przemilczac zbroni nacjonalistow ukrainskich," *Slowo Powszechne*, 17 December 1992.

45. Radio Warsaw, 25 January 1993.

46. *Gazeta Wyborcza*, 10 January 1994.

47. PAP, 20 June 1992. A similar poll carried out by the U.S.-based D-3 organization in June 1992 noted that 34 percent of Poles felt that Ukraine was most threatening, 13 percent of Russians, and 11 percent of Germans (Radio Warsaw, June 1992).

48. PAP, "Poles Do Not Like Their Neighbors," 8 September 1993.

49. Interfax (Moscow), 1 November 1992.

50. *La Stampa*, 4 March 1992.

51. See Leszek Moczulski, *U progu niepodleglosci* (On the Threshold of Independence) (Lublin: EMBE Press, 1990).

52. It should be stressed that the concepts of President Walesa and Moczulski are by no means identical. President Walesa sees a Central European alliance among the Visegrad Group, or "NATO-bis," as a means to bring Poland into the West. Moczulski's party, with a strong similarity to the pre–World War II Endecja, is highly nationalistic and sees a Polish-Ukrainian bloc as an anti-Western and anti-Russian third force.

53. PAP, 29 April 1992.

54. PAP, 14 September 1993.

55. *Polityka*, 17 October 1993.

56. PAP, 18 November 1992.

57. See Jan de Weydenthal, "Economic Issues Dominate Poland's Relations with Its Eastern Neighbors," *RFL/RE Research Report*, 5 March 1993.

58. *Zycie Warszawy*, 20 May 1992.

59. PAP, 22 May 1992.

60. See Jan de Weydenthal, "The Troubled Polish-Russian Economic Relations," *RFE/RL Research Report*, 5 March 1993.

61. See Rustam Narzikulov, "An Anti-Ukrainian Policy," *Segodnia*, 3 September 1993.

62. See *Gazeta Wyborcza*, 25 May 1993.

63. *Zycie Warszawy*, 25 May 1993.

64. PAP, 16 December 1991.

65. *Gazeta Wyborcza*, 13 January 1993.

66. PAP, 15 January 1993.

67. Radio Warsaw, 25 January 1993.

68. Reuters, 24 May 1993.

69. PAP News Wire, 24 May 1993 (emphasis added).

70. When Premier Suchocka, during a lecture in Lublin, stated that Ukraine was a priority of Poland (PAP, 18 August 1993), Foreign Minister Skubiszewski corrected the prime minister, noting that one cannot address Ukraine without dealing with Russia's interests. *Gazeta Wyborcza,* 1 September 1993.

71. Alexei Pushkov, "Ne sozdovaite vragov," *Moskovsie novosti,* 22 September 1993.

72. See *Rzeczpospolita,* 27 October 1993, p. 2.

73. See Owen Harris, "The Collapse of the West," *Foreign Affairs,* September/October 1993.

74. Tadeusz Konwicki, *Bohin Manor* (London: Faber, 1992).

75. Czeslaw Milosz, *Szukanie ojczyzny* (Warsaw: Znak Publishers, 1992).

76. See Stephen R. Burant, "Polish-Lithuanian Relations: Past, Present, and Future," *Problems of Communism,* May–June 1991.

77. PAP, 22 March 1990.

78. TASS, 25 September 1991.

79. Adam Krzeminski and Wieslaw Wladyka, "Czym Polska stoi?" (On What Poland Stands?), *Polityka,* 1 August 1993, pp. 1-6.

80. See Timothy Garton Ash, *In Europe's Name: Germany and the Divided Continent* (New York: Random House, 1993).

81. See Pawel Glogowski, "Polska byle jaka," from a conversation with Adam Bien, minister in Poland's ex-government-in-exile, *Tygodnik Solidarnosc,* 21 January 1994.

5

Looking West

Arthur Rachwald

Recent liberation from more than four decades of socialism *à la russe* has compelled Poland not only to search for democracy and a free market economy but also to thoroughly reexamine its national security priorities. Throughout the communist era, top national priority was given to unconditional subordination to Moscow's regional and global ambitions in order to preserve Poland's nominal independence (within the narrow confines of the Brezhnev doctrine of limited sovereignty). Together with other East European victims of post–World War II Soviet aggression, in 1948 Poland had to sign a bilateral security treaty with the Soviet Union that gave Moscow a commanding position in Poland's foreign and defensive affairs. The founding of the Warsaw Treaty Organization in 1955 augmented the Soviet Union's exclusive rights to the entire region even further. The communist leaders in Moscow acquired a multilateral platform for dictating their policies to unwilling clients and for infiltrating the defensive establishments of the East European nations. For this reason, countries of the Soviet bloc failed to develop their own defensive policies. Instead of focusing on their national defensive priorities, the East European allies, including Poland, had to assume a highly specialized and subordinate stance in the offensive strategy promoted by Moscow. The trust of Soviet leaders was the key to national security, since the main threat of foreign aggression was that of a Soviet disciplinary action intended to quell unauthorized domestic or foreign activities. Three times in its post–World War II history (1948, 1956, 1980-81), Poland had to face the realistic prospect of Soviet invasion.

To preempt the possibility of Soviet invasion and to secure some degree of independence at the price of integration within the communist bloc, Poland's foreign policy during the Cold War was that of unequivocal subordination to Moscow. This policy of "friendship" with the Soviet Union left a narrow margin for independent links with the nations of Western Europe and the United States. The first traces of an autonomous Polish engagement with the West emerged at the time of de-Stalinization in Moscow and the return to power of nationally minded communists in Warsaw. In 1956 Poland initiated bilateral economic relations with the United States and with the Federal Republic of Germany, bringing some measure of balance to its otherwise lopsided dependence on Moscow.

Abating global tensions fostered a gradual expansion of Poland's Western policies, but always within the parameters of Soviet priorities and limits, especially in all security-related matters. Thus, Poland championed denuclearization of Central Europe (the Rapacki Plan) in 1957 and a nuclear freeze in Central Europe (the Gomulka Plan) in 1964. Poland also took an active role in preparations for the Helsinki Accord in 1975 and in protracted negotiations for the reduction of conventional forces in Europe. Despite a sincere commitment to the alleviation of East-West hostilities, the Polish role was coordinated in Moscow as a component part of Soviet global and regional strategy. Still, the Polish effort to improve relations between the Soviet bloc and the West was in tune with a national search for security in a divided world. Although the politics of détente had a stabilizing effect on the communist order in Central Europe, it also relieved the danger of war and the likelihood of Soviet military intervention.

The dispute over the Polish-German border, the Oder-Neisse line, was a special case in Poland's relations with the Western nations. Broad international recognition of the western border was a key national security issue. Warsaw was never in a position to contradict Soviet policies, but it persistently strove to ensure Soviet backing of the border and to take full advantage of any opportunity to legalize its existence. This policy of "internationalization" of the Oder-Neisse line, that is, the policy of making the solution of any major East-West issue contingent on West German approval of Poland's western border, paid off in December 1970, when following the example set in 1953 by communist East Germany, the Federal Republic of Germany relinquished claims against former territories of the Third Reich. The Polish–West German treaty of 1970 was, perhaps, the most consequential foreign policy success of communist authorities in Warsaw.

The end of communist rule in Poland and the subsequent collapse of the Soviet Union with its East European empire presented Poland with a completely new set of international and domestic opportunities, including restoration of traditional ties with the nations of Western Europe and the United States. Poland had learned a painful lesson from unilateral dependence on Soviet Russia, and a complete reversal of the discredited spheres-of-influence policies in Europe was placed at the top of the national priorities list. Together with the other nations of Central Europe, Poland proceeded to dismantle its Eastern ties and moved forward with a policy of strengthening national independence through construction of a multilateral network of relations with the Western states and West European regional organizations. The European option, placed at the forefront of Polish foreign policy objectives, was justified as a historical return to Western civilization, as the best choice from the national security point of view, as the guarantee of development along a democratic and free market model, and as a precaution against excessive nationalism and religious intolerance. Krzysztof Skubiszewski, Poland's former foreign minister, explained in 1992:

> In moving closer to the Community, Poland is not just seeking material advantages. Like Greece, Spain, and Portugal, it wishes to guard against any risk of a return of totalitarianism and to guarantee the permanence of democracy which was recently regained. It is also seeking a definite and stable Europe. It is profoundly aware of its cultural affinity with Western Europe—is the pope not Polish?—it wishes to anchor itself once and for all to the group of nations to which it is bound by so many historical, and human ties.[1]

When the Soviet empire began to disintegrate, Poland and other nations of Central and Eastern Europe noted that they were left in a security vacuum between the integrated West and the mosaic of the frail, newly independent states still searching for a domestic political model and for a place in the international community of nations. Thus, Western Europe became a natural magnet for an independent Polish nation determined to solve its security problems not in isolation, but through association with the European Union (EU) and the North Atlantic Treaty Organization (NATO). Polish integration into the principal institutions of Western Europe is expected to secure an independent existence, which for the last two centuries has been threatened by the expansionistic ambitions of both Germany and Russia. The post–Cold War international situation is seen as a historical opportunity for Poland to reverse its drift to the East and to build lasting foundations for a place in an integrated Europe.

Integration into West European political, economic, and military structures is seen in Poland as a final stage of the anticommunist revolution that produced independence in 1989. The orientation toward the West and European integration have become the strategic linchpins of Polish foreign policy. The essential aim of this policy is to establish durable and indissoluble political, economic, and cultural ties with the Western world, and to ensure that the Polish presence becomes a permanent feature and a constituent part of the Western institutions. Assimilation with the Western world would secure development along the Western model and protect the nation from the military threats and socioeconomic turmoil prevalent in the East.

Poland approached the national security question in a comprehensive and multilateral manner, beginning with an effort to build good relations with neighbors, both East and West. Within the first two years of its independent existence, Poland signed treaties of friendship, inviolability of borders, renouncements of claims, and protection of minorities. The second element of the national security package is the building of a regional cooperation structure around the Visegrad Group, the Council of the Baltic States, and the Central European Initiative. Pan-European integration, the third and final tier of the national security architecture, includes an agreement with Poland on the association with the EU and the desire to join the Western European Union (WEU) and NATO, the only tangible collective security system in Europe that includes the United States.

The Polish push toward the West is not the product of an impulsive reflex after liberation from the Russian-dominated Soviet empire, but a result of the conviction that the experiences of the last two centuries must not happen again. Hardly any other European nation has suffered political and social abuses similar to the mistreatment of the Poles, who had their state dismembered, and their economy plundered by Russians and Germans alike, and who were several times subjugated to genocide, expulsion, Russification, and Germanization.

Left alone, or in between East and West, Poland would again find itself at the mercy of international developments that are far beyond national ability to control or prevent. The only realistic way to shield the country from another cycle of abuse and humiliation is through complete alignment with Western political, military, and economic institutions. Today Poland, free of both pompous nationalism and isolationist bent, is ready to welcome Western influence, since it is expected to enrich cultural heritage and strengthen statehood in the democratic tradition. This means that the country must be ready to rapidly assimilate a profusion of imperative changes and to take a positive attitude toward the integration process. Poland's ride to Europe has already been bumpy and full of tactical reverses and disappointments.

Moreover, Poland looks at the American military presence in Europe as a precondition to the maintenance of peace and stability. As a bulwark of democracy, only the United States can have a mitigating impact on the destructive nationalism of the European nations, fostering a climate of integration and cooperation especially between historical adversaries. The United States also provides an ultimate guarantee against the reassertion of rightist extremism in Europe, especially in Germany, and generates momentum in favor of the denuclearization of Ukraine and Belarus. Finally, the United States continues to counterbalance the conventional and nuclear power of Russia. Although weakened by the disintegration of the Soviet Union and the communist ideology, Russia continues to possess substantial military power far exceeding the capacity of all other European states.

In principle, Poland appears to be secure. The country is not alone as it was in 1939, and it is not threatened by war. However, there exists a potential for instability east of Poland in the territories of the former Soviet empire, especially in the destabilization of Russian-Ukrainian relations owing to national ambitions, territorial changes, and other political and economic rivalries. Equally threatening is the specter of Russian nationalism and the possibility that a post-Soviet Russia will sooner or later adopt the sphere-of-influence policies of its tsarist and communist predecessors. This is the only likelihood of an external threat to Poland, a threat that could be military as well as economic if deliveries of strategic raw materials and energy were reduced or halted and the country destabilized by a massive wave of refugees from the East.

The central issue of Polish security in the post–Cold War Europe is not whether the country is facing an identifiable external threat. Poland is sufficiently big and populous that no rational state in Europe would contemplate military invasion to change borders or to occupy the country. The danger does not exist in terms of partitions or attempts to impose an alien political or economic system as happened after World War II. The essence of Polish insecurity is in its location in the gray area between the Atlantic Europe and the East that today consists of several nations searching for statehood and Russia (still unable to define its own political identity). Consequently, Poland fears the instability of situations beyond its eastern border and the "absence of real external security boundaries affirmed by treaty and international law." Finally, as Marian Kowalewski and Lech Kosciuk have noted:

> positive direction of evolution of the international community is not
> necessarily a foregone conclusion: this refers to, among other things, such
> of its elements as NATO, CSCE, and the united Europe with its organi-

zations, not to mention the evolution of the military-political situation
directly in the area of Central Europe.[2]

In other words, Poland feels vulnerable because it has an incomplete sense of
belonging to the Western community of nations. It is a fundamental issue of
national identity and self-esteem, a declaration that the Polish nation belongs
to the Western civilization and has contributed to the development and security
of the Western world. This conviction has long historical lineage, for centuries
motivating generations of Poles to fight for "your freedom and ours." Poland
made a substantial military contribution to victory in World War II, one that
the Poles estimate to be next to the efforts of the United States, Great Britain,
and Soviet Russia. This pro-Western orientation is a powerful element of
national identity and was apparent in the program and actions of the Solidarity
union during its struggle for power. The Communist-Solidarity duel in Poland
was in essence a contest for Poland's place in the Western world.

The authorities in Warsaw realized that as a medium-sized state, Poland
has limited capacity to control its international security. According to the newly
formulated national security policy and defense doctrine, perhaps the most
important contribution to national independence would involve shaping a
system of international security that will eliminate threats.

> The basic principle of our country's foreign security policy is the treatment
> of Europe and North America as a single security sphere. The European
> security system that is gradually being formed may turn out to be the main
> guarantee of Poland's sovereignty and independence.[3]

Also, the document implicitly points out Russia as the most likely threat to
national security. Without identifying potential adversaries, it addresses the
possibility of "destabilization in our part of Europe." Moreover, "the basic
principle underlying the restructuring of the Polish Army and its balanced
deployment throughout the territory of the entire country are designed to
ensure the ability to provide defense in all directions in the event of a local
conflict." Considering the political, social, and economic situation in neighboring states, Poland has identified three levels of threat to its security: (1) countries
that at present are no threat at all or are only of minimal threat: Denmark,
Sweden, Lithuania, the Czech Republic, and Slovakia; (2) countries that are a
greater threat and that emerged from the former Soviet Union (the situation in
that region is still far from stable); and (3) Germany, wherein the threat lies in
Poland's economic weakness and technological backwardness. The danger of
military confrontation with Germany is practically nonexistent, but in view of

Germany's enormous economic and military potential and rising neofascist activities, Poland has to monitor closely internal developments in the West.[4]

Despite favorable international circumstances, Poland today is facing the old problem of having two powerful neighbors as well as a new one: Ukraine, a country that has at least the potential to become a powerful state, has adopted policies that have often clashed with the national interest of Poland. In the west, Germany is a powerful country pursuing an assertive economic foreign policy; at the same time the shadow of Russian imperialism is darkening. For these reasons, a pan-European solution of the national security issue has been placed on the forefront of the strategic objectives of all Polish governments since the 1989 revolution. What especially attracts Poland to NATO and the EU is the fact that these are voluntary international organizations and they are not dominated by a single hegemonic state. Since in the contemporary international system a country the size of Poland cannot act alone, membership in a union founded on common values is the best alternative to old spheres-of-influence politics.

Integration into the pan-European system is seen in Poland not as a self-centered national objective but as an action taken in the best interest of the entire continent. Poland's size and geostrategic location make it too important to be ignored without a detrimental impact on the Western nations of Europe. Poland's problems are Europe's problems. Only the West can guarantee Poland's independent existence, economic well-being, and democratic form of government. But an unstable or totalitarian Polish state, or Poland alone facing ethnic instability in the East, would only pass its problems over to the West, destabilizing Germany and the rest of Europe.

From the Polish perspective, membership in NATO would have at least three positive consequences: it would bring Poland closer to the United States; Poland's security would become a security concern of 16 other nations; and because NATO's political doctrine and military strategy are changing to address new concerns, integration of Poland and some other Central European states would bring a new raison d'être to this organization.[5]

As a temporary alternative to NATO, as well as for extra leverage in the West, Poland proceeded to build up bilateral relations with Germany. A united Germany firmly rooted in NATO and other key structures of the Western alliance is not a threat to Poland's security, and bilateral relations, including the possibility of military cooperation, create a security channel between Poland and NATO. Poland's security becomes the security of Germany, and the security of Germany is the security of NATO. For this reason, Germany has become Poland's most important international partner and a bridge to the West. Territorial issues ceased to poison mutual relations following the November

1991 bilateral treaty confirming that the "existing border between them is inviolable now and in the future" and reaffirming that both countries "have no territorial claims whatsoever against each other and will not assert such claims in the future."[6] Mutual relations have entered a new and historically unprecedented phase of good neighborly relations.

After centuries of bitter animosities and bloody confrontations, Germany has become the principal economic and political partner of Poland, as well as the main champion of Poland's pro-Western policies. Former Polish prime minister Hanna Suchocka in her foreign policy address pointed out the new mutual interdependence between the two nations. Germany, she said, "is today our liaison in contacts with the EC and NATO, at the same time the German road to the east leads through Poland."[7] For as long as Poland is refused membership in NATO, Germany provides a chance for Poland to sheltered under the Western security umbrella and an opportunity to confirm its view that the securities of Poland and Western Europe are indivisible.

During the period of transition, bilateral relations with Germany are critically important to the development of the Polish economy. The essential element for Poland's security as a democratic, pro-Western state is a healthy national economy. A politically viable and economically vigorous Polish state would become an attractive partner for the West and a solid example for Poland's eastern neighbors, including Russia. In this respect Poland plays a key role in the Central–East European region, and its ability to overcome its socioeconomic crisis may in the final analysis determine its place in the international community of nations.

This is not to say that all major issues dividing Poland and Germany have been solved and that mutual relations are without friction. The list of problems is long, and it includes such sensitive topics as the status of the German minority in Poland, the conditions of the Polish minority and the Polish guest workers in Germany, and many other, perhaps minor, but annoying, topics related to the whole spectrum of possible concerns between two neighbors. However, both states share similar interests in the European arena, including common stances on the simultaneous "widening" and "deepening" of Europe and a positive assessment of the American military presence. It is also important for Germany to cease acting as the eastern boundary of the Western security system. The addition of Poland and other Central European nations to NATO would change Germany's status as a front-line state.

The German view on enlarging NATO and promoting security guarantees is not entirely altruistic. The Germans are concerned that they have again become a frontline state, this time not against the Russian hordes but against "instability." Thus they would prefer to place a buffer of stability between themselves and the republics of the former Soviet Union. They could achieve this by having the East Central European states join NATO and the EU.[8]

Development of the German-Polish axis, combined with a conceptually different approach to security matters in Europe, has complicated Poland's relations with France, historically the main Polish ally in the West. France is opposed to any enlargement of NATO because it is an instrument for perpetuation of the American influence in Europe, and Paris views with apprehension bilateral relations between Germany and the nations of Central Europe. The political and economic void left by the disintegration of the Soviet bloc and the reunification of Germany opened the possibility of a revival of *Mitteleuropa* politics in Central Europe, providing Germany with an upper hand in the region and upsetting the balance between Germany and its western neighbors.

As seen from Warsaw, the security situation in Europe is exceptionally complicated and the direction of change may not necessarily be favorable to Poland. In the absence of international collective security guarantees for Central Europe, the entire region may find itself isolated from the West, frightened by Russia, and unstable to the point that some military consequences would be inevitable. Admission of the Central European states, in the Polish view, would enhance the security of the entire alliance, not only the security of Poland, the Czech Republic, and Hungary.

The Polish determination to become a member of NATO met with a reserved reception in the West. To begin with, the Poles assumed that the West owed them speedy integration in all major institutions of the West European alliance as a reward for Poland's contribution to the destruction of the communist system. Soon, however, Warsaw had to adjust its expectations and look at integration with the West as an end product of a long and frustrating process. Despite setbacks and disappointments, and frequent changes of the ruling coalition in Poland, the country has consistently attempted to pursue its way to unification with Europe. Only "evolutionary solutions to create one Europe, economically and militarily,"[9] have a chance of success, and Poland is not likely to discard or be diverted from its pan-European option.

The bottom line for Polish strategic calculations is that although NATO may not be admitting new members now, when it decides to, Poland would be the most obvious candidate. Regardless of Poland's membership, NATO is not able to remain indifferent to Poland's security concerns, since the alliance must approach the security of Europe as a whole rather than in a fragmentary manner. The nations of Central Europe constitute the most essential periphery of

NATO, and their stability is intertwined with the security of the West. Reemergence of a confrontational international system in Europe would not be in the best interest of any Western state.

At this point in time there is not a favorable climate in Europe or the United States to either expand the old or build a new political and military alliance, since it would generate a question of against whom such an alliance would be directed. Realistically, Poland could be threatened only by the reemergence of Russian imperialism, and admission to NATO could play on Russia's historical paranoia over hostile encirclement, isolation from the West, and the Polish-Russian rivalry over influence in Ukraine, Belarus, and the Baltic states. Such a move could rekindle the hostile image of the West in Moscow, and the clear impression that NATO was erecting for itself a sphere of influence at Russia's expense, reducing it to a predominantly Asian state. Last, but not least, the NATO nations are aware of practical obstacles, including cost, to be encountered on the road to integration of their military structures with the military establishments of the former members of the Warsaw Pact (as has recently been confirmed by the German experience of integration of the Bundeswehr with East German armed forces).

Poland's membership in NATO, according to the Western perception, could add external incentives to the domestic dynamics in Russia, especially its inability to overcome economic crisis, which would propel the country toward expansionism.

> Thus the essence of Poland's membership in NATO is not military but political. The West's goal today is not the containment of an eventual Russian aggression but its prevention, preferably by squashing it in its nascent stage, which can be achieved by supporting a democratic and peaceful evolution of Russia. At this point, the goals of the West and Poland coincide.[10]

Polish anxiety over membership in NATO is, perhaps, best illustrated by the "NATO-bis" idea mentioned by Poland's president, Lech Walesa, during his visit to Germany in May 1992. Poland, together with the Czech Republic, Hungary, Slovakia, and the Baltic states, would assemble a transitional military alliance in Central Europe to enhance regional security and to apply additional pressure on NATO to accelerate admission into its political and military structures. The NATO-bis would parallel the Visegrad Agreement of originally three and now (after the breakdown of Czechoslovakia) four Central European states in deciding, after liberation from the Soviet bloc, to cooperate in economic and some political matters to coordinate their efforts for membership in the European Union. As Jerzy

Milewski, secretary of the National Defense Committee, summarized, "the presidential idea of the creation of NATO-bis . . . would permit the increase of security of the eastern part of Europe before a European-wide system guaranteeing the political stability of our continent arises."[11]

With the possible exception of Moscow, the NATO-bis concept has never been taken seriously by either Western or Central European nations. Russians became alarmed at the prospect of a military consolidation of Central Europe. The Russian military publication *Krasnaya zvezda* castigated this idea and reiterated Moscow's insistence that the "efforts of all European states should be directed not at establishing new blocs or duplicating old ones, but rather at raising the effectiveness of the CSCE and developing its structures, so that it could in fact ensure real security for all its members."[12]

Since the breakdown of the Soviet empire the Russian government continues to insist that the optimal solution to all European security questions could be achieved through the Conference on Security and Cooperation in Europe (CSCE). This pan-European institution, which also includes the United States and Canada, is favored in Moscow because it would undermine the political and military cohesiveness of NATO, the EU, and the WEU as well as dilute the American position on the European continent. In fact, it could evolve into a kind of American-Russian condominium in Europe, placing all other states in a position of dependence on two nuclear superpowers.

To achieve this objective the Russians would like to transform the CSCE into a regional agency of the United Nations and to provide it with a military structure. In the Russian view, the CSCE should be the leading collective security organization in Europe, with NATO assuming a subordinate role. The United States is highly skeptical about this transformation, since it would dilute the American presence in Europe. The nations of Central Europe perceive the Russian insistence on the CSCE, which after all is a product of the Cold War, as an attempt to reconstruct the old spheres-of-influence policy on the continent, because such a pan-European system would incorporate security guarantees for Central and Eastern Europe provided by the nations of Western Europe and Russia. For the postcommunist nations of Eastern Europe this offer has too many similarities with the ideas brought out in the Yalta Conference of 1945.

Moreover, the Russians insist on a network of bilateral security agreements with the former members of the Warsaw Pact. As the most powerful country of the region, Russia would institutionalize its hegemonic position in a manner similar to the old bilateral and multilateral (Warsaw Pact) system of control over its western neighbors. The end result of the Russian offers would be a substantial strengthening of the Commonwealth of Independent States (CIS) and, eventually, a strategic alliance between NATO and the CIS, with the nations of Central and Eastern Europe caught up again between two powerful supernational institutions, a twenty-first-century version of the Holy Alliance.[13] Post-Soviet Russia is seen as rapidly evolving toward its traditional expansionistic foreign policy activism, despite, or perhaps because of, its inability to find solutions for the most basic political and economic problems at home.

The key element of contemporary Polish foreign policy is to take full advantage of the temporary weakness of Russia and completely reverse the international orientation of Poland from the Cold War period. Russia is not to be a component part of Poland's "strategic option," which is exclusively pointed toward the West, that is, the European Union, NATO, and the Western European Union. In other words, the Poles are united in the belief that nothing even remotely resembling the old bilateral relations with Moscow and the multilateral security system of the Warsaw Pact is to be reconstructed (as the Russian leaders would like to see). The Central–East European "security gap" is to be filled up entirely by multilateral strategic ties with the West.

Poland's foreign policy goals toward Russia include an elaborate list of such objectives, including diplomatic relations, political dialogue, the withdrawal of former Soviet troops from the region, the fostering of democracy, the explanation of the responsibility of the repression apparatus of the former Soviet Union for crimes committed against Poles, and, above all, economic cooperation to fill the gap left after the disintegration of the Council for Mutual Economic Assistance.[14] In short, while the Russian side insists on revival of its military ties with Central and Eastern Europe, the Polish side is willing to rebuild traditional trade links with Moscow. This policy, as put forward by Minister Andrzej Olechowski during his February 1994 meeting with Russian foreign minister Andrei Kozyrev in Kraków, is known as the "Partnership for Transformation," or the preferential treatment of bilateral trade.[15]

Also, Polish insistence on joining NATO and becoming a partner of the West is balanced with the security concerns of Russia and other independent nations of the former Soviet Union. Polish authorities repeatedly make it clear that in entering NATO Poland would not become a host to foreign American, German, or French troops, which could be seen as a risk to Russia and Eastern Europe. Actually, there are no foreign troops in several NATO states, including Denmark, Norway, and Portugal. Polish participation would consist of entering the defensive structures of the alliance, having influence on military decisions made in Brussels, and reorganizing of the Polish armed forces to meet NATO standards.

This does not mean that Poland is excluding the possibility of strategic-military cooperation with Russia. On the contrary, the Polish authorities emphasize the strategic importance of good bilateral relations with Russia as a preferential condition for membership in NATO. To overcome old patterns and customs, Poland is determined to distance itself from special bilateral or multilateral ties with Moscow that are dominated by the Russians. Instead, Poland wants to reroute its relations with Russia into the multilateral framework of cooperation within NATO, where Russian, as well as German, presence would be diluted and constrained by a large and complex international structure that also includes the United States.

For Poland it is a historical moment to adjust the country's geostrategic location from East, or in between East and West, to one unquestionably Western in its cultural, political, economic, and strategic meaning. It is a determined Polish view that the country would never be secured outside NATO, and that a consequent policy in this direction would leave the NATO states with no alternative to the extension of the Atlantic alliance into Central Europe.

To achieve this objective, however, the direction of Russia's domestic developments must be one of economic reform and democratization, since only a democratic Russia would forsake hegemonic schemes and give priority to friendly relations, based on the principles of equality, with the West. Two alternatives to democracy—return to authoritarianism or the breakdown of the Russian Federation—have ominous implications for Poland and the rest of Europe.

It is understandable, therefore, that Poland is alarmed by the full-scale departure from the policy of reforms in Moscow, by the nationalistic shift in Russia's domestic politics, and by the priority given to the resurrection of the Russian empire. Relations with Ukraine are of special importance for Poland. Consolidation of Ukraine's independence could have a constructive influence on the democratization of Russia, denying success to the Russian nationalists who continue to crave an empire. Poland is highly apprehensive about Russian policy aimed at the destabilization of Ukraine and other former republics of the Soviet Union. The muddy political and economic situation (frequently a result of Russian manipulation of supplies of raw materials) feeds the perception of immaturity of the newly independent states and creates an impression that their independence is undesirable from the point of view of global security.

Belarus and Ukraine, two buffer states between Poland and Russia, are in danger of being sucked in by Moscow, and a volatile situation around Russia's borders creates opportunities for Moscow to claim "particular interest" and "special rights" in the non-Russian states of the former Soviet empire. The most dreadful strategic prospect for Poland would be to find itself in direct proximity to a reborn Russian empire again in search of a window to the West. For this reason Ukraine is supportive of the Polish objective of joining NATO, since an independent Poland is the best safeguard of Ukrainian independence.

Polish diplomatic activities in Western Europe are closely related to the country's eastern policy. The iron principle in Polish relations with Eastern neighbors is that all newly independent states are fully independent and sovereign. It is in Poland's vital interest to see these countries self-reliant, economically self-sufficient, and evolving along the principles of democracy and a pro-free-market economic system. The independence of the Baltic States, Ukraine, Belarus, Moldova, and Kazakhstan is critically important for the independence of Poland and serves as a powerful brake on any messianic impulses of Russian nationalism.

But the idea of an immediate extension of membership to the nations of Central and Eastern Europe was put aside because of Western concern about the possibility of entanglement in ethnic and nationalistic conflicts in the East and the danger of isolating Russia. Instead of membership in NATO, the alliance proposed at the June 1990 Copenhagen meeting a new "security partnership" that would include all the NATO members, the former Warsaw Pact members, and the newly independent states of the former Soviet Union. The North Atlantic Cooperation Council (NAC-C) was established to coordinate the process of consultation and cooperation within this group of 38 states in Europe and Asia. Specific responsibilities of the NAC-C included:

- Organizing meetings of officials and experts to exchange views on security issues, military strategy, and doctrine, including arms control, nonproliferation, and conversion of defense industries;
- Intensifying military contacts between NATO military authorities and their counterparts in the Central and East European states;
- Encouraging participation of Central and East European experts in some NATO activities, including scientific and environmental cooperation;
- Expanding NATO information programs in Central and Eastern Europe; and
- Enhancing cooperation between Central and East European parliaments and the North Atlantic Assembly, the interparliamentary body of NATO countries.[16]

At the end of 1992, the NATO foreign ministers added one more role to the range of NAC-C activities, namely, joint involvement in peacekeeping activities sponsored by the United Nations or the CSCE.[17] The NATO response to the domestic conflict in Yugoslavia provided Poland with an opportunity to deploy its troops under the auspices of the United Nations and to benefit from a close military interaction with the military forces of the NATO states.

But even the military involvement in Yugoslavia did not alter the perception of NAC-C as nothing more than an occasional partnership between NATO and the Central and East European military establishments. This design for an exchange of opinions and ideas on an international platform not only completely failed to address the security issues of the region but also formally placed the security of Poland and other nations of Central Europe on the same level of priority as the security of some Eurasian nations, the former republics of the Soviet Union.

Sensing the general disappointment with the lack of opportunities provided by the NAC-C, and in order to address the question of NATO's mission in post–Cold War Europe, the NATO states adopted a new American proposal for cooperation with the post communist world on 10 January 1994. Known as the Partnership for Peace (PFP), this initiative invited former members of the Soviet bloc to adopt NATO's principles, values, and mission; to develop their military institutions and equipment along Western standards; and to demonstrate the capacity to act as a member of NATO. It also indicates that so far NATO has failed to modernize its vision of the contemporary international conditions in Europe and is unable to come out with long-range structural concepts. Instead it prefers partial and temporary solutions until a new vision of the regional security needs can be established.

From the Polish point of view, the PFP formula offers several benefits, together with some considerable disappointments, and for this reason it is known in Poland as "too small a step in the right direction"—an example of the American perfection of the art of stalling. On the one hand, the PFP is seen as a concrete first step in convincing the West that its security and the security of the rest of Europe are indivisible, and especially that stability of the Central European states is mandatory for the security of the NATO states. The alliance recognized the necessity of developing the crisis management capacity and assuming an active role in peacekeeping and peacemaking in the immediate proximity of the NATO area. The PFP demonstrates the ability of Poland and other nations of Central Europe to exert influence on the countries of Western Europe and the United States.

Also, the PFP indicates NATO's intention to eventually open its ranks and welcome other nations as members. It gives momentum to the process of integration and it prepares candidates for membership. It is a step forward from cooperation to participation, and for this reason it has a stabilizing effect on

Central Europe. It enables the participant to introduce NATO's technical standards and to accumulate indispensable military experience at various tactical levels, and it clears the path to getting closer to NATO's military structures. In this way, the PFP promotes the widening of NATO without sacrificing its other goal of deepening the alliance. This result has been achieved by de facto introduction of a two-tier structure of NATO (deepening for the existing members and widening through the PFP) and by endorsing the multipillar (NATO, PFP, WEU, CSCE) approach to European security.

Since the peace partnership is open to all European nations, it avoids the trap of "politically preselecting" some Central European countries at the price of isolating Russia.[18] The West averted the impression of drawing another dividing line in Europe, this time not along the Elbe but along the Polish eastern border. It is up to all European states that are not yet members of NATO to exercise the option of joining this organization, as has Russia, which after some initial procrastination decided to join the PFP. This step was welcomed in Warsaw and other capitals of Europe as a sign of Russian willingness to act as any other European nation rather than claiming special status and privileges.

When in May 1993 Russian president Boris Yeltsin visited Warsaw, the Polish authorities made the mistake of asking for his reaction to the idea of Polish membership in NATO. The Polish intention in approaching Yeltsin was not to create the impression of subordination to Moscow but to deprive radical and nationalistic groups in Russia of another argument against the reformers, to demonstrate Poland's concern that Russia's national security not be jeopardized, and to let the Russian leaders know that Poland does not want act against Russia.

Yeltsin voiced no objections at the time, but following the November confrontation between the president and the parliament in Moscow, the results of the December 1993 parliamentary elections, and the subsequent increase of the military's influence in Russian politics, he changed his mind. Russia began to voice strong opposition to any possible eastern extension of NATO. In order to avoid the impression of caving in to Russian pressure, yet taking into account Russia's concerns, the statement creating the PFP clearly stated that no third party had a right to veto NATO's decision on new membership. As U.S. senator Richard G. Lugar explained:

> But the starting point (and perhaps ending point, as well) for this effort appears in the first instance to be Russian-oriented. Partnership for Peace appears as much as a means for defining the limits of a cooperative security relationship with Russia as a vehicle for meeting the legitimate security interests of the West as well as those of the indigenous countries of Central

Europe. Put differently, the proposal appears designed in large part to ease President Yeltsin's supposed fears of a new European security policy of "neo-containment" aimed at Russia.[19]

Poland is actually in favor of Russian membership in the PFP or NATO, since membership in this regional military and political organization would strengthen democratic forces in Russia and remove the danger of a bilateral confrontation with Russia (unfavorable to Poland) or the elevation of Russia to the role of a co-guarantor of regional security with some special regional and global responsibilities. Such a development would create conditions similar to the Brezhnev doctrine of limited sovereignty for the members of the Soviet bloc, which had to subordinate their own national security to the regional and global ambitions of Moscow. Poland, probably more than any other Central European state, is apprehensive about a reawakening of Russian imperialism, since historically an independent Poland has always limited Russian influence in Europe. Consequently, speaking on the issue of Russian association with the PFP, Polish defense minister Piotr Kolodziejczyk concluded that Poland would "feel a little safer," since "no security system without Russia or, even worse, against Russia would be either permanent or safe."[20]

The Polish attitude toward Russia is full of ambivalence and uncertainty. It was the Russian empire that along with Prussia and Austria instigated the partition of Poland. In 1920 Bolshevik Russia invaded the newly independent Polish state, and some 20 years later conspired with Hitler to invade the country and to start World War II. Then, for over four decades, Moscow continued to impose political and military hegemony intended to facilitate the global ascendancy of the Soviet power.

Stabilization of Central Europe is possible only through cooperation with Russia, but as an equal partner and not as a guarantor. The right place for Russia in Europe is to act as any other continental state rather than usurp rights to determine the destiny of other nations. All major political parties in Poland are firmly convinced that the extension of NATO would contribute to the stability of the entire continent and in this way would benefit Russia, which is seen as one of the key pillars of the European order. The purpose of NATO today, in Polish opinion, is to bring closer to Russia a region of stability and prosperity rather than an anti-Russian military alliance. The anti-Soviet and anti-Warsaw Pact trust of NATO is no longer an issue unless Russia intends to resurrect the aggressive policies of the Soviet Union.

Finally, the PFP compromise between the Central European insistence on immediate membership and the Western reservation against prompt admission of the new members subverts French efforts to revitalize the WEU as the basis of a European defense identity without American participation. Lack of flexibility on the part of NATO on the new membership issue would play into the French objective of building an alternative to NATO and the American presence in Europe. Poland and other nations of Central Europe are strongly committed to the preservation of the American role on the continent and favor NATO over the WEU, although, having no choice, they had expressed interest in the WEU as an alternative road to NATO. As NATO Secretary General Manfred Woerner pointed out in his interview for *Gazeta wyborcza,* "If Poland joined the EC, and then the WEU, the question of NATO membership would immediately arise."[21]

Also, regardless of the membership in NATO, Polish security cannot be ignored by the West. It is impossible to imagine that a military confrontation in the center of Europe and involving a nation of some 40 million people could be confined to national borders. The security and stability of the Polish state are ipso facto a security issue of the West, and Washington's evasive political maneuvering is not likely to change West European support for Polish membership in NATO. To assure European stability Poland must enter NATO, or NATO would have to be replaced by another alliance, perhaps the WEU, that would be more in touch with the realities of European politics.

Still the PFP left in Central Europe an impression of big-power diplomacy, appeasement of Russian new imperialism, "dealing about us without us" as practiced in Munich and Yalta. The United States was using delaying tactics against the nations of Central Europe, offering paper guarantees,[22] similar to the security guarantees provided to Poland by France and Great Britain on the eve of the 1939 German invasion. Thus, the PFP creates the feeling that the West continues to pursue the discredited policy of appeasement, since expansion of NATO was ruled out by the Clinton administration to please Russia. The United States under the Clinton administration is repeating the old mistake of the Roosevelt administration of giving in to political blackmail and elevating relations with Russia to such a priority that everything else must be subordinated to it. The logical conclusion of this American attitude would be that Poland's admission to NATO would have to be negotiated with Moscow rather than with Washington. For this reason, the PFP plan is a vague and weak alternative to full membership in NATO, and it provides no meaningful security protection to Central Europe. It contributes, in France's opinion, to the "profusion of organizations with ill-defined and often redundant objectives."[23] However, the PFP has a

> significant political dimension as it is linked to the acceptance by participating states of important obligations to protect democracy in internal

relations and to observe international law in external relations. It gives particular emphasis to the commitment to restrain from a threat of the use of force against territorial integrity and political independence of states and to respect existing borders and solve disputes by peaceful means.[24]

In short, it has added some new political constraints to the imperial ambitions of Moscow, but it has failed to result in any significant improvement of the geostrategic position of Central Europe, including the expected alteration of the Russia-first foreign policy fixation embraced by the Clinton administration in Washington.

In the long run, the PFP is expected to act as a self-screening device for its participants. The organization is likely to open numerous opportunities for joint military operations and programs with NATO forces and is expected to be a trial of political commitment and military capability to operate according to the alliance's moral standards and military requirements. This will help to distinguish between active and nonactive members and generate new pressure for even closer affiliation, perhaps in the form of full membership, of the dedicated members with NATO.

The PFP, according to Poland's foreign minister, just opened the "door leading to the vestibule," and it should mobilize the Polish nation to take full advantage of the natural selection process to prepare for another leap toward the West. Poland has been more than ready to pledge commitment to peace, democracy, human rights, and restructuring of its military, and the country hopes for a speedy institutionalization of the PFP and integration with NATO. At this time the PFP includes all functions of NATO, including consultations regarding national security issues as envisaged under Article IV. The main exception is the lack of NATO's Article V, which provides for the common defense against a military attack on one of its members, but such an incident is most unlikely in post–Cold War Europe.[25]

Warsaw is not fully satisfied with the PFP, but the NATO-mania in Poland is not fading at all. The country has plans to mobilize its limited resources to enter the fast track in the race to NATO. This drive to Western Europe is supported by the great majority of people and strongly favored by the entire military establishment. Polish democracy is not fully developed and entrenched, and there is a temptation to use the armed forces for internal political objectives. Following the misuse of the Polish army in 1981 to impose martial law against Solidarity, the military cadres look to association with NATO as a guarantee against future abuses. Additionally, prospects for cooperation with NATO countries and eventual membership in this organization provide the armed forces with a special political status and justification for their demand that the military budget be increased to at least 3 percent of the gross national product.

Speaking at the signing ceremony in Brussels, Polish prime minister Waldemar Pawlak conveyed his country's frustrations and hopes when he said that

> even though the most recent NATO summit in Brussels did not fulfill all our expectations, we were happy to take note of NATO's declaration of openness to development of cooperation with the partner countries. We were also happy to take note of the prospect created at the summit of a future widening of NATO to include new members.

He added that the Poles

> regard the initiative as Poland's chance for strengthening its links to NATO . . . and as a chance for the future implementation of our strategic goal of Poland's integration with Western security structures.[26]

Already on 1 February 1994, the NATO fact-finding mission arrived in Warsaw to discuss bilateral implementation of the Partnership for Peace program.[27] Meanwhile, the Polish military establishment is preoccupied with the task of standardizing communication, command, firepower, and reconnaissance systems with those in NATO, and when resources become available the country will embark on bringing technological standards in line with NATO's.

Poland appears ready to become involved in a number of activities accessible through the PFP, including defense and budget planning; civilian control over the military; cooperation in peace missions conducted under the auspices of the United Nations and the CSCE; contributing military units to participate in joint operations; joint training, exercises, and maneuvers; search and rescue missions; and establishment of representation bureaus at NATO headquarters in Brussels and the military headquarters at SHAPE in Mons.[28]

In March 1994 Poland signed an agreement on military cooperation with the United States that provides for regular meetings at the level of chief of staff, the possibility of Polish military participation in American training sessions, and U.S. support for modernization of the Polish armed forces. Although no specific date for joint U.S.-Polish military exercises has been set, it is expected that by the end of 1994 American troops will take part in the Polish army's maneuvers. Also, a proposal has been submitted for an amendment to the defense appropriation bill that would commit the United States to "oppose, by applying the appropriate means, any attempts by the Russian Federation aimed at intimidation, using military force or economic blackmail, with the goal of restitution of spheres of influence on the territory of the former Soviet Republics, in the Baltic states, and in Central and East Europe."[29]

Consequently, the peace partnership offers some real opportunities for mutual cooperation, and a substantial increase in bilateral contacts would help advance Western interests in full integration with Poland and other Central European states. Polish soldiers are already active participants in six different UN operations, and Poland is the seventh largest contributor to the UN peacekeeping operations, which include presence in Golan Heights, Cambodia, Lebanon, and an infantry battalion in Croatia.[30] This is an indication that Poland is serious about a more active role in global affairs and about the professionalism of its military.

In the final analysis, the future of the Partnership for Peace might be decided in Moscow. If Russia becomes a stable and democratic state inclined to live by the internationally accepted norms of peaceful behavior, including respect for the sovereignty of its neighbors, the need for NATO and its extension through the PFP may cease to exist. If, however, Russian movement toward democracy and a free-market economy is derailed and the traditional Russian propensity toward expansionism prevails again, the United States, together with the other members of NATO, could very quickly transform the PFP into a meaningful military organization.

But the ultimate success or failure of Poland's Western policy depends on the performance of the Polish economy. Since the country remains committed to a democratic and free-market path of development, integration into the European Union is the central goal of its foreign policy. Poland intends to be an equal member of NATO with full rights, just as it wants to be an equal member of the European Union. The treaty on Poland's association with the European Community (EC) was signed in December 1991 and became effective on 1 February 1994. Poland signed the treaty for ten years in expectation that within six to ten years the country would qualify for a full membership in the European Union. As the *Economist* summarized: "The Hungarians, Poles and Czechs are embarrassingly impatient. They already have association agreements and free trade with the EU, but want full membership by 2000 at the latest."[31]

Immediately after regaining independence from the Soviet Union, Hungary, Poland, and Czechoslovakia decided to join forces in a coordinated effort to enter the West European market and formed the Visegrad Triangle. (There are now four countries in the group as a result of the 1 January 1993, division of Czechoslovakia into two independent states.) The principal purpose of this Central European organization has been to combine the forces of over 60 million people to apply pressure on the West, as well as to demonstrate that these particular postcommunist nations are a special case, since they have the capacity to cooperate, compromise, and coordinate their economic policies and strategic objectives. That is, they can provide evidence that their cultural and political values are identical to those of the West.

The Visegrad countries are also prepared to cooperate in military matters to ensure that the defense capabilities of these former members of the Warsaw Pact do not continue to deteriorate further and to ensure that research, development, and the quality and production of military equipment will correspond to NATO standards.

Conditions for their thrust to the West were specified at the October 1991 London conference, where the 12 members of the EC established a list of conditions for membership, including holding free elections to meet requirements of the Council of Europe. The next Western signal, which by no means was a commitment, was the June 1993 declaration of the Copenhagen EC summit, which acknowledged Central European interest in membership without, however, making any concrete commitment or suggesting any deadlines.

The associate status was initially seen as a significant accomplishment in the effort to move closer to the West, because in preparation for full membership it requires Poland to legislate the EC standards and defines the level of subsidies for agricultural products. However, the associate membership agreement also provides for uncompromising protection of the EC markets against the less expensive labor-intensive and agricultural products from Poland and other members of the Visegrad Triangle. At the same time, however, the new associate members have made their own markets vulnerable to penetration by the Western products, giving rise to accusations that the West is treating its Eastern neighbors as modern colonies or "Europe B."

The Central European states; in the opinion of the Polish Peasant Party, have provided new markets for Western products. Western competition has brought numerous domestic industries to bankruptcy. At the same time, Western investments in Central Europe are directed at labor-intensive and environmentally harmful economic sectors in order to circumvent higher labor costs and antipollution standards enforced in Western Europe.[32]

An additional complication on the road to economic integration with the West is the lack of loyalty among members of the Visegrad Group. The Czech Republic in particular is concerned that the agreement is an "artificial process created by the West," a product of Western pressure to group all Central European nations together, thereby creating a parallel regional economic organization subservient to the West. Instead of facilitating integration, the agreement institutionalizes segregation into Western and East-Central Europe. The

Czechs argue that the time has come for bilateralization of relations with the West to avoid construction of a substitute EC and a substitute NATO. While Poland and Hungary may need up to ten years to qualify for EU membership, the Czech state may need only three years. In the opinion of Czech premier Václav Klaus, it would be much easier for the EU to absorb some 10 million Czechs than over 60 million Central Europeans.[33]

Particularly because of the relative backwardness of Polish agriculture, Czech politicians perceive Poland as a rather weak candidate for full membership in the European Union, and they are willing to pursue alone their own interest in integration with the West. Only Warsaw and Budapest are striving for a "communal" bid for full membership and see the Visegrad cooperation as a natural transit route for Western support. Available data indicate that the economic situation in Poland, the Czech Republic, and Hungary is roughly identical, with Hungary leading in terms of gross domestic product per capita in 1991 ($2,974), followed by the Czech Republic ($2,128) and Poland ($2,040). However, the growth rate of economic output is the highest in Poland.[34]

Another obvious barrier to integration is resistance from some EU states, especially Portugal, Spain, and Greece, which fear for their privileged position among the more developed West European states such as Germany and France. There is also general concern that full integration of the Central European nations would be exceedingly expensive and, perhaps, unacceptable to Western taxpayers. Because the Central European nations rely heavily on agriculture, as members they would qualify for EU "structural funds," which would have to be increased up to 60 percent to avoid the disintegration of the common agricultural policy at the price of frustrating West European farmers.

In consequence, some Western nations, particularly Germany, are studying alternative solutions that would result in only partial admission to the EU and that would help the Central European states manage their economic situation sufficiently well to provide for a viable defense and relative economic prosperity. One such plan advocates a two-stage process that would first establish a pan-European free-trade zone and then in the second stage extend the single market to the Central European states. While rules regulating trade would be identical for all members of the European Union, "this new pact would involve no commitments on agriculture, fiscal transfer or the movement of workers—and no votes."[35]

Polish politicians and the general public are optimistic that by the year 2000 the country will no longer be a frontier state between the European Union and NATO and the East and that the dividing line between Poland and the West will be eliminated just as it was erased between Germany and France. The partial solution would probably be acceptable as another step forward, although this acceptance would come with loud complaints about duplicity and lack of understanding, immediately followed by another campaign for equal partnership.

It is apparent that despite frequent governmental changes, including the electoral victory of the leftist coalition, Poland remains committed to the idea of the European option. Integration into the European Union and NATO is at the center of its foreign policy objectives, mobilizing and uniting all relevant political and social forces in the country to pursue a policy of unilateral harmonization with Western standards. The Poles realize that the Partnership for Peace and associate membership with the European Community are the optimum solutions available at this time, and are not a substitute for full integration into the European structures. However, becoming a NATO and EU member is a process. Poland is determined to pursue its strategic objectives by demonstrating that the incorporation of the Central European nations into Western Europe would be in the best interests of the West. That is, without expansion to the east, NATO and possibly the EU would lose their international relevance. Poland's quest for membership in the Western structures is seen as a contribution to construction of a united Europe under unique circumstances not likely to be repeated in the near future. For Poland it is a historical opportunity that will determine national fortunes for a long time.

The prospect of union with the West is one the principal driving forces in Poland's domestic and foreign policies. The long chain of anticommunist revolts that began with the Warsaw uprising in 1944 and continued through the fall of the communist system in 1989 would never have come to full completion without confirming Poland's "Westernness" by securing for the country a permanent place in Western Europe. Poland is striving to become a permanent, durable, and indissoluble element in Western civilization, making sure that the Polish political system, economic structure, and cultural and moral values are identical to those of the Western world and that this state of affairs is fully reflected in the scope and purpose of the regional organizations that govern European politics. By becoming an indispensable constituent of the pan-European system, Poland could feel assured that the continuing transformation at home and of the entire region would proceed in the Western context and along the lines of Western cultural identity.

The historical essence behind the Polish drive to the West is to modify permanently the division of Europe into its eastern and western parts. The Iron Curtain produced division along Poland's western border, leaving the Polish nation under the culturally alien influence of a totalitarian political system rooted in the Byzantine legacy. The demise of the Russian empire, tsarist and Soviet, created a window of opportunity to merge with the West and to validate the Polish claim to being a Western nation.

Notes

1. "Poland Faced With the Changes in the EC," *Le Monde,* 22 May 1992, in FBIS-EEU-92-103, 28 May 1992, pp. 24-25.

2. Marian Kowalewski and Lech Kosciuk, "Problems of Military Security of Poland, Topic of the Month," *Wojsko i wychowanie,* no. 11, November 1992, 81-3, in JPRS-EER-92-172, 22 December 1992, p. 44.

3. "Security Policy and Defense Strategy of the Republic of Poland," *Polska zbrojna,* 13-15 November 1992, pp.4-5. Also Col. Marian Kopczewski, "Directions of Change in the Air Defense of Central European Countries Following the Transformation of Their Systems of Society," *Przeglad wojsk lotniczych i wojsk obrony powietranej kraju,* May 1993, pp. 39-44, in JPRS-EER-93-078-S, 4 August 1993, p. 13.

4. Tadeusz Mitek, "Wylacznie polska doktryna" (Exclusively Polish Doctrine), *Polska zbrojna,* 3 November 1992, p. 1.

5. Maria Wagrowska, "We and the North Atlantic Alliance: Why Join NATO?" *Rzeczpospolita,* 26-27 September 1992, p. 8, in JPRS-EER-92-151, 27 October 1992, p. 27.

6. The full text of the Polish-German treaty is included in *Gazeta wyborcza,* 14 November 1991.

7. Hanna Suchocka, "We count on understanding not only of unity of aims, but also of unity of interests," speech at Lublin Catholic University, 18 October 1992.

8. Michael Mihalka, "Squaring the Circle: NATO's Offer to the East," *RFE/RL Research Report* 3, no. 12 (25 March 1994): 7.

9. Polish president Lech Walesa interviewed on foreign policy issues by Warsaw Radio on 24 November 1993, in FBIS-EEU-93-226, 26 November 1993, p. 19.

10. Adam Bromke and Andrzej Micewski, "What Would Russia Say to This?" *Przeglad tygodniowy,* 14 February 1993, in JPRS-EER-93-023-S, 23 March 1993, p. 14.

11. Warsaw Radio Network, 2 November 1992, in FBIS-EEU-213, 3 November 1992, p. 19.

12. Manki Ponomarev, "A NATO Double in Eastern Europe. Illusion or Reality?: Notes of a Military Reviewer," *Krasnaya zvezda,* 20 October 1992, p. 3, in JPRS-UMA-92-041, 18 November 1992, p. 43.

13. For an explanation of the Russian policy toward Central and Eastern Europe, see "Russia's Kozyrev Addresses Partnership' Conference," Warsaw Polska Agencja Prasowa (PAP), 23 February 1994, in FBIS-EEU-94-037, 24 February 1994, p. 18.

14. Polish foreign minister Andrzej Olechowski, "Polska polityka wschodnia: My chcemy cieplejszych stosunkow z Rosja" (Polish East Policy, We Want Warmer Relations with Russia), *Rzeczpospolita,* 18 February 1994, p. 21.

15. "Olechowski Urges Cooperation," Warsaw PAP, 23 February 1994, in FBIS-EEU-94-037, 24 February 1994, p. 18.

16. "The North Atlantic Cooperation Council," Special Report, The Atlantic Council of the United States, vol. 4, no. 1, 15 March 1993.

17. Ibid.

18. German foreign minister Klaus Kinkel, quoted in "European Official and Media Comment on the NATO Summit," Special Memorandum, Foreign Broadcast Information Service, FB SM 93-10021, 21 December 1993, p. 2.

19. "NATO's Near Abroad': New Membership, New Missions," Speech to the Atlantic Council of the United States, 9 December 1993. For more comments see Jan Rozdzynski, "Wielka rosja ma wrocic" (Great Russia Is Returning), *Zycie,* 25 February 1994, p. 3; and Roger E. Kanet and Brian V. Souders, "Russia and Her Western Neighbors," *Demokratizatsiya* 1, no. 3 (1993): 32-53.

20. Quoted in "Minister on Russian Role in Security System," Warsaw Radio, 17 January 1994, in FBIS-EEU-94-011, 18 January 1994, p. 8.

21. Malgorzata Alterman, "On the Threshold of the Pact," *Gazeta wyborcza,* 17 March 1993, p. 6, in FBIS-EEU-93-055, 25 March 1993, p. 27.

22. "European Official and Media Comments," p. 9. See also "Walesa Says Partnership for Peace Unsatisfactory," *Rzeczpospolita,* 12 January 1994, in FBIS-EEU-94-008, 12 January 1994, p. 25.

23. "European Official and Media Comments," p. 6.

24. Polish foreign minister Andrzej Olechowski, in his address to the Polish Sejm on 21 January 1994, in "Foreign Minister Sees No Immediate Threats," FBIS-EEU-94-015, 24 January 1994, p. 30. For the review of Clinton's policy toward Russia, see Zbigniew Brzezinski, "The Premature Partnership," *Foreign Affairs,* March/April 1994, pp. 67-82.

25. "Olechowski Reviews Foreign Policy Concerns," *Czas krakowski,* 22-23 January 1994, 8, in FBIS-EEU-94-020, 31 January 1994, p. 8. Also, "NATO Partnership for Peace: Beyond the First Step," Special Report, Atlantic Council of the United States, vol. 5, no. 3, 21 March 1994.

26. "Pawlak's Speech on Signing Partnership,'" *BIURO PRASOWE RZADU. INFORMACJA,* 3 February 1994, in FBIS-EEU-94-024, 4 February 1994, p. 16.

27. Reported in FBIS-EEU-94-022, 2 February 1994, p. 12.

28. Ewa Kaszuba and Krzysztof Olszewski, "A Unanimous Choir and a Solo Singer," *Rzeczpospolita,* 10 January 1994, in FBIS-EEU-94-006, 10 January 1994, p. 22. "Bezpiecznstwo Polski jest w naszych rekach" (Poland's Security Is in Our Hands), interview with Minister of National Defense Piotr Kolodziejczyk, in *Polska*

zbrojna, 1 February 1994. Also, interview with Polish defense minister Piotr Kolodziejczyk, Warsaw TVP Television First Program Network, 23 January 1994, in FBIS-EEU-94-018, 27 January 1994, pp. 23-28.

29. Ewa Szymanska, "Military Cooperation With U.S.A.: Kolodziejczyk Signed Agreement With Perry," *Rzeczpospolita,* 26-27 March 1994, in FBIS-EEU-94-059, 28 March 1994.

30. Albert M. Zaccor, "Training Poland's Blue Berets," *Jane's Intelligence Review,* November 1993, p. 499.

31. "A Touch of Eastern Promise," *The Economist,* 26 March 1994, p. 58.

32. Krzysztof Wykretowicz, "An Equation With Four Unwanteds: A Four-Sided Triangle' That Fits None Too Well With a Constellation of 12 Golden Stars, or About the Square of a Circle," *Tygodnik solidarnosc,* 4 December 1992, in JPRS-EER-93-001-S, 29 January 1993, p. 1; and Maria Wagrowska, "Sygnal z Zachodu" (A Signal from the West), *Rzeczpospolita,* 30 March 1994, p. 2.

33. Czech premier Václav Klaus, in an interview given to *Le Figaro,* 11 January 1993, in FBIS-EEU-008-93, 13 January 1993, p. 7. Also, Michael Ludwig, "Poland and the Czech Dream of Good Luck," *Frankfurter Allgemeine,* 30 January 1993, in JPRS-EER-93-017-S, 4 March 1993, p. 1; and Jan B. de Weydenthal, "Poland Supports the Triangle as a Means to Reach Other Goals," *RFE/RL Research Report* 1, no. 23 (5 June 1992): 15-31.

34. *Gazeta wyborcza,* 13 October 1992, p. 18.

35. "Poor Men at the Gate," *The Economist,* 16 April 1994, p. 60; see also interview with Gregor Koebl, FRG consul general in Gdansk, in *Glos szczecinski,* 22-23 January 1994, in FBIS-EEU-94-021, 1 February 1994, p. 23.

Idealism or Realism: A Historical Dilemma or a False Dichotomy?

Ilya Prizel

The 1918 restoration of Polish statehood proved to be a false dawn. The Second Republic was overpowered by forces both from within and from without that had overtaxed the country's resources. Still, the two decades of interwar Polish independence were essential to the consolidation of the Polish nation as they would provide in the Polish national consciousness a sharp contrast to the communist era of the Soviet-controlled Polish People's Republic. Today, for the second time in this century, Poland has a historic opportunity to chart its own future as a sovereign state.

In a country where references to the past often overpower political discourse, the parameters of the national debate on Polish foreign policy since regaining independence are set by the weight of historical experience; these limits can be challenged but they cannot be ignored. As in 1918, postcommunist Poland is grappling with its geopolitical dilemma of being a medium-sized power between Europe's two giants, Russia and Germany. By virtue of its history, culture, and national mythology, Poland has emulated the West, which it admires; for similar reasons, it has shunned the East, which it fears. The rhetoric of pan-Europeanism notwithstanding, the newly independent Poland once again sees itself suspended between the East and the West. The ambiguity of Poland's international position in the "gray zone" of post–Cold War Europe has often been read in Warsaw as the ominous sign of an impending crisis. The policies pursed by the succession of postcommunist Polish governments have been built on the implicit axiom that Poland must achieve a clear definition of its place in Europe. Historically, Poland could be politically either of the West or of the East, but not both. This stark dichotomy held too true for interwar Poland; however, today it may ultimately prove a false choice.

Despite the fact that Poland's predicament as the weak link between Russia and Germany has remained constant, it would be a mistake automatically to assume that the so-called Polish dilemma must again be revisited with historically predetermined consequences. First, Poland itself is a profoundly different entity today from that of the interwar period. The delineation of Poland's eastern border along the "Curzon line" transformed the notion of Poland from that of a civilization locked in a *Kulturkampf* with Russia for supremacy over Ukraine, Lithuania, and Belarus to that of a nation-state pursuing its own interests, all but devoid of messianic distraction.

This physical as well as intellectual transformation has fundamentally altered the perception of Poland in the eyes of its Russian neighbor as well as those of its Western allies.[1] Although Russia remains vigilant in its determination to forestall any encroachment of NATO into what it considers its backyard, the existence of an independent Polish state, confined to ethnic Poland and devoid of a mission in Ukraine and Belarus, does not by itself challenge the fundamental Russian definition of self. True, for the Kremlin that definition still invariably includes Ukraine and Belarus, but it does not consider continued Polish sovereignty as anathema.

It would be equally deceptive to view contemporary Germany as a replica of either its Wilhelmine or Nazi predecessors. While it is evident that Germany faces a long and painful process of readjustment—from a divided semi-sovereign entity to that of Europe's natural leader—the current situation makes Germany an unlikely candidate for the resumption of its historic role as the anti–status quo power par excellence. Demographically, Germany is rapidly transforming itself into a country with one of the oldest populations in the world, with the number of pensioners increasing at a rate far faster than any other segment of its population. This shift in the nation's demographics will make any future adventurous German foreign policy difficult to sustain and unlikely. Moreover, Germany's political stability, which depends on the continuation of its "economic miracle," hinges on the country's ability to retain its position as the world's premier (or second-largest) trading nation. Among the OECD countries, Germany derives the largest portion of its GDP from foreign trade; this alone gives the Germans a vital stake in the stability of the international system. In view of the above, the notion that Poland is somehow once again a "Daniel in the lion's den" appears to be more a reflection of Poland's historical memory than of contemporary political and economic reality.

Perhaps the most important difference in the current Polish predicament is that the nature of a Russian-German axis has changed from that of the previous three centuries, where any rapprochement between Russia and Germany virtually by definition implied an anti-Polish conspiracy. While Russia sees Germany as its key advocate in the West and as a potential source of capital and technology, for its part Germany realizes that stability within the international system is unattainable if Russia is left outside that system. Furthermore, German industrialists consider Russia a potential market as well as a source of energy and minerals that they cannot afford to ignore. Germany recognizes that normalcy in Europe is contingent on relative stability in the former Soviet Union. However, despite the close special relationship between Moscow and Bonn, and despite a genuine symbiosis on a wide array of issues (with Russia supporting a permanent German seat on the United Nations Security Council and Germany supporting a permanent Russian membership in the Group of Seven group of industrialized states),[2] the relationship remains constrained by a variety of domestic and international forces, which by definition limit the potential of these two historically aggressive powers to returning to the pattern of Rapallo.[3]

There is little doubt that the international system is in the midst of a profound adjustment, in which Russo-German relations have reemerged as an important factor in European politics. For the first time since 1949, the Russo-German relationship is not subject to NATO supervision, which in effect diminishes the importance of Germany's Atlantic orientation altogether. However, the nature of that relationship is sufficiently different today from that which preceded World War II to suggest that a qualitatively new Bonn-Moscow axis has begun to emerge.

Historically, Russian-German alignments came into being only when Moscow and Berlin were eager to overthrow an international system which they had both deemed patently discriminatory against them. There is nothing in the contemporary reality of world politics—the occasional extremist rhetoric in Russia and Germany notwithstanding—that would suggest that Moscow and Bonn view the world through such prisms. Germany is thoroughly integrated politically, economically, and militarily into the international system. It has benefited greatly from that integration, and therefore any aggressive alliance aimed at the stability of the current international order would be contrary to Germany's vital national interests. Likewise, although Russia's position in the international system is far more amorphous, several factors seem to work against Moscow's resuming its role as a power determined to undermine the international order. Unlike the 1920s, when the Great Powers had sought to isolate Russia, the question of keeping Russia fully engaged in the international arena has been an axiom of NATO's policy; if anything, Poland and other former Soviet clients in Eastern and Central Europe have complained that the West was being overly "Russo-centric" in its post–Cold War Eastern policy. In an effort to integrate Russia into the international system, for example, the European Union established a special relationship with Moscow, and Russia was admitted as a full-fledged member of the political wing of the G-7.

Another factor that mitigates against Russia resuming direct aggressive policies against Poland is an apparent change in the perception of what constitutes a great power and what obligations that position entails. While the Russians continue to obsess over their great- power status, the definition of a "great power" in the post–Cold War world is different from that of the past. As Edward Luttwak observed in his insightful piece "Now that the Great Powers are Gone,"[4] what historically distinguished great powers from lesser states was their ability and willingness to use force to protect interests that were far from vital, as well as their willingness to continue to acquire more nonvital interests in the form of spheres of influence. By this criterion, it is clear today that Russia has neither the will nor the ability to play the role of a great power. Likewise, although the Russians have been increasingly assertive within the Commonwealth of Independent States (CIS), they have yet to take up the challenge of backing up the separatists in Crimea, a region that is of vital interest to Russia.

Today's Poland, while very important to the Kremlin for psychological as well as practical reasons, does not present itself as a Russian vital interest, unless it is perceived by Moscow as either a military threat or (more likely) an agent attempting to weaken its role in East Slavdom. In fact, as Luttwak argues, the reason that we are witnessing the emergence of "power vacuums" across the world is precisely because none of the historic Great Powers is willing, nor really able, to carry the burden that such status entails. Hence, for instance, whereas historically most great powers would have welcomed the Balkan crisis as an opportunity to expand their "sphere of influence," in the current environment the Balkans have become a "black hole" that all great powers, including the United States and its key NATO allies, are eager to avoid. Likewise, nationalist assertions notwithstanding, Russia has refrained from undermining the position of the world community in the Balkan crisis, and it has actually used its historic relationship with the Serbs in a constructive manner.

Clearly, it would be naive to assert that Russia has abandoned its great-power ambitions or that it is cured of its imperial proclivities. However, even if the traditional Russia imperialist vocation were to revive, it would likely be directed at the former republics of the Soviet Union in the "near-abroad" areas rather than at Poland, the country whose relentless quest for independence led the nineteenth-century Russian Slavophile Konstantin Aksakov to conclude that "Russia had swallowed Poland and poisoned itself in the process." While Russian geopolitical assertiveness vis-à-vis Poland is certainly possible, the cost of yet another attempt by Moscow to dominate it outright would far outweigh any possible gains the Russians could anticipate from the venture. In the past centuries, it was the tsars' repression of Poland that had earned Russia the moniker "the prison of nations" and made Russia into a pariah within the international system—a role that few within the Russian political mainstream today are eager to reclaim, the more so as the gains to Russia from any putative mastery over Poland are yet to be made clear.

It is no doubt unsettling for the Poles to remain in a "gray zone" on the fault line separating the affluent, integrated West and the sallow, impoverished Russia; however, Poland stands an even greater risk of becoming a victim of its own outdated perception of world politics. The ambiguity of Poland's present position as a Central European state par excellence may prove the best solution to its geopolitical dilemma. It will require patience and considerable diplomatic skill in Warsaw to build a workable foreign policy that balances Poland's interests in the West and in the East, without compromising them in either case; in the long run Poland stands to gain more as a bridge between the West and Russia than as an outpost of either.

The limitations on Polish foreign policy are well visible today: they are drawn by Russia's actions and NATO's reciprocal inaction. Four years into independence, Poland is beginning to leave behind the understandable early euphoria about the prospects for speedy reintegration with the West. There is a growing recognition in Warsaw that the West may in fact never come to share the urgency of the Polish pro-Western vision. Still, the reassessment of foreign policy under way since the beginning of 1994 need not involve a radical reorientation, even if it does portend change in the original expectations. An exclusive Russian orientation at the expense of Poland's Western ties would compromise Polish independence. Russia's powerful return to the arena of European politics, combined with the West's reluctance to undertake new commitments in Central Europe, feed into the historically justified Polish mistrust and fear of Moscow. Russia's staunch opposition to the eastward expansion of NATO, conveyed unequivocally to the Poles by foreign minister Andrei Kozyrev during his meeting with Polish foreign minister Andrzej Olechowski in Kraków in February 1994, has confirmed the traditional fears in Warsaw's thinking about foreign policy.

The Polish recognition of the changed realities of postcommunist Europe have translated into a policy of the minimum expectations and limits that the Polish side will put forth in its dealings with both the West and the East. It is fundamentally a reactive policy, leaving Poland few options but to adjust as best it can to the changing regional balance of power. If the best Polish hopes of being included in NATO come true while at the same time Russia becomes isolated from Europe, Poland will become an outpost of the West in the confrontation with Russia; if the worst Polish fears about Russian intentions become a reality while the West's commitment to East-Central Europe remains tenuous, Poland will be in the final analysis just as alone when confronted by the future Russian demands as it is today. In either case, the time of the great political opportunities attendant to the early post–Cold War transition reshaping Europe's strategic landscape will have been lost.

At its core, the Polish quest for inclusion in NATO is a repetition of the interwar quest for Western security guarantees. Likewise, Polish relations with Russia are the function of Moscow's position on the Polish bid for NATO membership. In the words of Foreign Minister Olechowski during his testimony before the Polish Senate's Commission on Foreign Affairs, Warsaw is determined to seek partnership with Russia provided that the core Polish strategic interests of striving for membership in the three main Western institutions (WEU, NATO, and the EU) are not hindered by Russia's policy.[5] In effect, rather than initiating policies that might induce Russia to take action favorable to Poland, the Polish foreign policy makers seem to have attempted to proscribe the actions Moscow cannot take because they would chip at the foundations of the newly restored Polish national sovereignty. It is unlikely that such proscription will be effective without leverage. This appears to be recognized by Olechowski's partial shift in emphasis in Polish-Russian relations from security policy issues toward the question of Poland's economic partnership with Russia.

Another indication that a new foreign policy line toward Moscow may be developing was Olechowski's implicit affirmation of the priority of Polish-Russian relations over Polish-Ukrainian relations. Olechowski rejected the Russian claim that the Poles displayed "imperial tendencies toward the East," but at the same time he hastened to convey to Kozyrev Warsaw's determination not to get involved in the Russian-Ukrainian dispute. As he put it, "it would be naive to expect that Poland can expand and strengthen the independence and sovereignty of states seeking independence [from Russia]. Whether or not they will want to integrate within the framework of the CIS will depend on them alone."[6]

The 1993 election and the transition in Poland from the center-right parties based on the original Solidarity movement to the postcommunist coalition marked the end of Krzysztof Skubiszewski's impressive stewardship over Polish foreign policy. Skubiszewski's tenure saw the drafting and negotiating of the bilateral treaty arrangements that would constitute the foundations of the new Polish foreign policy and whose limits are now being tested by Olechowski's team. This is a solid record of achievement on which the new foreign policy can be built.

The readjustment in the direction of Polish foreign policy that might seek more balance between the West and the East was underscored by the fact that the first foreign visit by Polish prime minister Waldemar Pawlak was his 14 March 1994 trip to Moscow. Reportedly, Pawlak was to meet with German chancellor Helmut Kohl in February, but at the request of the Polish government the Polish-German summit was postponed until April.[7] The new activism of Polish diplomacy in the East is best symbolized by the fact that Warsaw was the initiator of Russian foreign minister Andrei Kozyrev's visit to Poland, of Polish premier Pawlak's visit to Russia, and the visit to Moscow by leading Polish parliamentarians. At the same time, Foreign Minister Olechowski has amply demonstrated to his Russian counterpart that the new Eastern diplomacy would not mean the compromise of Polish national objectives; the talks have been frank and tough.

The direction of Polish-Russian relations will be determined decisively by the direction of political change in Russia. As observed by Bronislaw Geremek, chairman of the Sejm Commission on Foreign Affairs, after a visit to Moscow in the spring of 1994, the direction of Russian-Ukrainian relations will be for Poland a strong indicator of whether Russia intends to reclaim its imperial ambitions.[8] Geremek also observed that precisely at the time when Poland has been reclaiming its ties to the West it should not become the West's "border fortress," but rather that it should strive to build good relations with its eastern neighbors, especially Russia and Ukraine.[9]

Poland's aspirations to join NATO have remained in the forefront of the country's security policy. Still, the issue is not simply a political question, as, short of substantial foreign military assistance, Poland lacks resources to modernize and re-equip its army. Political considerations in Brussels and Washington mitigating against a speedy integration of Poland into NATO notwithstanding, the cost of equipment modernization that Poland would have to incur to meet NATO standards (estimated by Defense Minister Kolodziejczyk at $2.5 billion to begin with) remains prohibitive. The projected increase in the Polish defense budget, which is to reach 3 percent of the GNP in two to three years,[10] will not suffice without additional resources to bring the Polish army's equipment up to NATO standards.

In 1994 Western orientation has remained dominant in Polish foreign policy, with special emphasis on strengthening ties with the Western European Union, European Union, and NATO. At the same time, Poland has been making a serious effort to improve relations with Russia. In a report presented to the Sejm in May 1994, Foreign Minister Andrzej Olechowski emphasized that the national security and sovereignty as well as economic recovery of the republic ranked highest on the government's foreign policy agenda. In practical terms, argued Olechowski, Poland must improve relations with its eastern neighbors to "match its level of cooperation with the others."[11] At the same time, Olechowski expressed concern about the resurgence of Russia's pressure for influence and a "special role" in the region; he saw Poland's speedy integration with NATO and other Western institutions as the antidote to the latent Russian threat. In his report Olechowski spoke both of the "conservatism of the West," discerned in its fear of opening up to new members, and of the "conservatism of the East," which sees Polish membership in NATO as a security threat to Russian national interests. In economic terms, Poland has no alternative but to strive for full membership in the European Union in order to break out of discriminatory quotas imposed by the EU. However, in addition to the Western market, Poland should seriously explore its economic options in the East.

The lesson of the last four years of cooperation with the EU has been sobering for Warsaw, which all too often saw the lofty Western declarations on the need for integration give way to old-fashioned protectionism. The unequivocally pro-NATO policy has yet to yield the hoped-for results, while the time for developing a working relationship with Russia is quickly slipping away. It appears that in addition to the two "conservatisms" mentioned by Olechowski Poland has reached the point where its foreign policy needs to come to terms with its own historical constraints.

Despite the apparent deadlock, whereby Poland seems to be suspended in a gray zone flanked in the West by indifferent NATO and in the East by unstable and increasingly aggressive Russia, the historical dilemma of Polish geopolitics may well be a false dichotomy. It is certainly true that Russia hindered Polish accession to NATO[12] and there are vocal lobbies in Russia calling for a return to the simple world of the Cold War. However, it is also true that Russia itself appreciates how much its own economic recovery as well as its status as a great power is contingent on its returning to the international mainstream. Although on the emotional level they may find it hard to accept, Russian policymakers recognize nonetheless that Russia cannot attempt to return to the international mainstream while simultaneously insisting on the marginalization of its neighbor.

Poland should take comfort from the fact that the Kremlin has been compelled to face reality before when it reversed its veto over Austria's and Finland's membership in the European Union. Moscow recognized that EU membership for the Austrians and the Finns not only would not deepen Russia's isolation but would in fact add to the European Union two new member-states whose economies have extensive links to Russia and, therefore, whose presence in the EU would indirectly enhance Russia's presence. Likewise, on the question of Polish membership in NATO it would be simpleminded to assume that Russia's objection to it is capricious or irreversible. While the Kremlin may not be enthusiastic about NATO's eastward expansion, its objections can be nullified if indeed such an expansion were to be accompanied by a parallel integration of Russia into the international system.

It is noteworthy that during the spring 1994 meeting between Russia's defense minister, Pavel Grachev, and his German counterpart, Volker Ruhe, Grachev raised the possibility of Russia dropping its objections to NATO membership for the Visegrad Group in exchange for a "special relationship between Russia and NATO" under the rubric of "16 plus 1."[13] Although Grachev's offer was not fully explored, largely because of the lack of foreign policy direction in Washington, it would be a mistake to assume that all doors for Poland's NATO membership are closed. While much remains to be clarified, the idea that Russia may eventually accept Polish membership in NATO was revived by Sergei Blagovolin, a former national security advisor to President Boris Yeltsin and currently the director of a think tank associated with Yegor Gaidar. Blagovolin argued in *Novye Vremya* that Russia should in fact drop its opposition to Polish membership in NATO in exchange for a high-level strategic partnership with the United States, key European states, and key Asian states as a means of avoiding in Russia the sense of international isolation and of guaranteeing its global security.[14]

Admittedly, various Russian proposals on a new global security architecture remain ambiguous, and many Poles see any attempt by the Kremlin to establish a "special relationship" with NATO as a covert effort to create an ersatz Yalta system. However, it is significant that Moscow's policy parameter appears to have shifted from the historical disposition to create a sphere of influence along Russia's periphery as a means of isolating it from the outside world to the recent attempts to use the periphery as a means of bringing Russia into the international mainstream. This perceptible current change in the pattern of Russian foreign policy constitutes a unique opportunity for Poland to defy its historical geopolitical dilemma.

Jozef Pilsudski, the founding father of the Second Polish Republic, observed on his deathbed in 1935 that Poland, by virtue of having amicable relations both with Moscow and with Berlin, resembled a person standing on two shaky stools. For Pilsudski, the only real question was which stool would collapse first. In the initial phase of its post-1989 foreign policy, Poland remained wedded to this dictum. Foreign Minister Skubiszewski's assumption was that in light of the disintegration of the Soviet Union and the attendant chaos in Russia, Poland had been granted a historic opportunity finally to join the Western camp to which it has historical as well as cultural bonds. The rapid resurgence of Russian assertiveness in foreign policy, the continued Western "conservatism" vis-à-vis Poland, and a growing realization in Warsaw that Poland can neither forget its history nor escape its geography have by 1994 led to an attempt to reshape Polish foreign policy. Polish foreign minister Andrzej Olechowski has articulated the belief that while still striving to join the West, Poland must remember that it can be integrated into the international system not only against Russia but also with Russia. Speaking at the NACC meeting in Istanbul, Olechowski reflected Poland's new appreciation of that political reality when he observed:

> We are aware of the need of a solid partnership between NATO and Russia. The decision of the former Soviet Union not to participate in the Marshall Plan aimed at the rehabilitation of Europe after the second world war was one of the factors clinching the division of Europe. . . . A cooperative relationship between Russia and NATO inside and outside "Partnership for Peace" is important for both sides of Europe and the World.[15]

The recognition in Warsaw that the more Russia is itself integrated into the international system the greater are the prospects of Poland's own integration with the West may finally put to rest the historic Polish dilemma as to which of the "two stools" supporting Poland will give way first.

•

Notes

1. There is ample literature on how Poland's ongoing feud with Russia during the Second Republic alienated Poland from the West European powers. See A. J. P. Taylor, *The Origins of Second World War* (London: Hamilton, 1961), or Jan Karski, *The Great Powers and Poland, 1919-1945: From Versailles to Yalta* (Lanham, MD: University Press of America, 1985).

2. See Jim Hoagland, "Germany and Russia are Getting Together," *The International Herald Tribune,* 17 May 1994.

3. See Ilya Prizel, "Germany and Russia: The Case for a Special Relationship," in *Postcommunist Eastern Europe: Crisis and Reform,* ed. Andrew A. Michta and Ilya Prizel (New York: St. Martin's Press, 1993).

4. Edward N. Luttwak, "Now that the Great Powers are Gone," *The International Herald Tribune,* 6 July 1994.

5. Maria Graczyk, "Wschod pragmatykow," *Wprost,* 6 March 1994.

6. Ibid.

7. Jacek Maziarski, "Wizyta przyjazni," *Lad,* 3-4 April 1994.

8. Slawomir Popowski, "Potrzeba przelomu: Rozmowa z Bronislawem Geremkiem," *Rzeczpospolita,* 13 April 1994.

9. Ibid.

10. Wieslaw S. Debski, "Rozne odcienie Partnerstwa: Rozmowa a Jerzym Szmajdzinskim, przewodniczacym Komisji Obrony Narodowej Sejmu RP," *Trybuna,* 15 April 1994.

11. Eliza Olczyk and Jerzy Pilczynski, "Polityka zagraniczna 94: Trwale bezpieczenstwo ponad wszystko," *Rzeczpospolita,* 13 May 1994.

12. It is noteworthy, however, that during the debate over the prospects for the Visegrad Group's membership in NATO, few paid attention to the profound lack of enthusiasm on Capitol Hill to extend American security guarantees to any new state.

13. Hoagland, "Germany and Russia."

14. Sergei Blagovolin, *Novye Vremya,* no. 7 (1994), pp. 7-14.

15. The statement of Polish foreign minister Andrzej Olechowski at the NACC Ministerial Meeting, Istanbul, 10 June 1994.

INDEX